GOVERNMENT ONLINE

1/8/96

"GOVERNMENT ONLINE"

Max Lent

HarperPerennial

A Division of HarperCollins*Publishers*

HarperCollins books may be purchased for educational, business, or sales promotional use. For information, please write: Special Markets Department, HarperCollins Publishers, Inc., 10 East 53rd Street, New York, NY 10022.

FIRST EDITION

ISBN 0-06-273301-X

95 96 97 98 99 ❖/RRD 10 9 8 7 6 5 4 3 2 1

Contents

Chapter 10: The Departments 81

Contents

Chapter 11: Independent Establishments and Government Corporations   157

Part III: Nongovernment Online Sources of Government Information

Part IV: State and Local Online Services **237**

Chapter 16: Government Online Sources of Government Information **239**

List of Illustrations

Acknowledgments

Many people have contributed information to this book. These include people I have never met, but corresponded with through the Internet, CompuServe, government agencies, nonprofit organizations, and through the mail. To all of you, I say thank you. Jock Gill, Jack Fox, David Lytel, and others in President Bill Clinton's administration, deserve recognition for their generous sharing of information.

This book would not exist if it were not for the pioneering efforts of government employees who had the vision to see that providing citizens access to government electronically was efficient, cost effective, and democratic. We owe these inspired public servants our gratitude and respect.

I wish to express my sincerest gratitude to my agent, Sallie Governeur, whose skills, professionalism, good nature, and advocacy are unparalleled. Maron L. Waxman deserves credit for seeing the value of *Government Online* and deciding that it was worthy of publication while she was working at HarperCollins. Erica Spaberg's inspired editorial advice kept the manuscript on course. Patricia Leasure's thorough editing of the final drafts of the manuscript was greatly appreciated. Roger Vershen of Page Studio graphics designed the symbols used throughout this book.

Without the friendship, love, and financial support of my wife, Tina Olsin Lent, I would not have had the luxury of developing the concept for this book or completing the manuscript. She provided me with emotional and intellectual support whenever I needed it. She cleaned the house, fed the cats, shopped for groceries, and cooked meals when it wasn't her turn. And she put up with more computer tech talk than a mate should have to endure. To her, I offer my love and eternal indebtedness.

Introduction

README.1ST

The world's largest producer of information, the United States Government, wants to share with you a vast part of the information it collects and produces. Much of this information is available to anyone electronically, and mostly for free. State and local governments are also placing huge quantities of information at your electronic fingertips. All you have to do to gain access to these storehouses of information is instruct your computer and modem to connect to government online services. The objective of this book is to provide logical, practical, and easy-to-use instructions to find and use government online information.

Can I Really Do This?

If the thought of using your computer and a modem to connect to government computers is enough to conjure up visions of FBI agents knocking at your door to confiscate your computer, you may be surprised by what you are about to read.

Many Federal Government agencies and state and local governments *prefer* that you use your computer, rather than a letter or a personal call, to contact them. Why? A letter requesting information from a government agency must be answered with a letter or a telephone call. A letter requires the time of a person to research the information you request and the time to write a response. The response requires paper, an envelope, postage, and the U.S. Postal Service for delivery to you. A voice telephone call to a government agency requires that someone answer the call, look up the information that you request, and provide it to you. In most cases, the information that you request was requested by others, probably by hundreds or thousands of other callers. To the person answering these "frequently asked questions," or FAQs, the job of providing the same information over and over again can become boring, if not mind-deadening. Computerizing the information that is most commonly requested and making it available 24 hours a day eliminates thousands of redundant inquiries and replies. With computers responding to redundant information requests, office staffs are freed up to spend more time with unique requests and to provide better service. Moreover, the methods for obtaining information electronically will likely expose you to new additional useful information you may not have known was available.

Getting information electronically provides instant gratification. Gone are the days (or weeks) of frustration while waiting for a big, brown envelope from a government agency to show up in your mailbox. Using *Government Online*, you can quickly determine if the information you need is available online. If the information is available, you can—using your computer, modem, and telephone line—obtain the information within minutes. Not only will you have nearly instant access to the information, you will have access to it in a form that can be used with your computer's wordprocessing, spreadsheet, database management, or image-processing software.

Many Federal and state agencies and local governments, have established electronic bulletin boards (BBSs) and Internet services to more efficiently and economically disseminate information to the public, other agencies, and personnel within agencies. Some of these systems simply post information that you can read, while others maintain files and programs that you may download (transmit files from their computer to your computer). You may also upload (transmit files from your computer to their computer) files and messages to many of these bulletin boards. The reports of the success and cost savings of these systems has caused a proliferation of new electronic bulletin boards and Internet services.

Although you can access an online government agency like the Department of the Treasury's Internal Revenue Service or the Pentagon, don't think for a moment that you can change your tax status or start a nuclear war. The electronic bulletin boards reached by the phone numbers listed in this book usually reside in desktop computers that have no connection whatsoever to government mainframe computers or computers containing top secret information. Security on government computers connected to the Internet is sufficient to prevent intentional or accidental misuse. So, don't worry about getting into a situation where you would be seeing information that you shouldn't see, or executing software that you shouldn't execute, or downloading restricted-use software or information.

However, there is one big difference between government-run online services and nongovernment ones. Deliberate attempts to damage a government online service by uploading software containing viruses or attempting to crash it (cause the electronic bulletin board or computer to shut down or destroy data) could result in extremely serious penalties including fines and prison time. As long as you don't intentionally try to cause mischief, you need not concern yourself with these issues.

Most of the electronic bulletin boards (BBSs) listed and described in this book can be accessed using no more than a computer, modem, telecommunication software, and a telephone. The computer you use to call government-operated BBSs need not be of any special type. An Apple™, Commodore™, IBM™ (or IBM™ compatible), Power PC™, and most other computers will work just fine. If the computer you use is a mainframe computer directly connected to the Internet, you may have even quicker access to government online services. Most government BBSs use IBM compatible equipment. There are few, if any, telecommunication software programs that will not work with these BBSs. If you have successfully called a local electronic bulletin board with your computer, you won't have difficulty calling government BBSs. Accessing government online services through the Internet may require state of the art computer hardware and software. If you are just learning to use computers, be patient. Accessing government online services is much easier than you may expect. Step-by-step instructions in the following sections will walk you through the process.

Who would find government online information services useful? Accountants, bankers, corporate executives, economists, educators, engineers, farmers, information brokers, investors, lawyers, librarians, physicians, pilots, researchers, scientists, and many other professionals make use of electronically obtained government information. If your profession isn't listed, don't feel left out. Access to government online services and information has been greatly democratized in the last few years. More services are being provided to more people than ever before. Now that public libraries, secondary schools, and other community-related institutions and organizations have begun providing public access to government online services, nearly everyone can benefit.

Not All Government Online Services Are Equally Valuable Resources

Some online services are modest systems offering common public domain and shareware programs and electronic messaging services and not much else. If there is government information that you would like to access by computer, that is not currently online, write to the agency director and request that the information be made available. If you would like to see an online government agency offer more information online, write a letter to the director of the agency and the SYSOP (systems operator) of the existing online service. Tell them what you want and why. You should also mention whether you would be willing to pay for such information or if you believe that access to the information should be free. Chances are that you will find the person you write to responsive and willing to assist.

Commercial services also provide access to Federal and state government information. One of the benefits of using commercial services to access government information is that they often format the information to meet the needs of their clients. This service can be especially valuable to database users and legislative data searchers. However, this efficiency comes at a price. Before paying a commercial service for government information, call the government agency that supplies the information and ask if it is available directly from them for a lesser fee or free. Sometimes commercial services simply collect the free data from the government and resell it.

Other Sources of Government Information

Not all online services providing access to government information are government run. Community-oriented Free-Net electronic bulletin board systems provide a wealth of local information and a way for individuals to communicate with each other and local government. Additionally, Free-Net users can communicate with physicians, psychologists, dentists, teachers, and other professionals to seek advice and share experiences. These community-based electronic bulletin boards are unique in that they are, as Free-Net originator Tom Grundner of Case Western Reserve University calls them, "Electronic cities." Instead of seeing the usual bulletin board menu items, such as files or message sections, Free-Net users choose from a menu that lists items like post office, administration building, school house, university circle, court house, hospital, and government house. Tom Grundner's fresh approach to online information sharing has spread to many cities around the world and has become the model for electronic cities of the future.

One of the pathways to reach government online services is through the Internet. The Internet is a huge, global computer network where users can access information, exchange e-mail, exchange public messages, and exchange files—including government information. For example, you can use the Internet to send mail to and receive mail from the President, Vice President, and some members of the U.S. Congress. It also has many other government-related uses. For example, I retrieved copies of Russian and American Cold War documents on display in an exhibition at the Library of Congress through the Internet. This exhibit was, perhaps, the first gallery exhibit made available online. More recently, I connected to the White House using a World Wide Web (WWW or Web) browser (a graphical hypertext navigational tool and a means of viewing documents containing text, images, sounds, and even video online), and listened to the meow of Socks, the White House cat.

The Internet is not easy to use. Even the well-written, well-researched, and readable texts on the Internet, like Ed Krol's *The Whole Internet*, Brendan Kehoe's *Zen and the Art of the Internet*, John R. Levine and Carol Baroudi's *The Internet for Dummies*, and John R. Levine and Margaret Levine Young's *More Internet for Dummies*, have difficulty overcoming the image of the Internet as an unapproachable morass of technical jargon and arcane commands. It is only the value of the resources available through the Internet that makes it worthwhile to learn the jargon and commands. Luckily, the number of commands needed to use the Internet effectively are relatively few. The jargon becomes second nature with experience. Commercial and noncommercial providers of Internet access are offering ever easier ways to get online and navigate the Net or Iway, as it is often called.

The future of government online information has great potential, but it is still in its infancy. More information needs to be made available in a more standardized way. Access needs to be easier and more intuitive. Although WWW browsing tools like NCSA Mosaic promise to provide easy access and navigation of the Internet, it is still barely operational and prone to frequent failures. Using NCSA Mosaic efficiently usually requires a direct (and costly) Internet connection. Only those people who can afford to access the Internet through a Point-to-Point Protocol (PPP) or better connection are able to use NCSA Mosaic or similar tools. And even a PPP connection is sluggish. Until the arrival of the Information Superhighway, those without expensive computer hardware and software resources will be left by the roadside. The larger population of computer and modem owners, those without direct Internet access, are limited to using electronic bulletin boards or text-based Internet services. An immediate shift from using electronic bulletin boards to NCSA Mosaic or other Internet servers to deliver government information would be a big mistake. It would cut off the free flow of government information to those who have limited computer resources—all those people who have computers and modems, but don't have, or can't afford, access to the Internet. For now, NCSA Mosaic is a flashy, elitist technology that benefits the technologically wealthy at the expense of the technologically poor. Between now and the arrival of the Information Superhighway at your doorstep, you may want to encourage your elected officials to install new and enhance older electronic bulletin boards with state-of-the-art hardware and software.

Ensuring that you have easy access to more information is partly up to you. If you want easier access to more and better information, ask for it. If you want to maintain access to existing online information services, let the service providers know that you appreciate their efforts. Send them some affirming electronic mail. Inform your Federal, state, and local elected representatives that you use and appreciate access to government online information. If you want to correspond with representatives electronically, call them and ask for their e-mail and Fax addresses. If they don't have an e-mail address or Fax number, ask why not. The more people call and ask, the more likely the representatives will go online.

How to Use This Book

With *Government Online*, you can quickly locate and use government online services. If you know exactly what you are looking for, the index may be the best place to start. If you don't have a specific information need in mind, browse through the book and read the descriptions and annotations of individual entries. If you don't know exactly what you are looking for, but know that you are interested in a specific branch of the U.S. Government, investigate the online services offered by the agencies within that branch.

The following is a list of the information requested from government online service providers:

I. Name of online service.

II. Government agency.

III. Acronym for online service.

IV. Internet addresses. (This section lists the electronic addresses of online services.) Address examples:

A.	telnet	fedworld.gov
B.	ftp	jplinfo.jpl.nasa.gov
C.	Gopher	gopher.financenet.gov
D.	WWW	URL (Uniform Resource Locator)
	1. http://www.financenet.gov	
E.	CompuServe	GO CABB

V. E-mail addresses. (E-mail addresses listed here may be for an auto-mailer. Auto-mailers respond to your e-mail by sending you a response. Some auto-mailers are quite sophisticated and respond to specific requests like requesting files or indexes. Others will only send you information on what message to send if you want more information. In other cases, the e-mail address may be the address of the system administrator. E-Mail addresses may also be used to subscribe to list servers, also known as Listservs. E-mail addresses are written like the following example: "info@financenet.gov.")

VI. Log on. (This provides you with information on how to log on to an online service. For example, if you connect to an anonymous ftp server you will usually use the word *anonymous* as your identification and your e-mail address as your password. However, this is not uniform or consistently used on all systems. Log on instructions found here will help you log on correctly. Unless otherwise noted, all log on procedures are standard BBS log on procedures.)

VII. Contact person & title.

VIII. Contact person's voice phone number.

IX. Mailing address.

X. Description. (The descriptions are usually drawn from information provided by the service provider. If you see the description enclosed within quotation marks, I have copied it directly from material provided by the information provider.)

XI. Annotation. (The annotation contains my comments on the quality of the online service, usage tips, and descriptions of additional useful information. Text in quotes was provided by the service provider.)

Where data was not available, the list category was removed to conserve space. Some online service providers only supply limited or no information about themselves and their personnel. Others, because of the type of service or the means of dissemination, do not supply specific resource information.

Why BBS Modem Speeds Are Not Listed in Government Online

You may have noticed that the speeds of the modems used by the electronic bulletin boards are not listed. There are several reasons for this. If you set your modem software to operate at your modem's maximum speed, it will most likely fall back to a slower speed if you connect to an online service operating at a slower speed. If you are using an older modem that operates at speeds below 1,200 bps (bits per second, also known as 'baud'), you may find that it won't be able to connect to some BBSs. Although the technical capability exists, some SYSOPs refuse to let users of 300 baud modems connect to their systems. The trend is for government agencies to upgrade their old modems to newer, faster ones whenever possible. As this book went to press the typical speed for modems was 14,400 bps, with 28,800 bps rapidly becoming the norm. If you are contemplating purchasing a modem, buy the fastest that you can afford. The faster modem will save you money in the long term by lowering your long-distance telephone costs and decreasing the amount of time spent on file transmissions.

Most technical terms and jargon are defined as they are discussed. If you encounter an unfamiliar term, refer to one of the how-to books described from time to time in the narrative or in the bibliography.

The list of government-related acronyms in the Appendix will help you decipher many of these you will encounter in your exploration of government online services.

Why I.P. Addresses Are Not Listed in Government Online

What is an I.P. address you may ask? I.P. is an abbreviation for Internet protocol and represents an electronic address numerically. I.P. addresses look like this: "192.231.192.1." Nearly all of the electronic addresses you find listed in *Government Online* are domain addresses. Domain addresses are translated into I.P. addresses when they are passed through the Internet. A domain address looks like this: "vice.president@whitehouse.gov." Domain addresses are more commonly used than I.P. addresses, probably because they are easier to recognize and remember.

PART
I

WHAT YOU NEED TO GET STARTED

Chapter I
THE BASICS

HOW THIS BOOK IS ORGANIZED

The organization of *Government Online* is based on the structure of the U.S. Government and follows the organization used in the *U.S. Government Manual* (now available online), a widely used and accepted government reference.

Federal government agencies are divided into three branches of the government: the Legislative, Executive, and Judicial. The listing within these branches is hierarchical, meaning that the agencies are presented in descending order of power and authority. There are also agencies within agencies, but *Government Online* does not list or describe subagency hierarchies. Independent agencies are listed alphabetically, as are online services within an agency.

I. Legislative

  A. The Congress

    1. Agencies Overseen by the Congress

II. Executive

  A. The President

    1. The Executive Office of the President

    a) Agencies Overseen by the President

III. Judicial

  A. The Supreme Court of the United States

    1. Courts Overseen by the Supreme Court

IV. Independent Establishments and Government Corporations

 V. States (alphabetically by name)

  A. Governor

    1. Legislative Bodies

    a) State Government Agencies

     1) Counties

     2) Cities

The following illustrations graphically represent the organizations of the U.S. Government.

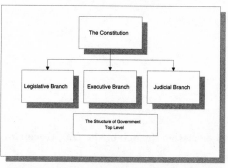

The Branches of the U.S. Government

```
┌─────────────────────────┐
│                         │
│    Legislative Branch   │
│                         │
└────────────┬────────────┘
             │
┌────────────┴────────────────────────────┐
│                                          │
│   The Congress                           │
│   Senate & House                         │
│   Architect of the Capitol               │
│   United States Botanic Garden           │
│   Government Accounting Office            │
│   Government Printing Office             │
│   Library of Congress                    │
│   Office of Technology Assessment        │
│   Congressional Budget office            │
│   United States Tax Court                │
│                                          │
└──────────────────────────────────────────┘
```

The Legislative Branch of the U.S. Government

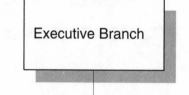

Executive Branch

The President
Executive Office of the President
White House Office
Office of Management and Budget
Council of Economic Advisors
National Security Council
Office of Policy Development
Office of National Drug Control Policy
National Critical Materials Council
Office of the U.S. Trade Representative
Council on Environmental Quality
Office of Science and Technology Policy
Office of Administration
National Space Council
The Vice President

Departments

The Executive Branch of the U.S. Government

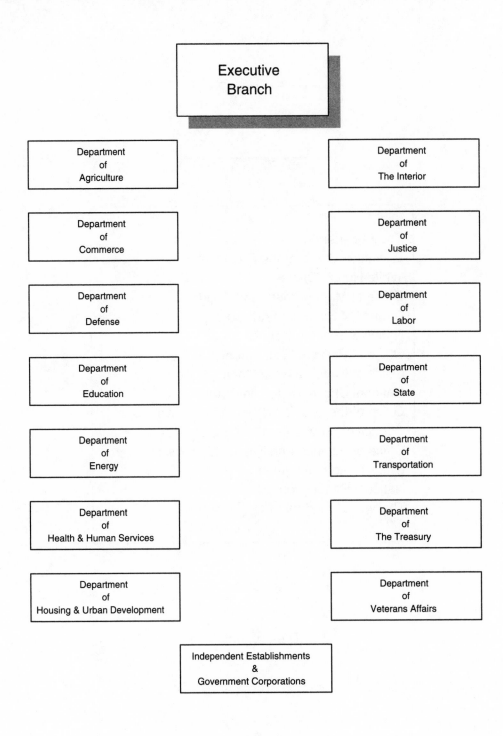

The Departments of the U.S. Government

```
                    ┌─────────────────────────┐
                    │                         │
                    │    Executive Branch     │
                    │                         │
                    └─────────────────────────┘
                                 │
              ┌──────────────────┴──────────────────┐
┌──────────────────────────────────┐  ┌──────────────────────────────────┐
│ ACTION                            │  │ National Foundation on the Arts and │
│ Administrative Conference of the U.S. │ │ Humanities                        │
│ African Development Foundation    │  │ National Labor Relations Board    │
│ Central Inteligence Agency        │  │ National Mediation Board          │
│ Commission on Civil Rights        │  │ National Railroad Passanger Corporation │
│ Commission on National and Community │ │ National Science Foundation       │
│ Service                           │  │ National Transportation Safety Board │
│ Commodity Futures Trading Commission │ │ Nuclear Regulatory Commission     │
│ Consumer Product Safety Commission │  │ Occupational Safety and Health Review │
│ Defense Nuclear Facilities Safety Board │ │ Commission                      │
│ Environmental Protection Agency   │  │ Office of Government Ethics        │
│ Equal Employment Opportunity      │  │ Office of Personnel Management     │
│ Commission                        │  │ Office of Special Counsel          │
│ Export-Import Bank of the U.S.    │  │ Panama Canal Commission            │
│ Farm Credit Administration        │  │ Peace Corps                        │
│ Federal Communications Commission │  │ Pennsylvania Avenue Development     │
│ Federal Deposit Insurance Corporation │ │ Corporation                       │
│ Federal Election Commission       │  │ Pension Benefit Guaranty Corporation │
│ Federal Emergency Management Agency │ │ Postal Rate Commission            │
│ Federal Housing Finance Board     │  │ Railrod Retirement Board           │
│ Federal Labor Relations Authority │  │ Resolution Trust Corporation       │
│ Federal Maritime Commission       │  │ Securities and Exchange Commission │
│ Federal Mediation and Conciliation │  │ Selective Service System          │
│ Service                           │  │ Small Business Administration      │
│ Federal Mine Safety and Health Review │ │ Tennessee Valley Authority        │
│ Commission                        │  │ Thrift Depositor Protection Oversight Board │
│ Federal Reserve System            │  │ Trade and Development Agency        │
│ Federal Retirement Thrift Investment │ │ U.S. Arms Control and Disarmament │
│ Board                             │  │ Agency                             │
│ Federal Trade Commission          │  │ U.S. Information Agency            │
│ General Services Administration   │  │ U.S. International Development      │
│ Inter-American Foundation         │  │ Corporation Agency                 │
│ Interstate Commerce Commission    │  │ U.S. International Trade Commission │
│ Merit Systems Protection Board    │  │ U.S. Postal Service                │
│ National Aeronautics and Space    │  │                                    │
│ Administration                    │  │                                    │
│ National Archives and Records     │  │                                    │
│ Administration                    │  │                                    │
│ National Capital Planning Commission │ │                                    │
│ National Credit Union Administration │ │                                    │
└──────────────────────────────────┘  └──────────────────────────────────┘
```

Independent Establishments and Government Corporations

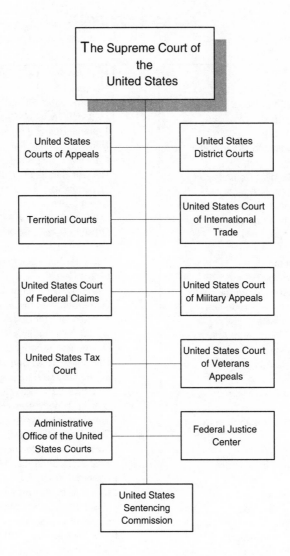

```
                    ┌──────────────────────┐
                    │  The Supreme Court of │
                    │          the          │
                    │     United States     │
                    └──────────────────────┘
                              │
      ┌──────────────────┐    │    ┌──────────────────┐
      │  United States    │───┼────│  United States    │
      │ Courts of Appeals │   │    │  District Courts  │
      └──────────────────┘    │    └──────────────────┘
                              │
      ┌──────────────────┐    │    ┌──────────────────┐
      │                   │   │    │ United States Court│
      │ Territorial Courts │──┼────│ of International   │
      │                   │   │    │       Trade        │
      └──────────────────┘    │    └──────────────────┘
                              │
      ┌──────────────────┐    │    ┌──────────────────┐
      │ United States Court│  │    │ United States Court│
      │ of Federal Claims  │──┼────│ of Military Appeals│
      └──────────────────┘    │    └──────────────────┘
                              │
      ┌──────────────────┐    │    ┌──────────────────┐
      │ United States Tax  │  │    │ United States Court│
      │      Court         │──┼────│ of Veterans        │
      └──────────────────┘    │    │      Appeals       │
                              │    └──────────────────┘
      ┌──────────────────┐    │    ┌──────────────────┐
      │  Administrative   │    │    │                   │
      │ Office of the United│──┼────│ Federal Justice   │
      │   States Courts    │   │    │     Center         │
      └──────────────────┘    │    └──────────────────┘
                              │
                     ┌──────────────────┐
                     │  United States    │
                     │   Sentencing      │
                     │   Commission      │
                     └──────────────────┘
```

The Judicial Branch of the United States Government

WHAT IS AN ONLINE SERVICE?

Practically speaking, an online service is an electronic means of distributing information to many people from one source. It is also a means for many people to concentrate information in one place. Online services often provide a central place where many people can share files and messages electronically. Assume, for the moment, that you represent a U.S. Government agency and you have a list of the names, addresses, Fax numbers, and telephone numbers of the members of the U.S. Congress that you want to make available to the public and government employees. You could make that information available instantly and provide access to the data around the clock using an online service. When the information is online, consumers of the information have a means of obtaining it quickly and inexpensively whenever they need it with little or no human intervention.

Suppose you, as a consumer, had compiled a list of all of the legislators in your state and you wanted to share it with others. An online service could provide you with the means to electronically send that information to a central point to store and distribute it. Other users of the online service would then have the opportunity to electronically request that copies of your data be sent to them without your intervention.

The term "online service" may often be used synonymously with the term "electronic bulletin board" or "bulletin board system" (BBS). How the terms differ is that an online service may include electronic bulletin boards and many other similar, but technically different, services. The term BBS usually refers to a specific kind of online service.

The term "online" refers to either a service or a part of a service that is available for electronic access. Most online services are constantly available. When a file is removed from an online service and is placed in storage, it is said to be off line. When an online service is turned off or becomes unavailable, it is said to be off line. In the context of this book, online refers to electronic bulletin boards, Internet services, and Fax on demand services.

A bulletin board service or BBS is usually a computer and a modem connected to a telephone line. This computer will use some kind of BBS software that enables it to answer the telephone and respond to commands from your computer. BBS software enables the BBS computer to exchange files and messages with you. BBSs vary a great deal in size, scope, and complexity. This description is based on a typical microcomputer-based BBS. Mini and mainframe computers may also provide similar services, but may not operate exactly the same way and may not use BBS software. Fortunately, the variety of computers and software programs operating online services are usually not important to online service users.

Usually?

I apologize for using the word *usually* so often. The reason for this is that there is a wide variety of hardware and software used to connect to and operate online services. The technical details are generalized for a reason. I want you to get online and start using government information as quickly as possible. If you become hungry for detailed technical information regarding telecommunications, consult some of the books listed in the bibliography.

HOW TO GET ONLINE

There are four essential items you need to get online from your home or business:

- Computer
- Telecommunication Software
- Modem (2,400 baud or faster)
- Telephone Service

Computers

The age, model, or power of the computer you use to get online is of little importance. Even old CP/M computers will work. In some cases, you don't even need a computer. It is possible to connect with an online service with nothing more than a terminal that has a keyboard and a modem and access to a telephone line. Of course, you won't be able to upload or download files

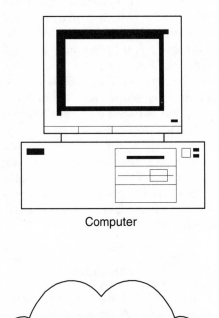

Computer

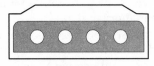

Modem

Online Service

Basic Computer Components Required to Connect to Online Services

using just a terminal. Having a computer with floppy disk drives or a hard disk is necessary for storing files. To download or upload files, you will need software to instruct your computer and modem to perform these tasks. Products that perform this function are often labeled as communication, telecommunication, or terminal software.

Telecommunication Software

The following are examples of communication software for MS-DOS™ and Apple™ computers:

MS-DOS™ and Microsoft Windows™ Computers

CrossTalk™ for DOS and Windows from DCA, 1000 Alderman Drive, Alpharetta, GA 30202-4199. 404-442-4930.

HyperAccess™ from Hilgraeve, Inc., Genesis Centre, 111 Conant Avenue, Suite A, Monroe, MI 48161. Voice 313-243-0576, Fax 313-243-0646, BBS 313-243-5915.

PROCOMM PLUS™ for Windows from Datastorm Technologies, Inc., P.O. Box 1471, Columbia, MO, 65205. Voice 314-443-3282, Fax 314-875-0595, BBS 314-875-0503.

Smartcom II™ from Hayes Microcomputer Products, Inc., P.O. Box 105203, Atlanta, GA 30348. 800-934-2937.

Apple™ Computers

CrossTalk™ for DOS and Windows from DCA, 1000 Alderman Drive, Alpharetta, GA 30202-4199. 404-442-4930.

Microphone II™ from Software Ventures Corporation, 2907 Claremont Avenue, Berkeley, CA 94705. 510-644-3232.

Smartcom™ from Hayes Microcomputer Products, Inc., P.O. Box 105203, Atlanta, GA 30348. 800-934-2937.

White Knight™ from The Freesoft Company, 105 McKinley Rd., Beaver Falls, PA 15010. 412-846-2700.

Confused and Lost?

If terms like computer, modem, and terminal seem like a foreign language to you, don't despair. There are books that will take you, painlessly, from not knowing anything about telecommunications to being moderately fluent. My favorites are published by Ziff-Davis Press:

- *How Computers Work* by Ron White
- *How to Use Your Computer* by Lisa Blow
- *How Networks Work* by Frank Derfler, Jr., and Les Freed
- *All About Computers* by Jean Atelsek
- *How to Use the Internet* by Mark Butler
- *How Macs Work* by John Rizzo and K. Daniel Clark

These books really are for beginners. They have lots of nicely drawn, easy-to-understand illustrations that demystify and simplify complex subjects.

If you own a computer with Microsoft Windows™ software installed, you already have a software program that will enable you to connect to online services. It is the Terminal program located in your Accessories Group. If you buy a new modem it will, most likely, come with telecommunication software that you can use to call government online services. Don't confuse proprietary software provided by commercial online services like America Online™, CompuServe™, Delphi™, and Prodigy™ with basic telecommunication software. The software you need will allow you to connect to any online service, not just one commercial service. Often the telecommunication software supplied with modems and operating systems is minimal, but just powerful enough to get you online. That is all you will need to connect to most government and nongovernment online services.

Modems

As with computers, government online services don't care what kind of modem you use. However, your computer will care. When shopping for a modem, look for one that is compatible with your computer. An internal modem designed for an Apple™ computer will not fit or work in an MS-DOS™ compatible computer. External modems will probably work with any computer, as long as you have the appropriate connecting cable and compatible software to operate it.

HOW TO LOG ON TO AN ONLINE SERVICE

Before calling an online service, you should have the following information about yourself handy:

Name, company, address, daytime and evening telephone number, password, and mother's maiden name.

With few exceptions, every BBS listed in this book will require that you fill out a questionnaire the first time you connect "log on" to the service. You will be asked to provide a password to use the next time you log in to the service. The password maximum length is usually eight characters.

Password Tips

• Don't tell anyone else your password.
• Don't use the same password for every online service.
• Don't use your name, telephone number, Social Security number, date of birth, driver's license number, your spouse's name, your children's names, your pets' names, your house number, or your street name as your password.
• Do use a mix of numbers and characters like 1XDR2GTY. This password is much harder to decipher than MAXLENT, but it is also harder to remember. (I've never used this password.)
• Do record your password on paper. It may be a factor of age, but I have been known to forget my password before I even logged off an online service. Some online services will pause after you enter your new password and display a message instructing you to copy the password onto paper.
• Do not provide credit card numbers unless you are absolutely sure it is appropriate. For example, some government agencies may require that you set up an account with them so that you may purchase documents online. Verify their request with a voice phone call before supplying credit card information.

Instruct your communications software to call the telephone number of the online service. This usually means providing a telephone number to the software so that it can place the call. If the telephone number is a long-distance call for you, add whatever long-distance code your telephone company requires in front of the area code. In my case, I must add the numeral 1 in front of the area code. If you are calling from an office that requires special numeric codes to reach an outside line, you will also have to include those codes as part of the telephone number.

Why So Much Security?

The same kind of mind that writes graffiti everywhere, shoots holes through the images of deer on highway signs, dumps poisonous chemicals along the roadside, and starts fires in national forests is at work in the computer world. There are creeps out there who delight in sneaking around online services looking for any opportunity to destroy them, erase files, create electronic viruses, lie, cheat, steal, and generally wreak havoc just for the perverted fun of it. They will use every trick they know to obtain someone else's name and password to log on to an online service. Once there, they will use whatever destructive tools they have. If they discover your name, telephone number, and password, they will use it instead of their own. They would much rather have you investigated or get the blame for their mischief.

SYSOPs are onto criminal intruders. They now have an arsenal of tools, like caller identification, to trace and locate bogus callers. Each new generation of BBS software has better safeguards against criminal intrusion. The simple childish techniques of breaking into BBSs have been checked. Only the advanced techno freaks still have some success breaking into government computers, but even these criminals are being caught now. When they are caught, the penalties are severe.

SYSOPs who request personal information like your mother's maiden name, are requesting it to protect you from becoming a victim. Someone knowing your name, telephone number, and address will not be able to call a SYSOP and request your password without knowing at least one additional highly personal piece of information.

Once connected, you will probably see an opening screen describing the online service you are connected to. If you don't, depress the Escape or Enter key on your keyboard a couple of times. Some BBS software programs require a signal from you before they display their opening or welcoming message. Sending Escape or Enter key codes provide that signal.

You will probably be asked to type your name. Some remote computers will request first and last names separately. Other online services may ask you to write your entire name on one line. Some online services will not ask for your name. (This is one of the many annoyances of nonstandardized software.) Type your name if requested. Assuming that you have never called this online service before, you will probably receive a message asking if your name was typed correctly. If you respond with a Y or yes, you will receive a message saying that your name was not found, followed by another message asking if you would like to register as a new user. Often, you will be asked to type the character "c" to represent that you want to register as a new user. Sometimes, depressing the Enter key will be all that is required.

Answering the registration question negatively will probably result in a good-bye message quickly followed by your computer being disconnected from the remote computer. Answering positively will result in your being asked a series of questions about yourself. These questions are rarely excessively personal. However, you may be asked for your mother's maiden name. The reason for requesting such a personal question is security. If you forget your password and call the SYSOP to request it, the SYSOP needs to be able to ask you a question to which no one else knows the answer. This is a means of verifying who you are. When the SYSOP knows for sure that you are who you say you are, they will provide you with your password. Don't be surprised if you also receive a lecture about the necessity of copying your password onto paper and storing it in a secure place. Telephone calls to SYSOPs regarding lost passwords are nuisance calls. If you had to answer a few thousand of these calls a year, you, too, would probably tire of it quickly. Don't blame the SYSOP for being a little testy when you call the second or third time about a lost password. Write your password on a piece of paper and avoid the aggravation.

Bulletins about the BBS will probably be displayed next. On some BBSs you will be given a choice of reading the bulletins or not. You may even be shown a list of bulletins and asked which, if any, you wish to read. BBS bulletins offer the SYSOPs an opportunity to introduce you to the BBS and inform you about changes such as the addition of a new telephone number, new files, new services, and general BBS news.

Once you have logged on and registered, you are free to explore the BBS. In most cases, you will be allowed to read and write electronic mail, move around and explore the BBS, upload or download files, and more.

The main menu is probably what you will see next. This menu will offer you a variety of choices including:

Files

File Directories: File directories are directories of files accessible for downloading from the BBS to your computer.

Download a File: When you find a file that you want to download, you use this command to tell the BBS to send you the file.

Download Batch: This feature is the same as above, but permits you to download more than one file per download command. Use this command to download a batch of files. Not all BBSs offer this service.

Upload File: Selecting this option permits you to upload a file to the BBS. Some government BBSs don't permit uploads.

Upload Batch: Selecting this feature enables you upload a batch of files with a single upload command.

Message Area

Comment to SYSOP: Selecting this option enables you to send a private or personal message to the SYSOP without having to use the messaging command directly.

Read Messages: Read messages tells the BBS that you want to read messages posted by other BBS users. This selection will offer you additional selections for choosing subject areas, dates, and message numbers within those subjects.

Enter Messages: This feature enables you to leave or post a message.

Quick Message Scan: This feature enables you to scan groups of messages by one of several parameters. For example, you could scan for messages from a specific person, about a particular subject, or since a specific date. In the scan mode, message titles will be displayed. Some BBS software programs permit you to tag messages for later reading.

Utilities

Help: Selecting the help option will provide you with information about the BBS and how to use BBS software commands.

Mode/Graphics: This option enables you to toggle from graphics mode to text mode. Graphics mode will often provide colorful, attractive menus with shaded boxes and some graphics. Text mode may still show boxes, but they will be simple line drawings. Text mode displays screens of information faster. If you are paying long-distance phone charges, use the text mode to save time and money.

Transfer Protocol: Using this command

tells the BBS what protocol you want to use to exchange files. Examples are ZMODEM, KERMIT, and XMODEM.

View Settings: This command displays the settings you have selected and permits you to change the settings.

Bulletins

Bulletin Listing: This is the area where BBS SYSOPs post bulletins about the BBS. For example, a SYSOP may announce new features, new files, or any other information that the SYSOP believes you should know about.

Questionnaire: This is usually the questionnaire that you fill out as a new user of a BBS. However, some SYSOPs may use this area as a means of asking you for an evaluation of the BBS and the files stored on the BBS.

Gateway

The existence of this command option means that the BBS provides a means of connecting with another BBS while logged onto the current BBS. An example of this is the gateway on FedWorld BBS. Through FedWorld you can gateway to more than 130 other BBSs.

Doors

Doors are areas of a BBS that have been set up as sub-BBSs. For example, a government BBS may have an area set aside just for government employees. Without permission granted by the SYSOP, you may not be able to access certain doors.

Conference

Join a Conference: Some BBSs have hundreds or even thousands of conferences dedicated to specific topics. By being divided into conferences, a large BBS can be easier to use. You can go quickly to the topic you are interested in by joining a conference. In some cases you may be able to join more than one conference.

Abandon a Conference: This command enables you to disassociate yourself from a conference.

Log Off

Good-bye (Hang Up): There is little mystery to this command. It simply means that you no longer wish to be connected to the BBS. On some BBSs you will be asked if you would like to leave a comment for the SYSOP before the connection is broken. This is an excellent opportunity to tell SYSOPs what you think of their BBS.

UNDERSTANDING SYSOPS

Systems Operators, more commonly called SYSOPs, are the people who operate bulletin board systems. Sometimes they have complete responsibility for the operation of a BBS. Other times, they may be part of a team that oversees the operation of a BBS. Government BBSs are sometimes run by independent contractors who do not use the term SYSOP. In these cases you may find that the person who operates the BBS or online service has the title of systems administrator, military officer, or contact.

SYSOP personalities range from megalomaniacs to benevolent gurus. The personality type of the SYSOP determines the look, feel, content, ease-of-use, and every other aspect of a BBS. The megalomaniacs usually introduce their BBS with several pages (or screens) of warnings about what will happen to you if you misuse their BBS. They will threaten you with the wrath of the entire government should you disobey their rules in any way. After reading the warnings, you may be

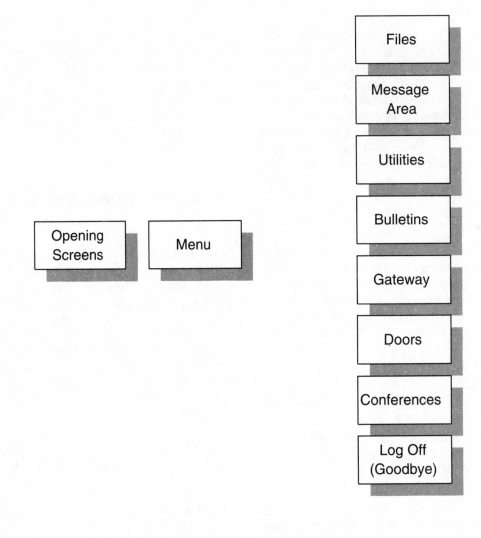

Files

Message
Area

Utilities

Bulletins

Gateway

Doors

Conferences

Log Off
(Goodbye)

Opening
Screens

Menu

How Electronic Bulletin Boards Are Organized

required to fill out an extensive, overly personal questionnaire. Even filling out the questionnaire probably won't get you access to their BBS right away.

You may have to wait until the SYSOP calls you or sends you a postcard to verify who you are. Finally, when you gain access to a megalomaniac's BBS you will find that there was little if anything there worth gaining access to. The files will, most likely, be old and out of date. There will be few, if any, messages to read or respond to, if there is a message section. Even after you have obtained access to the BBS, you will probably find that you have only limited access. Limited access means that parts of the BBS are reserved for only those persons having the personal blessing of the SYSOP. The SYSOP, spending every available minute on security and restrictions, probably didn't take the time to make their BBS worth using. There are few BBSs that still operate this way. Most are fossils from the Cold War who have never heard of Total Quality Management or reengineering.

Benevolent guru SYSOPs have the attitude that making government information available to you, the taxpayer, is their number one priority. They want you to have unrestricted access to their BBSs. They want you to have easy access to files, messages, bulletins, and press releases. They collect every public access document they can find and make it available to you. They may even measure their success in the numbers of new users who register to use their BBSs. Instead of telling you that you are being watched, they ask for your suggestions on how to make their service better. BBSs run by benevolent gurus will be the ones you tell your friends and colleagues about. They will be the ones that you write to your elected officials to praise. You are in luck, because there are more of these than any other. The BBSs that fall between the two extremes are moving in a positive direction. You can expect to see government BBSs improve in obvious ways in the future.

The best SYSOPs are client driven. They respond well to comments, suggestions, and constructive criticism. Let these SYSOPs know what you think. Leave them messages letting them know if you were able to find what you were looking for. Let them know what you like most and least about their BBSs. Be kind with your suggestions. Don't assume access to government BBSs is a right to which you are entitled. Government BBSs often exist as random acts of kindness on the part of government employees with vision and compassion. Don't assume that government BBSs are run by huge staffs with million dollar budgets. The staff may be one person. The equipment used for the BBS may have been scrounged and kept running with nothing more than tender loving care. Many of the government BBSs you call may be under-budgeted or have no budget at all. Government BBSs are often run by overworked and underpaid government employees whose main work responsibility probably has nothing to do with the BBS. These employees may be putting in unpaid hours to keep the BBSs functioning. Some are providing BBSs because they are thrilled at the prospect of making government work better. Support them. Sometimes a kind word from a happy client is just the boost beleaguered SYSOPs needs to make their labor worthwhile.

FILE COMPRESSION

To save hard disk space and speed up the transmission of files over phone lines and networks, online files are often compressed. File compression is a mathematical means of reducing the amount of storage space a file occupies. Compressed files will have file extensions like ZIP, ARJ, LZH, and ARC. The most common file type you will encounter on government BBSs will be ZIP. Should you download a file that is compressed you will need software to decompress it on your computer. If you plan to compress a file before transmitting it, you will need software to perform that as well. Files with the extension ZIP have been compressed with a program called PKZIP. To find a copy of the file compression software, look in the utility file directories of BBSs. File compression programs will most often have an ".EXE" extension. To use this type of file, download it and put it into a new directory and name that directory something like UTILITIES. Next execute (start) the program as you would any other program. The ".EXE" file will decompress and probably produce a number of new files which can then be used to compress or decompress files. A compressed file may contain more than one file. The process of combining many files into a single file for transmission to a remote computer is also a convenient feature of file compression programs. Apple™ computer users use Apple™ specific compression utilities and they use folders rather than directories to store files. Since most government BBSs contain files and programs written in or for MS-DOS™ computers, Apple™ computer users may feel left out. However, most compressed files can be decompressed by Apple™ specific software.

Connecting to Internet online services introduces additional complexities to the file compression process. The computers used to provide Internet online services are not often MS-DOS™ or Apple™ compatible computers. These online service providers may be using mini or mainframe computers using a UNIX operating system.

If you connect to a UNIX-based online service, there are a few commands and tips that you will need to know. The use of upper- and lowercase letters in the commands is important. For example, to list the files within a directory the command is (lowercase) ls not LS or Ls or lS.

ls takes the place of the DIR command in DOS and lists the files in the directory.

ls -l will list the files along with their sizes and date created. cd is the command used to change directory. This command works similar to the MS-DOS™ command cd.

File compression systems you may see on UNIX computers may have extensions like:

Extension	Compression Program
.pit	PackIt
.Sit	Suffit
.Z	compress
.z	pack
.ZIP	PKZIP
.zoo	zoo210

Each of the above compression schemes requires a specific program to decompress it. If you are using a UNIX-based computer system, ask your system administrator or technical support technician for advice on how to use these programs. Additionally, Ed Krol's *The Whole Internet* has a well-written section on this subject.

FILE TRANSFER PROTOCOLS

At some point in your exploration of government online services, you will find files that you will want to download. Instructing the remote computer to send you a file is easy and straightforward. The catch is that your computer and the remote computer must be using the same process in order to

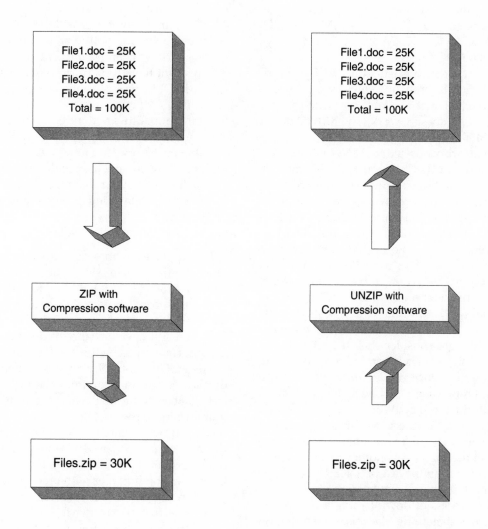

File1.doc = 25K
File2.doc = 25K
File3.doc = 25K
File4.doc = 25K
Total = 100K

File1.doc = 25K
File2.doc = 25K
File3.doc = 25K
File4.doc = 25K
Total = 100K

ZIP with
Compression software

UNZIP with
Compression software

Files.zip = 30K

Files.zip = 30K

Compressing and Expanding Files

exchange files. These processes are known as file transfer protocols. The most commonly used protocol is ZMODEM because of its speed and reliability. Other protocols you may encounter include XMODEM, 1K-XMODEM, KERMIT, 1K-XMODEM-G, YMODEM, YMODEM-G, and ASCII.

If you are connected to a BBS by phone, ZMODEM is probably your best choice. If ZMODEM is not available as a choice, or if ZMODEM doesn't work, try XMODEM or KERMIT.

If you are connected to a BBS or online service through the Internet, KERMIT may be the only file transfer protocol that works, if any transfer protocol works. For example, if you connect to FedWorld through their telephone number, you can use ZMODEM or any of the other protocols they list to successfully download files from FedWorld. If you connect to FedWorld through an Internet service provider and use TELNET to connect to FedWorld, KERMIT will probably be the only protocol that works. If this is not complex enough, consider this. It is possible to use an Internet service provider to connect to the Internet. Once you are there, you can use a program called TELNET to connect to FedWorld. From FedWorld you can use their Gateway to connect to BBSs outside of FedWorld. The BBS you connect to may permit connecting to yet another BBS. To download a file from the last BBS, KERMIT will be the most likely protocol to work.

The process of downloading a file from a BBS goes something like this, depending on the way a BBS is set up:

1. Select a file and then use an instruction, like the character "D", to start the download process.
2. The remote computer will then display a list of download protocols available. Often, you will be asked to select a file transfer protocol when you register as a new user. That protocol will remain in effect until it is manually changed.
3. Select one that is compatible with your software and press Return.
4. The remote computer will then display a message telling you to start your download. (If you are using ZMODEM you may not have to perform the next steps. ZMODEM will continue the process for you.)
5. Tell your software to receive a file.
6. Your software will display a list of available protocols. If your software permits, you may assign a specific protocol to each entry in your dialing directory.
7. Select the matching protocol and press Return.
8. The file transmission will begin.

If you get error messages that eventually cause the file transmission to abort, try using another protocol. XMODEM or KERMIT are your best second choices. If these also fail, try using a slower speed connection. If even this fails, you still have a chance of downloading text information using the ASCII protocol.

The ASCII protocol provides a means of displaying files in a continuous flow. To collect what is being displayed, set your communications software to capture whatever is displayed on the monitor to a file. Next, tell the remote computer to perform an ASCII transmission. If you have been having problems downloading files with other protocols, you can expect to see garbled characters from time to time during the transmission. ASCII protocol will not reliably transmit programs. It only works with plain text files. On noisy telephone lines, the ASCII protocol will often transmit patches of garbage characters during a transmission.

Uploading files is basically the same procedure, but you have to tell the BBS that you are sending a file and then send it using the same procedures.

Chapter 2
THE INTERNET

Government agencies are connecting to the Internet at a rapid pace. Over the course of a few months, I have seen government agencies show up in the world of online services as electronic bulletin boards and then quickly evolve into Internet service providers. Once on the Internet, they quickly move on to provide information through a hypertext searching tool used to explore the Internet, the World Wide Web (WWW). More recently, government agencies have been bypassing the electronic bulletin board phase and going directly online by establishing a WWW home page.

Everyone seems to be talking about the Internet, but few people can describe it without considerable cogitation. The Internet is hard to describe because of its vastness and complexity. However, there are ways to visualize it in human terms.

One way of visualizing the Internet is to compare it to the global structure of voice telephone service. Visualize all of the telephones in your neighborhood connected by telephone lines to all of the telephones in your city. Visualize all of the telephones in your city connected by telephone lines to all of the telephones in your state. Visualize all of the telephones in your state connected by telephone lines to all of the telephones in the U.S. Visualize all of the telephone lines in the U.S. connected by more telephone lines to all of the telephones in the world. The result of this exercise should be a mental image of a global matrix of hundreds of millions of telephones connected by as many or more wires to other telephones.

To imagine the Internet, replace the image of telephones with computers and the image of telephone lines with network cables. The result should resemble the matrix formed by the telephone system. If you want to exercise your gray matter to the maximum, try to visualize the computer networks also connected by telephone lines—which they often are. If you still have any space left for visualizing, imagine all of the computer networks interlinked interactively with all of the cable television installations in the world. The Internet is often described as a network of networks, and that description fits our visualization.

At the human level, you don't often visualize the entire telephone network every time you make a telephone call. Likewise, at the human level, it is not necessary to visualize the entirety of the Internet to connect to it or use it. Whether you are connecting to a BBS, a corporate mainframe computer, or the Internet, you are still one person using an electronic means of communicating. What differs is the scale of resources available.

If you use your computer to connect to a politician's local electronic bulletin board

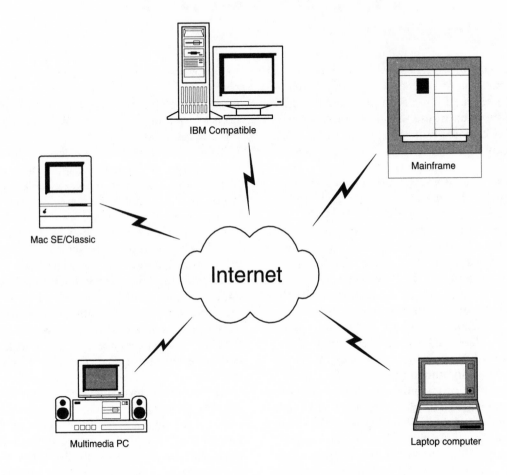

IBM Compatible

Mainframe

Mac SE/Classic

Internet

Multimedia PC

Laptop computer

Accessing the Internet

The Internet Is Not the Information Superhighway

The Internet and the Information Superhighway are not the same thing. The Internet exists and is growing. The Information Superhighway does not exist, except in political rhetoric. You will recognize the Information Superhighway when it reaches your house. It will provide you with open access to something like the Internet at speeds many times (preferably hundreds of times) faster than what is currently available.

It will provide you with an easy-to-use interface. It will offer a wide range of advanced applications. It will be free or very inexpensive. Insider rumors say that the Information Superhighway is years away, if it ever happens at all. Some say that the technology does not yet exist to create the Information Superhighway. What may keep it from happening is expense. Who will pay for the infrastructure and the support it will require is in question. The U.S. Government is more likely to cut back on funding for such projects in its current rush to cut spending. Corporations will want to recoup the expense of such a project quickly. That translates into expensive user fees. The Information Superhighway is a super idea. It is too soon to predict if it will ever exist. In the meantime, expect to see the term incorrectly applied to government and commercial products and services.

and post a message about a law soon to be voted on, your message may not be read by more than a few hundred people locally (or a few thousand if the BBS is linked to a national BBS network). If you post the same message somewhere on the Net, your message might be read by hundreds of thousands or more. There is a price to be paid if you want to use the Internet rather than a local BBS. The BBS probably doesn't charge for access. Full Internet access can be costly. Electronic bulletin boards are easy to use. The Internet is not.

If the Internet is difficult to define, hard to use, and costly to access, you may ask why is the world scrambling to use it or be a part of it? In a word, the answer is resources. There are so many resources on the Internet that you could easily spend the rest of your life interacting full-time with one small part of it. From subjects like AIDS to Zebra Mussels, the Internet is an ever-expanding storehouse and disseminator of information and exchange of discussion. It is becoming a means of commerce. If you are willing to invest the time and money to gain access to the Internet, you will be rewarded by a cornucopia of data flowing through your computer.

The popularity of the Internet has lead to a decline in its usefulness. Establishing connections with popular government Internet resources, like FedWorld, used to be instantaneous. Now, making that same connection may not be possible during the day because the Internet is clogged with others seeking the same resources. If you find the Internet too slow for your needs, try calling the dial-up BBS of the relevant government agency you are interested in contacting instead. BBSs are often easier to reach with a telephone line connection than an Internet connection. Additionally, file download speeds are often much faster through a dial-up connection than through indirect Internet connections.

INTERNET TOOLS

Once in a while, I read weekly news magazine stories about scientists working on a theory that promises to unify all of the theories of physics. While the endeavor sounds noble, it is far too remote for me to relate to. What I would like to see is the same amount of effort and time spent on a unified computer theory. I dream of the day that someone like Microsoft's president, Bill Gates, will wake up thinking about my theory. He will say to himself, "Why do computer users have to learn a new language, new commands, new file structures, new file names, new file name extensions, and new jargon when they connect their home computers to mainframes and to the Internet?" With a jolt, he will sit up in bed and jot a reminder to himself, on his personal digital assistant, to unify all computer commands for all operating systems or replace all of the commands with icons. He will add that all names, addresses, telephone numbers, Fax telephone numbers, Internet addresses, and E-mail addresses that a computer user accrues should be stored in one software application that is accessible by all other applications. Are you listening, Bill?

For now, we are stuck with the fact that every computer operating system has a unique set of commands that perform day-to-day tasks like deleting files, opening directories, saving files, and so on. Leaving the security of your home or office to explore the Internet, you will encounter computers that will require you to learn unique, and often confounding, commands. Fortunately, just like traveling in foreign lands, knowing a few important phrases, like "where is the bathroom?" will be enough to get you where you want to go.

The Internet has tools that are particularly useful in tracking down government online resources. (Here we go again; new words to memorize.) These tools can be grouped into several categories.

Searching Tools

Wide Area Information Servers (WAIS): WAIS provides a means of searching online databases by keywords.

Archie: Archie enables you to find the location on the Internet of a file that you know the name of.

Veronica: A means of searching for specific Gopher directories and files.

Navigating Tools

Gopher: Gophers are menus of menus of menus. Gophers are an easy way to navigate around the Internet by simply making selections from menus.

NCSA Mosaic: Mosaic is an emerging means of graphically browsing the WWW. Still primitive and crash prone, it promises to be a major influence on how the Internet of the future will look, especially for those who can afford PPP/SLIP, ISDN, or better Internet connections.

TELNET: telnet is a means of connecting your computer to another distant computer so that the distant computer behaves as though it were your computer.

World Wide Web (WWW): The World Wide Web or WWW is a hypertext means of navigating the Internet. You select highlighted or underlined keywords to move from one resource to another.

File Acquiring Tools

File Transfer Protocol (FTP): FTP is a means of transferring files through the Internet. FTP enables you to connect to another computer through the Internet, log on, and then exchange files. Using FTP creates an impression that the remote computer is just another disk drive on your computer.

The most common commands you will

use are ASCII, binary, cd, dir, D, and get. Once you have logged on to another computer, you will probably want to explore the directories listed. To display a list of directories and files in the current directory, type "dir." To change directories, use the "cd" command followed by the directory name. Before starting a download procedure for a binary file (a file with a ".bin", ".zip", or other extension reflecting that the file is compressed or contains binary codes), type "binary" and press the "Enter" key. If the file you want is an ASCII or text file, type "ASCII" and press "Enter." Next, type "get" and the name of the file and press "Enter." The file will be transmitted. If you are using an intermediate host, like a university computer, to log onto the Internet, you may be able to use the "D" command followed by the file name to download a file directly to your computer. Some commercial FTP programs make exchanging files with an FTP host a simple matter of dragging and dropping filenames between windows.

E-mail: Some government information providers will send you files in response to e-mail requests. This means that you can obtain government information even if you don't have direct or full access to the Internet. For example, you could send an e-mail message requesting a file to a government information provider through CompuServe, America Online, a local electronic bulletin board, or other online service provider, and receive the file as an e-mail message.

Information Exchange Tools

LISTSERV: List servers are subscription services. They enable you to join a community of other Internet users to share information on a specific topic. When you subscribe to a list server, electronic mail generated by every subscriber is sent to every other subscriber including you. When you respond to a message, your response is then sent to every other subscriber of the list server.

The best list of list servers I found was compiled by Stephanie da Silva at MIT. It is archived and available by anonymous ftp from rtfm.mit.edu under the directory /pub/usenet/news.answers/mail/mailing-lists. For WWW users, the URL is: http://rtfm.mit.edu/pub/usenet/news.answers/mail/mailing-lists/. Be warned, da Silva's list comes in 14 sections and is about 125 pages long. Although it is long, its length testifies to the number of list servers there are to choose from. The variety and range of subjects covered by list servers is awesome.

USENET: USENET is a collection of bulletin boards called newsgroups. Unlike Listservs, the information posted on USENET must be searched out and read or subscribed to. However, when you subscribe to a USENET topic, you will not receive the information by electronic mail. Instead, you will use a USENET reader to scan through posting summaries and select those postings you want to read.

If you hunger for more depth and detail about Internet tools and procedures, I recommend that you read *The Internet for Dummies* by Levine and Baroudi, *More Internet for Dummies* by Levine and Young, and *The Whole Internet* by Ed Krol. Krol's book is a required desk reference. You may find that other how-to books will help you to understand the Internet with less effort, but Krol's book will be the one you will need to get you through difficult problems. Don't enter cyberspace without it. If you don't have time to read a book on using the Internet, buy a copy of Peter Kent's *10 Minute Guide to the Internet*. Kent puts every basic command you will need to get real work done on the Internet in one small concise book. I have it open, on my desk, every day.

Mosaic

As you overcome the barriers to accessing the Internet there will be still more challenges ahead. You will probably hear converts extolling the virtues of Mosaic. Don't get overly excited by what you hear. Mosaic is a graphical hypertext browser designed to navigate the World Wide Web. What it does is provide you with a means of exploring the Internet by using a mouse. It is basically a point-and-click navigation tool. It is colorful, it can play audio, and it can display video. Mosaic shows great promise, but in its first manifestations it is often unstable and extremely slow when used through dial-up Internet providers.

The National Center for Supercomputer Applications's (NCSA) NCSA Mosaic, during the writing of this book, was in Alpha testing. In the world of product development, Beta testing follows Alpha testing. Only after Beta testing is complete is a full product usually introduced. A working final version of the

---

The NCSA on Mosaic

"NCSA Mosaic is a network navigational tool that allows the user access to networked information with the click of a button. The Internet is the primary source of this world wide information. With more and more people using the Internet the amount of information available is literally exploding. NCSA Mosaic was designed to provide the user transparent and seamless access to nearly all of these information sources and services. NCSA Mosaic gives the user a mechanism that will retrieve and display a wide variety of data types. These data types typically include text, image, movie and audio files."

NCSA Mosaic still may not be available by the time you read this. Versions of NCSA Mosaic, licensed by the University of Illinois at Urbana-Champaign, are available as commercial products from several companies. When I use the term Mosaic I am referring to NCSA Mosaic and licensed products based on NCSA Mosaic generically.

NCSA Mosaic was available for MS-DOS™ Windows, Apple™ Macintosh, and Digital Equipment Corporation™ (DEC™) computers at the time *Government Online* was compiled.

Are you excited by NCSA's description of NCSA Mosaic? I was, at the start of what turned out to be a complex, expensive, mostly unsuccessful, and often perilous experiment using it. NCSA Mosaic suffered the usual ills of first-generation software and emerging technology. I suffered misleading sales pitches, uninformed or non-existent customer support, computer crashes, lost data, and frustration attempting to use NCSA's and commercial versions of NCSA Mosaic. I also experienced moments of near ecstasy when Mosaic worked correctly. Visiting the White House home page and listening to the White House cat, Socks, meow was conceptually exciting and fun. However, it took two days of attempts to connect to the White House WWW server and it was not possible to explore all of the White House pages during a single session, because the versions of Mosaic software I was using crashed frequently.

Using the current versions of Mosaic on home-based computers is slow and tedious even using a 28,800 bps PPP connection. Until connections to the Internet are speeded up or replaced by the Information Superhighway, Mosaic is a useful tool only to those who can afford high-speed connections to the Internet.

For now, Mosaic is a spectacularly beautiful, but horribly slow and often maddeningly unreliable emerging technology. If you are more interested in getting work done than looking at totally cool formatted text with audio and graphics, use electronic bulletin boards or text-based Internet connections while the Information Superhighway, WWW, and Mosaic evolve a little more.

USENET

To visualize USENET, imagine a supermarket bulletin board that has been organized into sections dealing with specific topics. On this imaginary bulletin board you might find a "for sale" section and beneath that you might find an "autos for sale" section and beneath that you might find an "autos for sale-Fords" section. To visualize USENET, imagine all of the people connected to the Internet—tens of millions—using an electronic version of a bulletin board. Imagine expanding the topics to include discussions, graphics, sounds, and more. Imagine this electronic bulletin board uncensored. You now have in your mind a conceptual picture of USENET. There were more than 10,000 topics listed on USENET when I last checked and the number shrinks and grows daily, but mostly grows.

Bear in mind that USENET is not the best Internet resource for online government information. USENET's content is mostly discussion about topics. You may find USENET useful for posting messages searching for information, especially government online information.

If you have access to the Internet, you probably have access to USENET. If you don't have access to the Internet, but would like to access USENET, explore local BBSs. Some of them subscribe to some, or all, USENET groups. If you belong to a commercial online service like CompuServe, America Online, or Delphi, check with customer service to find out what, if any, access you have to USENET.

USENET NEWSGROUPS: The following list of USENET groups was assembled from a list of USENET groups obtained from the Internet. The list was then searched for keywords such as "gov" and "politics." The resulting list was further narrowed by editing out groups that didn't seem to have Federal or state government subject matter. You may come up with a different list that better fits your needs by searching the list of USENET groups by different keywords.

    alt.politics.bush
    alt.politics.clinton
    alt.politics.democrats
    alt.politics.democrats.clinton
    alt.politics.democrats.d
    alt.politics.democrats.governors
    alt.politics.democrats.house
    alt.politics.democrats.senate
    alt.politics.economics
    alt.politics.elections
    alt.politics.libertarian
    alt.politics.media
    alt.politics.org.ccr
    alt.politics.org.cia
    alt.politics.org.covert
    alt.politics.org.fbi
    alt.politics.org.misc
    alt.politics.org.nsa
    alt.politics.org.un
    alt.politics.usa.constitution
    alt.politics.usa.misc
    alt.politics.usa.republican
    bit.listserv.govdoc-l
    clari.nb.govt
    clari.news.usa.gov.financial
    clari.news.usa.gov.foreign_policy
    clari.news.usa.gov.misc
    clari.news.usa.gov.personalities
    clari.news.usa.gov.politics
    clari.news.usa.gov.state+local
    clari.news.usa.gov.white_house
    nptn.govt.governors-office
    nptn.govt.memory.house
    nptn.govt.memory.house-102

nptn.govt.memory.senate
nptn.govt.memory.senate-102
nptn.govt.public-officials

CHEAP INTERNET CONNECTIONS

Cheap is good. Free is better. The first place to look for free access to the Internet is at your local public library. If they don't have access, ask a reference librarian to help you locate local and national Internet providers. Computer clubs, local BBSs, educational institutions, telephone companies, and computer retailers are also good sources of information. If you are enrolled in, or teach at, an educational institution, you may already have access to the Internet. If you are an alumnus of a college or university, check with their computer department to see if you qualify for a free or inexpensive Internet account. If you are employed by a corporation, your employer may already have access to the Internet. If your employer has access to the Internet and maintains a local area network, your gaining access to the Internet may only be a matter of requesting an account. If you access the Internet through an employer's computer, keep your access work-related.

The names and telephone numbers of commercial Internet access providers are advertised and listed in computer magazines and some of the books mentioned throughout *Government Online*. More advertisements may be found in your local newspapers and magazines and national computer magazines. Also, contact:

- local computer stores
- telephone companies
- library reference or science librarian
- computer clubs and organizations

PDIAL

Another source of information about Internet access providers is Peter Kaminski's list of Internet service providers, PDIAL. However, when I checked Kaminski's list recently, almost a year had passed since it was updated. He describes his list as "...a list of Internet service providers offering public access dialins and outgoing Internet access (ftp, telnet, etc.). Most of them provide e-mail and USENET news and other services as well."

To obtain Kaminski's list follow Kaminski's instructions. "...send email containing the phrase 'Send PDIAL' to 'info-deli-server@net-com.com'.

To be put on a list of people who receive future editions as they are published, send email containing the phrase 'Subscribe PDIAL' to 'info-deli-server@netcom.com'.

To receive both the most recent and future editions, send both messages."

You may also find the PDIAL file available from BBSs.

While shopping for an Internet service provider, ask what kind of Internet service connection they provide. The most commonly advertised providers offer indirect connections, PPP/SLIP connections, and ISDN connections.

An example of an indirect connection is one where you use your computer and a modem to connect to the provider's computer by phone line. Once connected, you use Internet software on the provider's computer to access the Internet. This type of connection is likely to be the least expensive, but not provide full access to the Internet.

PPP/SLIP connections enable you to have full access to the Internet, including Mosaic, at a higher cost. A high-speed modem is strongly recommended for this type of connection.

ISDN connections are still more expensive to use and require high-cost, specialized telecommunication hardware, but provide faster full connection to the Internet.

The best buy of this group is the PPP connection. Flat fee rates of $20 per month or less are not unusual for PPP service in large cities. Software necessary to connect your computer to a PPP service provider can be purchased for as little as $100 and is sometimes included as part of a sign-up package.

Chapter 3
COMMERCIAL ONLINE SERVICE PROVIDERS

The following commercial online services provide some government information directly or indirectly from government agencies. The trend is for the commercial online services to offer partial access to the Internet, thus providing access to government online services. Delphi was one of the first of the commercial online services to offer Internet access. However, not all of the commercial online services listed below offer direct access to the Internet. What they may offer you is indirect access through their online service. It is their online service that connects to the Internet. They may ask you to use their software to access services like USENET. They may also censor what newsgroups you have access to. To have direct access to the Internet requires at least a Point-to-Point Protocol (PPP) or better connection.

America Online
America Online, Inc., 8619 Westwood Center Drive, Vienna, VA 22182-2285
Voice: 800-827-6364

CompuServe
CompuServe Information Services, 5000 Arlington Centre Boulevard, P.O. Box 20212, Columbus, OH 43220
Voice: 800-848-8199

Delphi
Delphi Internet Services Corporation, 1030 Massachusetts Avenue, Cambridge, MA 02138

Voice: 800-522-3567

GEnie
GEnie, P.O. Box 6403, Rockville, MD 20848-6403
Voice: 800-638-9636

Prodigy
Prodigy Services, Co., 445 Hamilton, White Plains, NY 10601
Voice: 914-448-8811

Chapter 4

COMMERCIAL ONLINE INFORMATION PROVIDERS

Before you decide to pay a commercial online information provider for government information, call the government agency providing the information to see if it is available online for free. However, commercial online information providers can often save you time and money by providing you information quicker and in a format that may be more usable than what is provided directly from government agencies.

The following list of commercial online information providers is not provided as an all-inclusive list. These companies were the ones that I saw mentioned most often or were described to me by government agencies. Check with your public library's reference librarian to find other similar services.

NATIONAL

BRS

8000 Westpark Drive, McLean, VA 22102
Voice: 703-442-0900. Fax: 703-893-4632

DESCRIPTION

"BRS Online Products (BRS), a division of infoPro Technologies, is one of the world's preeminent electronic information services. Through its four principal product lines—BRS Online Service, BRS Colleague, BRS After Dark (available only in North America), and BRS Morning Search (available only in Europe)—BRS offers convenient, timely and cost-effective access to information in medicine, the biosciences, science, health, and related interdisciplinary areas."

Counterpoint Publishing

84 Sherman Street, Cambridge, MA 02140
Voice: 800-998-4515 or 617-547-4515. Fax: 617-547-9064
Internet: fedre@internet.com

DESCRIPTION

Counterpoint Publishing, Inc., provides fee-based access to the Federal Register through

Gopher/WAIS, NNTP (Usenet News), and telnet.

DIALOG
Information Services, Inc.

One Commerce Square, 2005 Market Street,
Suite 1010, Philadelphia, PA, 19103
Voice: 215-587-4400. Fax: 415-858-7076

DESCRIPTION

"Contained in the DIALOG information collection are millions of documents drawn from more sources than any other online service—from scientific and technical literature—from full-text trade journals, newspapers, and newswires.... Compiled from the world's most respected and authoritative information sources, DIALOG databases can provide you with instant answers from just one source."

HandsNet

20195 Stevens Creek Blvd., Suite 120,
Cupertino, CA 95014
Voice: 408-257-4500

DESCRIPTION

HandsNet provides, in addition to a wide range of information, documents from The Corporation for National Service.

Mead Data Central

860 Clinton Square, Rochester, NY 14604
Voice: 800-554-8986

DESCRIPTION

Mead Data Central provides government online information through their Lexis & Nexis online services.

STN International

Chemical Abstracts Service, 2540 Olentangy River Road, P.O. Box 3012, Columbus, OH 43210-0012
Voice: 800-753-4227

DESCRIPTION

"STN International, the scientific and technical information network, is an online service providing direct access to more than 160 scientific and technical databases."

"STN databases offer information on a wide variety of technical topics, including government regulations."

West Publishing
Corporation

620 Opperman Drive,
Eagan, MN 55123-1308
Voice: 612-687-8000

DESCRIPTION

"WESTLAW™ is the nation's premier computer-assisted legal research (CALR) service with over 5,000 databases and extensive editorial enhancements. Researchers can use WIN™ , a natural language search method, voice activation access or Boolean searching to conduct research on WESTLAW™." I have listed West Publishing Corp. primarily because the United States Supreme Court refers inquiries about their online data to West Publishing Corp.

STATE

Arizona

Arizona News Service, Inc.

P.O. Box 2260, Phoenix, AZ 85002

DESCRIPTION

Arizona News Service, Inc., provides online access to Arizona state government information. They offer legislative bill information online.

California

Legi-Tech

1029 J Street, Suite 450,
Sacramento, CA 95814
Voice: 916-447-1886. Fax: 916-447-1109

DESCRIPTION

"Legi-Tech has been an industry leader in online legislative tracking for over a decade. Via a computer, modem and modem communication software, our subscribers have access to exceptionally accurate and timely legislative information from California, New York and Washington, D.C. Online users include trade associations, lobbyists, law firms, public interest organizations, as well as state and local government entities. These groups have the ability to view bill statuses, histories, summaries, introductions, full text, committee

and floor analyses, calendar information, plus much more."

Florida

Florida Business Network

516 North Adams Street, P.O. Box 784,
Tallahassee, FL 32302
Voice: 904-224-7173. Fax: 904-224-6532

DESCRIPTION

The Florida Business Network provides fee-based access to an on-line database of Florida government legislation.

Louisiana

LEGISCON

P.O. Box 1643, Baton Rouge, LA 70821
Voice: 504-343-9828

DESCRIPTION

LEGISCON provides full text of Louisiana Legislature bills, amendments, and substitutes as well as other online information services.

Michigan

CONGWER News Service, Inc.

630 Michigan Tower, Lansing, MI 48933
Voice: 517-482-3500. Fax 517-482-4367

"CONGWER News Service publishes daily legislative reports in Ohio—since 1906—and in Michigan—since 1962. The emphasis is on reporting legislative activities, but both reports include coverage of virtually all state and government activities, including the courts. A weekly report on the Supreme Court of Ohio is published in Ohio. Both states also publish special reports, directories of state government officials and elections materials including overnight election results and candidate directories."

New Jersey

Government News Network

Capitol Information Service, Inc.,
172 West State Street, P.O. Box 2041,
Trenton, NJ 08607

DESCRIPTION

The Government News Network provides on-line information on and coverage about the New Jersey Legislature and Office of the Governor.

New York

Legi-Tech of New York

1 Steuben Place, Mezzanine Level,
Albany, NY 12207
Voice: 518-434-2242. Fax: 518-433-0689

DESCRIPTION

See Legi-Tech under California.

Ohio

CONGWER News Service, Inc.

17 S. High St., Suite 630,
Columbus, OH 43215
Voice: 614-221-1992. Fax: 614-221-1992

DESCRIPTION

See CONGWER under Michigan.

Oklahoma

Oklahoma Business News Company

Leroy A. Ritter Publisher, 605 NW 13th,
Suite C, P.O. Box 1177,
Oklahoma City, OK 73101
Voice: 405-521-1405. Fax: 405-521-0457

DESCRIPTION

Oklahoma Business News Company provides online information on Oklahoma State Legislative activities.

Oklahoma Stateline, Inc.

1615 N. Lincoln Blvd.,
Oklahoma City, OK 73104
Voice: 405-235-6661. Fax: 405-235-6676

DESCRIPTION

"StateLine is a database retrieval system for the timely recall of governmental information for the State of Oklahoma as well as seventeen other major States and Congress. All operations are menu driven for ease of use. On-line help is provided by a single key for any field throughout the entire array of functions. StateLine is compatible with virtually all computers ranging from personal computers to corporate mainframes. The system is updated continually with legislative, committee and state agency information. Custom report generation is available for customer specific legislation."

Legi-Tech

508 East Union, Olympia, WA 98051
Voice: 360-754-2534

DESCRIPTION

See Legi-Tech under California.

Chapter 5

WHERE TO LOOK FOR MORE INFORMATION

New sources of public access government online information are rapidly becoming available. The speed of the proliferation is much faster than the speed of the process of book publishing. That means that information you are looking for may be available, but not yet listed in this book. Finding new online information resources can be as easy as asking for directions. Where and whom you ask for directions may determine whether you are successful.

If you have an idea of what kind of information you are looking for, the next step is to find out what government agency collects that information. A call or visit to your public library reference desk is often the most efficient and successful means of obtaining this information. Once you have found the name and telephone number of the agency, call them and ask if they provide public access to electronic information. If the person you speak with doesn't under-stand your question, ask to speak with someone from their dataprocessing or public affairs department. If there isn't a data-processing department, ask to speak to the person who is in charge of the agency's computers. It is important to phrase your question clearly. Receptionists may not be famil-iar with terms like *online*, *electronic bulletin board*, or *BBS*.

If you don't have access to the Internet, calling government agencies directly may be your most successful method for locating public access government online services. If you are lucky enough to have access to the Internet, experiment with some of the vari-ous search tools like Archie, Jughead, Veronica, or some of the Mosaic search tools.

There is a WEB search tool available from Stanford University called Yahoo. It has a URL of: htp://akebono.stanford.edu/yahoo, and it is one of the best.

Chapter 6

HOW CURRENT IS GOVERNMENT ONLINE?

While every effort was made to make *Government Online* current when it went to press, you should know that new government online services are being added almost daily. A few of the resources described here may have closed down and many new resources will have come online by the time you read this. This makes it impossible for a published book on the subject of online services to be up-to-date by the time it is printed. Even with these reservations, *Government Online* is probably the most complete published directory of its kind. Using the tools and resources found here, you will be prepared to search out the newest resources available.

You can make the next edition of *Government Online* even better by letting me know if you discover new government online services. Tell me about those that have closed down and any errors you may come across in the listings.

Are you a government employee? If so, does your Federal, state, or local government agency provide a public access online service that is not listed in *Government Online*, but should be? Send me information about your online service and your agency and I will contact you regarding your entry. There is no charge for being included in *Government Online*.

Do you know of foreign public access government online services? If so, I would like to hear from you. The next edition of *Government Online* may include public access online services from foreign countries.

My address is:

Max Lent
Government Online
24 Wellington Avenue,
Rochester, NY 14611-3018
Internet address:
maxlent@max.roc.servtech.com

If you need technical support or advice about software, hardware, or online services, call the manufacturers or the online service providers. Posting a message in the appropriate USENET news group may also be helpful.

PART

II

FEDERAL GOVERNMENT ONLINE SERVICES

Chapter 7
THE LEGISLATIVE BRANCH

THE CONGRESS

United States Senate
United States Senate Gopher

🌐 Internet address(es): Gopher gopher.senate.gov; ftp ftp.senate.gov; WWW Gopher://Gopher.Senate.GOV:70/1

DESCRIPTION

The United States Senate maintains a Gopher on the Internet at gopher.senate.gov. It was still in the development stage when this book was being researched. It was not as well organized or useful as the House of Representatives Gopher. However, there were still valuable and unique files there worth perusing.

United States Senators Online

The following are United States Senators who have Internet e-mail addresses:

Name	State	E-mail Address
Bingaman, Jeff	NM	senator_bingaman@bingaman.senate.gov
Craig, Larry	ID	larry_craig@craig.senate.gov.
Jeffords, Jim	VT	vermont@jeffords.senate.gov
Kennedy, Ted	MA	senator@kennedy.senate.gov
Leahy, Patrick	VT	senator_leahy@leahy.senate.gov
Robb, Charles	VA	senator_robb@robb.senate.gov
Simon, Paul	IL	senator@simon.senate.gov

United States Senate WWW Pages

🌐 Internet address(es):
http://www.ai.mit.edu/projects/iiip/Kennedy/homepage.html

💻 E-mail addresses: kennedy-webmaster@ai.mit.edu

👥 Contact person & title: Kennedy—Chris Casey, technical staff, office of Senator Kennedy; Cambridge—Todd Marinoff, technical staff, office of City Clerk, Cambridge, MA.

💻 Contact person's e-mail address:
Eric Loeb—loeb@ai.mit.edu
Kennedy Chris_Casey@kennedy.senate.gov

☎ Contact person's voice phone number: Loeb—617-253-0771

✉ Mailing address: Eric Loeb, 3 Leonard Ave, #1, Cambridge, MA 02139

DESCRIPTION

"The Kennedy page is the first senate WWW page. It was built in May 1994 over the course of 1 week. It was built because in March 1994 we established an ftp archive for the senate office, and as a result Chris Casey was able to convince the Senate computer systems folks to establish a Gopher for the U.S. Senate. We hoped, then, that building a web page for Senator Kennedy's office would similarly accelerate the webification of the Senate."

ANNOTATION

Senator Kennedy's Web page is impressive. Once there, you will find a portrait of Senator Kennedy along with press releases, legislation, and Massachusetts-related information. Look for the Boston area map of WWW resources. It is a very impressive use of WWW technology.

House of Representatives

House of Representatives Gopher

🌐 Internet address: The Gopher address for the House of Representatives is:

Gopher: gopher.house.gov

House of Representatives WWW Pages

🌐 Internet address: The House of Representatives WWW addresses are:

http://www.house.gov

http://thomas.loc.gov

The following is from the White House FAQ document:

Charlie Rose, the Chairman of the Committee on House Administration is pleased to announce that the text of legislation introduced in the U.S. House of Representatives is now available on a W.A.I.S server located at the House Information Systems data center. The database contains the text of House bills beginning October 1993 and is updated daily. H.I.S. is happy to provide this information to the Internet community.

The server may be accessed from the directory at quake.think.com or using the following information:

WAIS   Server: diamond

Port: 210

Name: USHOUSE_house_bill_text_103rd

WWW   URL: "wais://quake.think.com/INFO?USHOUSE"

The following information was captured

from the House of Representatives Gopher. By the time you read this information the list may have changed.

"WELCOME TO THE U.S. HOUSE OF REPRESENTATIVES' GOPHER SERVICE

The U.S. House of Representatives' Gopher service provides access to information about Members and Committees of the House and to other U.S. government information resources. This Gopher serves staff of the U.S. House of Representatives and constituents throughout the world. It was built using the Gopher software from the University of Minnesota. Maintaining the menus on this Gopher server is coordinated by the House Administration Committee Internet Working Group in cooperation with service units and divisions throughout the House of Representatives. Posting and maintaining information in Committee folders is the responsibility of the individual Committees.

Since the information offered by the system will be viewed by both Congressional staff members and users outside the Congress from workstations with varying ranges of characteristics and capabilities, the format of documents on the Gopher service will, for the most part, adhere to the 'lowest common denominator'—plain ASCII text.

The U.S. House of Representatives does not provide anonymous FTP or telnet.

If you have suggestions or comments regarding the U.S. House of Representatives' Gopher service or if you need to report operational difficulties with the system, please con-tact the House Internet Working Group at the Internet address:

househlp@hr.house.gov

Thank you for your interest."

"UNITED STATES HOUSE OF REPRESENTATIVES CONSTITUENT ELECTRONIC MAIL SYSTEM

We welcome your inquiry to the House of Representatives Constituent Electronic Mail System. Currently, forty-one Members of the U.S. House of Representatives have been assigned public electronic mailboxes that may be accessed by their constituents. The nature and character of the incoming electronic mail has demonstrated that this capability will be an invaluable source of information on constituent opinion. We are now in the process of expanding the project to other Members of Congress, as technical, budgetary and staffing constraints allow.

A number of House committees have also been assigned public electronic mailboxes. The names and electronic mailbox addresses of these committees are listed below after the information about participating Representatives.

Please review the list of participating Representatives below, and if the Congressional District in which you reside is listed, follow the instructions below to begin communicating by electronic mail with your Representative. If your Representative is not yet on-line, please be patient.

United States Representatives Online

U.S. Representatives Participating in the Constituent Electronic Mail System:

Name	State	District	E-mail Address
Barton, Joe	TX	6	barton06@hr.house.gov
Boehlert, Sherwood	NY	23	boehlert@hr.house.gov
Boucher, Rick	VA	9	jshoumak@hr.house.gov
Sanders, Bernie	VT	-	bsanders@igc.apc.org
Camp, Dave	MI	4	davecamp@hr.house.gov
Canady, Charles	FL	12	canady@hr.house.gov

Conyers, John	MI	14	jconyers@hr.house.gov
DeFazio, Pete	OR	4	pdefazio@hr.house.gov
Deutsch, Peter	FL	20	pdeutsch@hr.house.gov
Dickey, Jay	AR	4	jdickey@hr.house.gov
Ehlers, Vernon	MI	3	congehlr@hr.house.gov
Eshoo, Anna	CA	14	annagram@hr.house.gov
Furse, Elizabeth	OR	1	furseor1@hr.house.gov
Gejdenson, Sam	CT	2	bozrah@hr.house.gov
Gingrich, Newton	GA	6	georgia6@hr.house.gov
Goodlatte, Bob	VA	6	talk2bob@hr.house.gov
Hastert, Dennis	IL	14	dhastert@hr.house.gov
Hoke, Martin	OH	2	hokemail@hr.house.gov
Istook, Jr. Ernest	OK	5	istook@hr.house.gov
Johnson, Sam	TX	3	samtx03@hr.house.gov
Lantos, Tom	CA	12	talk2tom@hr.house.gov
Manton, Thomas	NY	7	tmanton@hr.house.gov
Miller, George	CA	7	fgeorgem@hr.house.gov
Pastor, Ed	AZ	2	edpastor@hr.house.gov
Paxon, Bill	NY	27	bpaxon@hr.house.gov
Pomeroy, Earl	ND	-	epomeroy@hr.house.gov
Ramstad, Jim	MN	3	mn03@hr.house.gov
Roberts, Pat	KS	1	emailpat@hr.house.gov
Rose, Charlie	NC	7	crose@hr.house.gov
Shays, Christopher	CT	4	cshays@hr.house.gov
Skaggs, David	CO	2	skaggs@hr.house.gov
Stark, Pete	CA	13	petemail@hr.house.gov
Stearns, Cliff	FL	6	cstearns@hr.house.gov
Taylor, Charles	NC	11	chtaylor@hr.house.gov
Walker, Robert	PA	16	pa16@hr.house.gov
Watt, Mel	NC	12	elmail@hr.house.gov
Zimmer, Dick	NJ	12	dzimmer@hr.house.gov

INSTRUCTIONS FOR CONSTITUENTS

The list above includes the electronic mail addresses of members who are participating in the program. However, if your Representative is taking part in the project, we request that you send a letter or postcard by U.S. Mail to that Representative at the address listed above with your name and Internet address, followed by your postal (geographical) address. The primary goal of this program is to allow Members to better serve their CONSTITUENTS, and this postal contact is the only sure method currently available of verifying that a user is a resident of a particular congressional district.

In addition, constituents who communicate with their Representative by electronic mail should be aware that Members will sometimes respond to their messages by way of the U.S. Postal Service. This method of reply will help to ensure confidentiality, a concern that is of utmost importance to the House of Representatives.

COMMITTEES OF THE U.S. HOUSE OF REPRESENTATIVES PARTICIPATING IN THE ELECTRONIC MAIL SYSTEM.

Subcommittee on Labor-Management Relations Committee on Education and Labor: slabmgnt@hr.house.gov

Committee on Natural Resources: natres@ hr.house.gov

Committee on Science, Space, and Technology: housesst@hr.house.gov

COMMENTS AND SUGGESTIONS

You can send comments about our service to the Constituent Electronic Mail System Comment mailbox:

comments@hr.house.gov

We will make every effort to integrate suggestions into forthcoming updates of our system. Please note, that the intended purpose of this mailbox is to support public inquiry about the House Constituent Electronic Mail System. Messages intended for Members of Congress should be sent directly to the appropriate Member of Congress at their electronic mail or postal address.

UPDATES AND ADDITIONAL INFORMATION

From time to time, you may want to send another e-mail message to congress@hr. house.gov to see the most recent version of the list of Members and Committees using Constituent Electronic Mail. The information is also available on the U.S. House of Representatives' Gopher server at

gopher.house.gov

in the folder Congressional Information.

To learn more about information available electronically from the House, send an e-mail message to

househlp@hr.Xhouse.gov

Thank you again for contacting the House of Representatives' Constituent Electronic Mail System. We are excited about the possibilities that e-mail has to offer, and will be working hard to bring more Members on-line and to expand our services.

This message will be updated as necessary.
Honorable Charlie Rose (D-NC)
Chairman
Committee on House Administration"

ANNOTATION

If you need a current list of e-mail addresses for the House of Representatives, send a request to congress@hr.house.gov.

GENERAL ACCOUNTING OFFICE

General Accounting Office Watchdog BBS

🖳N Acronym for online service: GAO BBS

🖳) Online service number(s): 202-371-2455, FedWorld BBS 703-321-8020

🌐 Internet address(es): telnet fedworld.gov

🏛 Government agency acronym: GAO

👥 Contact person & title: Tom Luttrell, SYSOP

☎ Contact person's voice phone number: 202-512-7476

📠 Contact person's Fax phone number: 202-371-2442

✉ Mailing address: General Accounting Office Watchdog BBS, P.O. Box 1736, Washington, DC 20013

DESCRIPTION

"This Bulletin Board is a pilot project dedicated to identifying misconduct and wrongdoing related to Federal Government funds and programs. GAO invites you to leave related messages or related files. Mail, voice or Fax reports are also accepted by the GAO Fraud Hotline."

Have you personally observed government agencies wasting money? If you have, this is the place to report it. You can't download files or exchange private messages here, but you can change the way the government works if you have knowledge of fraud or misconduct within the Federal Government.

Government Accounting Office Policy BBS

⌨N Acronym for online service: GAO-Policy BBS

⌨) Online service number(s): 202-512-4286, FedWorld 703-321-8020

🌐 Internet address(es): telnet fedworld.gov then gateway to GAO-Policy

🏛 Government agency acronym: GAO

👥 Contact person & title: Rick Gist, SYSOP, and Vicki Gullixon, co-SYSOP

☎ Contact person's voice phone number: Gist—202-512-4487, Gullixon–202-512-7970

✉ Mailing address: Government Accounting Office, GAO-Policy BBS, 441 G Street, NW, Washington, DC 20548

"The purpose of this BBS is to provide access to the latest electronic data that is maintained by GAO's Office of Policy. For example, GAO's policy manuals and policy guidance publications are maintained by the Office of Policy and will be placed on this BBS. Since GAO's reports (Blue Books) are not maintained by the Office of Policy, we are unable to put them on our BBS. Please note that most of GAO's reports (Blue Books), starting about May of this year, will be placed on GPO's BBS."

If you are not a GAO employee, you will find that you will not have access to all aspects of the GAO-Policy BBS. Some of the menu commands will simply not work when you press a key. This is not a problem, but a known means of separating public areas from GAO areas.

The files sections listed on the GAO-Policy BBS were:

- Policy Manuals—GPPM & CM
- Policy Guidance—Gray Books
- Recommendations Data
- Misc. Data
- Customer Requested Data
- Computer Utilities
- GAO History Trivia Answers

A list of all of the files on the GAO-Policy BBS is available in the file ALLFILES.TXT. This file takes about a minute to download at 14,400 bps.

The Federal Bulletin Board

⌨N Acronym for online service: Federal BBS

⌨) Online service number(s): 202-512-1387

Internet address(es): DIALOG Information Retrieval System 800-334-2564 (File Code 166, GPOPRF)

E-mail addresses: Telex—710-822-9413 (International Orders)

Government agency acronym: GPO

Contact person & title: Superintendent of Documents

Contact person's voice phone number: Telephone orders for books, subscriptions, and CD-ROMs 202-783-3238; for other electronic products call 202-512-1530

Contact person's Fax phone number: Inquiries and ordering publications 202-512-2250; subscriptions 202-512-2233; electronic products 202-512-1262

Mailing address: U.S. Government Printing Office, North Capitol and H Streets, NW, Washington, DC 20402

DESCRIPTION

"The Federal Bulletin Board is a service of the U.S. Government Printing Office (GPO). This bulletin board service enables Federal agencies to provide the public with immediate, self-service access to Government information in electronic form at reasonable rates.

The mission of the GPO is the production or procurement of printing for Congress and the agencies of the Federal Government. GPO also disseminates information to the public through the Superintendent of Document's publications, and depository library programs. Established as the official printer of the Nation, GPO is part of the legislative branch of government.

Through its documents program, GPO disseminates what is possibly the largest volume of information in the world. The Superintendent of Documents offers approximately 12,000 titles to the public at any given time. These are sold principally by mail order and through government bookstores across the country.

Primary Focus: GPO's primary mandate is to facilitate the printing of Congressional work in an efficient and cost-effective manner. The Congressional Record and Federal Register are printed daily. Although it is often referred to as the "Nation's largest publisher," GPO neither initiates or exercises control over the publications it sells. Virtually all government publications are issued by Congress and the various agencies of the Federal Government. GPO prints or procures the printing of these publications and distributes them through its sales and/or depository library programs.

Through GPO, government agencies can create electronic information products, such as CD-ROMs and personal computer diskettes. The Federal Bulletin Board, operated by GPO, enables Federal agencies to provide the public with immediate access to a variety of government information in electronic formats at reasonable rates. In addition, the GPO Electronic Information Access Enhancement Act of 1993 (Public Law 103-40) requires GPO to establish an electronic directory (locator) for Federal electronic information and a system of online access, beginning with the Congressional Record and the Federal Register. These online services are to be available in the summer of 1994."

The following is a listing of the pages accessible on the Federal BBS:

Page Name	Page Description
40_CFR	40 CFR
40_CFR_COMPRESS	40 CFR, Compressed Files
ABOUT_GPO	General Information about GPO
ACCESS	GPO Access Legislation Info
ACCESS_EPA	Access EPA, Info Resources
ACCOUNT	Account/Registry Information
ACCOUNT_INFO	Edit Account Info (Password..)
AD_NOTES	Administrative Notes
AGENCY01	Federal Agencies Information
ATSDR_FRC	PHS, ATSDR FR Cites
BBS_ACCESS	Access Privileges & Charges
BBS_SERVICE	Service Availability
BBS_USER_DOC	Download the User's Guide
BBS_VALIDATION	Becoming a Validated User
BESTSELLERS	Order GPO Bestsellers
BESTSELL_TEXT	GPO Monthly Bestsellers
BOOKSTORES	GPO Bookstores
BYE	QUIT (Logoff the Board)
CATALOGS	Order FREE GPO Pub Catalogs
CDROM_CATALOG	Order CD-ROM Titles from GPO
CLASSIFICATION	SU/DOC Classification Manual
CONGRESS	Congressional Info Libraries
COURTS	Supreme Court/Federal Courts
DEPOSITORY_LIBS	Depository Library Program
DEPOSIT_ACCOUNT	Opening a GPO Deposit Account
DEP_LIB_PROGRAM	Depository Library Program
DOE_DISKETTES	Order Other DOE Files on Disk
DOE_HMER	DOE Historical Energy Review
DOE_MER	DOE Monthly Energy Review
DOE_SEDS	DOE State Energy Data System
DOE_SEPE	DOE State Price & Expenditures
DOJ_ADA	Americans with Disabilities

DOS_ADMIN	Administrative/Reference
DOS_ASIA_PACIF	East Asian & Pacific Affairs
DOS_BKG	Background Notes
DOS_DISPATCH	Dispatch Magazine
DOS_DPB	Daily Press Briefings
DOS_DTN	Defense Trade News
DOS_ENVIRON	Environment
DOS_EURO_CANADA	European/Canadian Affairs
DOS_HUMAN_RTS	Human Rights Country Reports
DOS_LATIN_AMER	Latin American Affairs
DOS_NARCOTICS	Narcotics Control
DOS_PER_DIEM	Foreign Travel Per Diem
DOS_SEC_STATE	Secretary of State Files
DOS_SPECIAL	Special Publications
DOS_TERRORISM	Terrorism
DOS_TEXTILES	Textile Agreements
DOS_TRADE	Trade Expansion
DOS_TRAVEL	Travel Abroad
DOWNLOAD	Download Files
EMAIL	Send & Receive Electronic Mail
EMAIL_LIST	List of Useful E-Mail Addresses
EMAIL_STATE	Send E-Mail to State Department
ENERGY	Energy Department
ENVIRON_CATALOG	Order FREE Catalog on Environ
EPA	Environment' Protection Agency
EPAFR_COMPRESS	EPA FR, Compressed Files
EPA_AQD	EPA FR Air Quality Designat'ns
EPA_CDROM	Order EPA CD-ROM Titles
EPA_DISKETTES	Order EPA Info on Diskette
EPA_FR	EPA FR Files (Prior to 7/1/93)
EPA_FRC	EPA FR Cited Material
EPA_FRS	EPA Daily FR Subset
EPA_FRS2	EPA Daily FR Subset
EPA_LEAD	EPA Lead Documents & Regs

EPA_TRI	Toxic Release Inventory, 1990
EXIT	EXIT (Logoff the Board)
FAC	Foreign Assets Control/Treas
FAC31CFR	FAC, Title 31, CFR
FAC_31FR	FAC Federal Register Files
FAC_BRO	FAC Country Brochures
FAC_MISC	FAC Press Releases/Misc Docs.
FAC_SDN	FAC Specially Design'd Natl's
FDA	Food & Drug Administration
FDA_FR	FDA Federal Register Files
FED_REGISTER	Federal Register/CFR et al.
FED_REGISTER2	Additional FR/CFR Files
FILE_LIBRARY	Search for Files
FILE_LIST	File Listing
FIND	Go List
FORUMS	Forums/SIG's
FREE	Free Information Libraries
FREE_LIBRARY	Free Files
FUTURE_TEXT	Coming Attractions
GOTO_LIST	GO TO ...
GOVMANUAL	Government Manual 1993/94 Menu
GOVMANUAL_DISK	Order Government Manual-disk
GOVMANUAL_FILES	Government Manual 1993/94 Files
GOVMANUAL_PAPER	Order Government Manual-paper
GPOINFO	General Information about GPO
GPO_ACCESS	GPO Access Legislation
HCFA	Health Care Financing Admin
HCFA_CDROM	Order HCFA CD-ROM
HCFA_DISKETTE	Order HCFA Files on Diskette
HCFA_FR	HCFA Federal Register Files
HCFA_PAPER	Order HCFA Publications
HOT	Hot/New Titles from GPO
HOTELEC	Hot Electronic Titles from GPO

HOT_TEXT	What's Hot!
INFO_CENTER	GPO Information Center
JUSTICE	Justice Department
MAIL	Send & Receive Electronic-Mail
MAIN	Return to MAIN Menu
MAIN_LIBRARY	The MAIN Library (Overview)
MAIN_MENU	Return to the MAIN Menu
NEWELEC	New Electronic Titles from GPO
ORDER	Order Products from GPO
ORDER_TEXT	Ordering Products Online
PERF_REVIEW	National Performance Review
PHS_FR	Public Health Service/HHS
READ_EMAIL	Read E-Mail Messages To You
README	README.DOC for Current Library
REGIONAL_LIBS	Regional Depository Libraries
REGISTRY	Enter/Edit Registry Info
SC_92	Supreme Court Opinions 1992/93
SC_92ORD	Supreme Court Orders, 1992/93
SC_93	Supreme Court Opinions 1993/94
SC_93ORD	Supreme Court Orders, 1993/94
SENATE_01	Senate Sbcmte Regs & Govt Info
SINCE_LAST_ON	Files Since Last On
STATE	State Department
STATE01	Files: Public Affairs, Geog..
STATE02	Files: Global Issues, Travel..
STATE_CDROM	Order Foreign Affairs on CDROM
TODAYS_FILES	Today's Files
TRADE	National Export Strategy
WHATS_HOT	What's New and Hot!
WHITE_HOUSE	White House (Menu)
WH_HOUSE	White House (File Library)
WRITE_EMAIL	Write an E-Mail Message
YESTERDAY	Yesterday's Files"

Huge and gigantic are appropriate words to describe the Federal BBS of the GPO. Exploring all of the subject areas created more than 200 pages of screen capture. Although this is primarily a fee-based document distribution system, there are many files available for free. For example, you can obtain a copy of the Declaration of Independence (DECL_IND.TXT) and the Constitution of the United States (CONSTITN.TXT) without opening a charge account. These documents are located in the section "LIB GOVMANUL 1993/94 U.S. Government Manual."

Be prepared to learn yet another new file structure system when you log on here. An excellent user guide (USER.DOC) is available if you find yourself confused by the navigational commands. If you have an interest in U.S. Government documents, you owe it to yourself to explore the Federal BBS.

LIBRARY OF CONGRESS

Automated Library Information Exchange

🖥 Acronym for online service: ALIX

💻) Online service number(s): 202-707-4888, FedWorld BBS 703-321-8020

🌐 Internet address(es): telnet fedworld.gov, telnet locis.loc.gov, or ftp seq1.loc.gov.

💻 E-mail addresses: FLICC@mail.loc.gov

🏛 Government agency acronym: LOC

👥 Contact person & title: Erik Delfino

☎ Contact person's voice phone number: 202-707-4848

📠 Contact person's Fax phone number: 202-707-4818

✉ Mailing address: Library of Congress, 101 Independence Avenue, SE, Washington, DC 20540-5510

DESCRIPTION

A forum for exchange of information on:

- innovative library and information center automation programs
- solutions to library and information center automation problems
- microcomputer experience and techniques

ANNOTATION

ALIX looks as though it is primarily designed for the use of librarians associated with the Library of Congress, but power users of libraries will like what they find here. There are messaging areas where you can exchange information with librarians and researchers on libraries and their use. You can read job postings, newsletters, and other informative notices about the Library of Congress. You can also download files and search databases through ALIX, but you cannot access the Library of Congress electronic card file from within ALIX.

LC MARVEL

🌐 Internet address: Gopher marvel.loc.gov, telnet marvel.loc.gov, ftp ftp.loc.gov, WWW gopher://marvel.loc.gov

💻 E-mail address: lcmarvel@loc.gov

DESCRIPTION

"The Library of Congress (LC) Machine-Assisted Realization of the Virtual Electronic Library (MARVEL) is a Campus-Wide Information System that combines the vast collection of information available about the Library with easy access to diverse electronic resources over the Internet. Its goal is to serve the staff of LC, as well as the U.S. Congress and constituents throughout the world. It is available on the Internet and uses the Gopher software from the University of Minnesota. Since information offered by the system will be viewed by both staff members and users outside of the Library from workstations with varying ranges of characteristics and capabilities, the format of most documents on LC MARVEL will, for the most part, adhere to the "lowest common denominator"—plain ASCII text. In some cases files will be listed that are not in ASCII format (i.e., graphic images and computer software programs) which can be saved, but not viewed through text-based Gopher clients. When accessing LC MARVEL using a graphical Gopher client, users will have the ability to call viewers to display graphics files (GIF and JPEG), WordPerfect (W51), and postscript (PDF) documents. The posting of information on LC MARVEL will be coordinated by the 'LC MARVEL Coordinators Team' in cooperation with service units and divisions throughout the Library. LC Management is now considering the assignment of departmental responsibility for individual LC MARVEL menus and their contents. If you have suggestions regarding the addition of data to LC MARVEL or would like to make comments on any aspect of the system, please contact the LC MARVEL Design Team at the Internet address: lcmarvel@loc.gov. Please report any operational or technical problems to the same Internet address."

ANNOTATION

Although you can reach LC MARVEL using the WWW, you may find using a Gopher or ftp connection useful. When you visit LC MARVEL take an extra couple of minutes to explore the online exhibition area.

OFFICE OF TECHNOLOGY ASSESSMENT

Office of Technology Assessment FTP Server

Internet address(es): ftp otabbs.ota.gov

Log on: Using the OTA ftp server, login as anonymous and use your e-mail address as your password.

E-mail addresses:

"OTANEWS Listserv Now Available.

OTA has introduced an electronic mailing service to provide news about recently released OTA publications to those with access to Internet e-mail. The purpose: to provide more timely delivery of our press releases and report briefs—and to cut mailing costs.

When an OTA publication is released to the public, we will distribute an electronic version of the report brief or news release to readers who subscribe to OTANEWS.

HOW TO SUBSCRIBE

To subscribe to OTA's electronic mailing list, you must have e-mail access to the Internet. Then follow these easy steps:

l) Address an e-mail message to listserv@ota.gov

2) Leave "subject" blank. Go to the body of the message.

3) In the message space, type "subscribe OTANEWS your e-mail address." For example:

subscribe OTANEWS jmcdonald@ota.gov

4) Send the message.

5) You will get a confirmation that your subscription has been entered. If you encounter difficulties, send an e-mail message to postmaster@ota.gov

The information you receive about newly released OTA publications will include order information as well as instructions for downloading the publication from the OTA ftp server if it is available electronically. For more information about the OTANEWS listserv, call the OTA Congressional and Public Affairs Office, (202) 224-9241, or e-mail cpa@ota.gov."

Government agency acronym: OTA

Contact person & title: Martha Dexter, Director, Information Management

Contact person's e-mail address: mdexter@ota.gov

Contact person's voice phone number: 202-228-6233

Contact person's Fax phone number: 202-228-6098

Mailing address: Office of Technology Assessment, U.S. Congress, Washington, DC 20510-8025

DESCRIPTION

"OTA is a nonpartisan analytical agency that serves the U.S. Congress. Its purpose is to aid Congress with the complex and often highly technical issues that increasingly affect our society.

Files on the ftp server may also be viewed via the Library of Congress Gopher, MARVEL (marvel.loc.gov). Select U.S. Congress from the Main Menu, then Other Legislative Support Agencies.

OTA press releases (only) are posted on FedWorld and Capaccess (National Capital Area Public Access Network).

FedWorld (online 703-321-8020 or telnet fedworld.gov), select OTA-PRES from the Library of Files.

Capaccess (online 202-785-1523 or telnet cap.gwu.edu) type 'go ota.'

If you access the Capital Area Public Access Network login as 'guest' and use the password 'visitor.'"

ANNOTATION

On my first visit to the OTA BBS I found a personally valuable file dealing with osteoporosis that I downloaded for my wife. Watch this resource carefully. As government becomes more wired to its constituents, OTA may become a major information disseminator.

OTA may have an electronic bulletin board online by early 1995 says Martha Dexter.

Chapter 8
THE EXECUTIVE BRANCH

THE PRESIDENT

The following is the electronic mail addresses for the President of the United States.

The President of the United States:

> president@whitehouse.gov

THE VICE PRESIDENT

The following are the electronic mail addresses for the Vice President of the United States:

> vice.president@whitehouse.gov

or:

> vice-president@whitehouse.gov

ANNOTATION

Don't expect the President or Vice President to drop you a personal E-mail note in response to your E-mail message to either of them. Most likely, you will receive a com-puter-generated generic note by E-mail or through the U.S. Postal service if you provide your street address. However, don't let this dissuade you from letting the President and Vice President know your thoughts on important issues by E-mail. This is your opportunity to speak out. Although your E-mail may not receive the personal attention you would hope for, it will still be recognized and counted. To be most effective, keep your E-mail messages short and to the point, and include your mailing address and telephone number, no matter whom you write to.

THE WHITE HOUSE

The White House offers several information resources on the Internet. The address for the White House WWW server is:

> http://www.whitehouse.gov/

A frequently asked questions (FAQ) file is available through an automated E-mail response system. To obtain the FAQ file send an E-mail message to:

> faq@whitehouse.gov

There is no need to include text in your message. The recipient is an autoresponder that does not read messages, only return addresses.

What you will get in response is a 31K (approximately) text file describing various ways to use E-mail to contact the Federal Government.

The file I received covered the following topics:

- Sending E-mail to the White House
- Sending E-mail to congress; ftp and Gopher
- Searching and retrieving White House documents
- Signing up for Daily Electronic Publications
- President's Saturday Morning Radio Address
- Submitting Updates to the FAQ

The following information was obtained by sending an E-mail message to:

publications@whitehouse.gov

By including the words "send info" in the text of the message, we received the following:

"Welcome:

Welcome to the White House automatic mail response system. To send requests to the response system, simply enclose them in the body of a message addressed to publications@whitehouse.gov.

In order to be correctly processed, requests must be in the message BODY, not in the Subject line

Commands:

The following commands are recognized:

help	Will send you this file.
topic STRING	Will send you a list of files and file numbers with the specified string in their title.
send file NUMBER	Will send you the specified file. The file number is returned as part of a "topic" request.
send index	Will send you the complete file index from the server. This file is approximately 400kb in size.
uuencode	Will turn on binary transfer mode for UNIX style uuen code.

Example of retrieving a document:

%-> mail publications@whitehouse.gov
Subject:
topic nafta
EOT
%->

Once the message has been sent with a topic request, a reply will arrive with matching files listed, such as:

>## Regarding your request:
> topic nafta
>
>To request copies of matched files, note the file number and request the >file by number using the "sendfile" command. E.g.:
>sendfile 12031
>
>Matching Filenames:
>——
>File-#   Name
>158737   pub/political-science/
                .cap/nafta (53 bytes)
>168963   pub/political-science/
                nafta/full-text/surge.txt
                (3401 bytes)
>169033   pub/political-science/
                nafta/full-text/.cache
                (6029 bytes)
>168966   pub/political-science/

nafta/full-text/

chap-03.txt (94543 bytes)

Supposing you want a copy of the 'surge.txt' file, you would send a request to the publications server as follows:

%-> mail publications@whitehouse.gov

Subject:

send file 168963

EOT

%->

Anonymous FTP:

The publications area is available for anonymous FTP over the Internet. To access a file, FTP to whitehouse.gov, and log in as user 'anonymous'. The FTP area is set up such that files are stored under the same name as used by the mail responder; that is, the file in the example above can be found in the FTP area as file:

pub/political-science/nafta/full-text/ surge.txt

Comments:

Comments relating to this service can be mailed to publications-comments@white-house.gov

Other sources of White House information quoted from the White House FAQ document include:

1. On USENET/NETNEWS, electronic publications are found on a variety of groups:

Direct Distribution

alt.politics.clinton

alt.politics.org.misc

alt.politics.reform

alt.politics.usa.misc

alt.news-media

alt.activism

talk.politics.misc

Indirect Distribution

misc.activism.progressive

cmu.soc.politics

assocs.clinton-gore-92

2. On CompuServe: GO WHITEHOUSE.

Also, see the Democratic Forum: Go Democrats

CompuServe's White House Forum is devoted to discussion of the Clinton administration's policies and activities. The forum's library consists of news releases and twice-daily media briefings from the White House Office of Media Affairs. CompuServe members can exchange information and opinions with each other in the 17 sections in the forum's message area. The message board spans a broad range of topics, including international and United Nations activities, defense, health care, the economy and the deficit, housing and urban development, the environment, and education and national service.

CompuServe's Democratic Forum (GO DEMOCRATS) is the Democratic Party's online information service covering the activities of the Clinton administration. The SYSOPs of the Democratic Forum work for the Democratic National Committee, and are directly involved in managing the forum and responding to online questions. The Democratic Forum provides access to documents from the White House Office of Media Affairs, with vigorous discussion and debate in the message sections about the impact of the Clinton Administration's policies and proposals. The Democratic Forum also holds a regular weekly online conference with special guests on current topics.

3. On America Online: keyword WHITEHOUSE or THE WHITEHOUSE or CLINTON

On America Online, the posts are sent to the White House Forum, located in the News & Finance Department of the service or accessible via keywords: 'white house' or 'Clinton'. The White House Forum on America Online contains the press releases from the White House, divided into the categories 'Appointments,' 'Budget,' 'Congress,' 'Education,' 'Economy,' 'Foreign Policy,' 'Health Care,' 'Housing,' 'Labor,' 'Law and Order,' 'Meetings & Speeches,' 'Proclamations,' 'Technology,' and 'Vice President'. The area features a message board so you can discuss the releases with other AOL members, a searchable database for easy retrieval of releases that interest you, a Library for longer releases from the White House, and a library to which members can upload files of interest for other members.

America Online now offers full access to the Usenet Newsgroups, Gopher and WAIS servers mentioned throughout this document.

4. On Prodigy, jump WHITE HOUSE MEMO.

On Prodigy, WHITE HOUSE MEMO contains all the public documents released by the White House. This service is offered as a PLUS feature.

5. On The WELL: type whitehouse

6 On MCI: type VIEW WHITE HOUSE

MCI Mail users access daily information on the administration's programs provided by the White House through MCI Mail bulletin boards. The available boards are: WHITE HOUSE ECONOMIC, WHITE HOUSE FOREIGN, WHITE HOUSE SOCIAL, WHITE HOUSE SPEECHES and WHITE HOUSE NEWS. A listing of these boards can also be obtained by simply typing VIEW WHITE HOUSE at the COMMAND prompt.

7. On Fidonet: See Echomail WHITE-HOUSE

8. On Peacenet or Econet: See pol.gov info.usa.

9. On The Meta Network: Go Whitehouse

On The Meta Network, material is posted in the White House conference and is accessible via keywords (matching on document titles and subject categories) as well as full text search. Discussions on specific initiatives take place in special interest forums, e.g. health, technology, and reinventing government.

10. On GEnie: Type WHITEHOUSE or WHRT, or MOVE 1600

GEnie's White House RoundTable has been established to distribute and discuss the official press releases and files relating to the White House and the Clinton Administration. The files library holds all of the press releases on the official mailing list, and the Bulletin Board has categories set up with topics relating to all aspects of the Administration and Executive Branch of government. Letters to the White House can be entered easily online with a menu option on the WHITEHOUSE page.

If you don't have access to these accounts or if you would prefer to receive the releases via E-mail, then this section details how to sign up for this service. The server is not set up to answer E-mail letters, comments, or requests for specific information. To reach this MIT server, send E-mail:

To: Clinton-Info@Campaign92.Org
　　　Subject: Help

The server works by reading the subject line of the incoming message and taking whatever action that line calls for. If you want to sign up to automatically receive press releases, then your subject line would begin with the word RECEIVE. You can then specify what kind of information you are interested in receiving. The categories of information are:

ECONOMY
　　Get releases related to the economy such as budget news, technology policy review, etc.
FOREIGN
　　Get releases related to foreign policy such as statements on Bosnian airdrop, Haitian refugee status, etc.
HEALTH
　　Get releases related to health care policy, without receiving any other social issues. Use this instead of social.
SOCIAL
　　Get releases related to social issues like National Service (Student Loan) program, abortion, welfare reform, etc.
SPEECHES
　　All speeches made by the President and important speeches made by other Administration officials.
NEWS
　　Transcripts of press conferences released by

the White House Communications office, as well as the President's remarks in photo ops and other Q&A sessions.

ALL

All of the above

So, if you wanted to sign up to get releases related to the economy, your e-mail message would look like this:

To: Clinton-Info@Campaign92.Org

Subject: RECEIVE ECONOMY

When you send a signup message to the clinton-info server, it sends you back a status message letting you know what distribution streams you are signed up for. If you ever want to check on what groups you are signed up for, send the following message:

To: Clinton-Info@Campaign92.Org

Subject: STATUS

You can stop receiving e-mail releases by sending a REMOVE message to the clinton-info server. The word REMOVE would be followed by whatever distribution stream you wanted to drop. If you wanted to stop receiving messages about the ECONOMY, then your mail would look like this:

To: Clinton-Info@Campaign92.Org

Subject: REMOVE ECONOMY

You could substitute SOCIAL, FOREIGN, HEALTH, SPEECHES, NEWS, or ALL for ECONOMY in the above message and you would be dropped from that distribution list. If you send the subject line REMOVE ALL, then you will be taken off the e-mail distribution system altogether and will not receive further releases of any kind.

You can also ask for help from the automated server. Send an e-mail query as follows:

To: Clinton-Info@Campaign92.Org

Subject: HELP

The server will respond by sending you a detailed form that will guide you through the process of signing up for the various distribu-

tion streams. As you will quickly discover, there is an automatic form processing interface that parallels quick and easy subject line commands discussed here. More detailed help is available by sending an e-mail query as follows:

To: Clinton-Info@Campaign92.Org

Subject: Please Help!

Finally, if you want to search and retrieve documents, but you do not have access to the retrieval methods discussed in section II, you can do this via e-mail through the MIT server. You can obtain the WAIS query form by sending an e-mail query as follows:

To: Clinton-Info@Campaign92.Org

Subject: WAIS

Once you have identified the documents that you want, be careful not to request them all at once, because you may be sent a message containing all the documents and this message may be too big for some mail delivery systems between the e-mail server and you.

E-MAIL SUMMARY SERVICE

The Extension Service of the U.S. Department of Agriculture provides a daily summary of White House electronic publications.

1. Subscriptions

To subscribe to the USDA Extension Service White House Summary service, send a message to:

almanac@ESUSDA.GOV

In the body of the message, type:

subscribe wh-summary

To unsubscribe from the USDA Extension Service White House Summary service, send a message to:

almanac@ESUSDA.GOV

In the body of the message, type:

unsubscribe wh-summary

2. Document Retrieval

To request a specific document from the daily summaries, send a message to:

almanac@ESUSDA.GOV

In the body of the message, type:

send white-house ##### (where ##### is the request number for the document)

3. Document Search
A user-friendly search facility is also available to search the White House documents archived at ESUSDA.GOV. To search, send a message to:

almanac@ESUSDA.GOV

In the body of the message, type:

search white-house keyword1 keyword2

4. Catalogue of Summaries and Documents
Back issues and the catalog of the summaries or the documents contained at ESUSDA.GOV can also be retrieved through our almanac server. To get the summary catalog, send a message to:

almanac@ESUSDA.GOV"

In the body of the message, type:

send wh-summary catalog

5. Further Information

If you have any questions about Almanac, please contact:

wh-admin@ESUSDA.GOV"

OFFICE OF MANAGEMENT AND BUDGET

Online service number(s): FedWorld 703-321-8020

Internet address(es): telnet fedworld.gov then search the files section for OMB.

Contact person & title: Paul Tisdale

Contact person's voice phone number: 202-395-3080

Mailing address: Office of Management and Budget, Executive Office Building, Washington, DC 20503

DESCRIPTION

The Office of Management and Budget maintains files in the FedWorld files section.

ANNOTATION

The following is a list of the files that I found in the OMB Library:

File Name	Size	Date	Description
A-130725.TXT	160K	07/22/94	REVISED OMB Circular A-130 as pub. in Fed. Reg on 7/25/94. This ASCII text file contains the full text of a notice published in the July issue of the Federal Register regarding OMB Circular A-130. Contains information on phases 1 and 2. A-130

A-130725.WP5	179K	07/22/94	REVISED OMB Circular A-130 as pub. in Fed. Reg on 7/25/94. This WordPerfect 5.1 file contains full text of a notice published in the July 25th issue of the Federal Register regard ing OMB Circular A-130. Contains informa tion on Phases 1 and 2. A130
A-16.TXT	19K	05/31/94	A-16 Surveying, Mapping, Spatial Data
A11_FY96.EXE	238K	08/11/94	OMB Circ A-11 for FY96 Budget ASCII-self extract
A11_FY96.TXT	976K	07/24/94	OMB Circ A-11 for FY96 Budget ASCII
OMB-REG.TXT	24K	10/12/94	Regulations Under Review at OMB 10/12/94

COUNCIL OF ECONOMIC ADVISORS

ANNOTATION

The Council of Economic Advisors documents will be available electronically through the Government Printing Office starting in the Spring of 1995. They do not provide any online services directly to the public.

OFFICE OF THE U.S. TRADE REPRESENTATIVE

ANNOTATION

The Office of the U.S. Trade Representative provides an automated Fax service at 202-395-4809. The documents available are press releases, statements, and testimonies. Request document 20000 for a catalog of available documents. Call 202-395-6186 if you experience difficulty using the automated Fax system.

OFFICE OF SCIENCE AND TECHNOLOGY POLICY

National Coordination Office for HPCC Home Page

- Parent agency: National Coordination Office for High Performance Computing and Communications

- Internet address(es): WWW URL http://www.hpcc.gov/

  Gopher Internet server: gopher.hpcc.gov

  Log on: (none — we don't provide ftp service)

- E-mail addresses: (none — we have no autoresponder)

- Government agency acronym: NCO HPCC

- Contact person & title: Sally E. Howe, Ph.D., Assistant Director for Technical Programs

NCO HPCC

📭 Contact person's E-mail address:
howe@hpcc.gov

☎ Contact person's voice phone number:
(301) 402-4100 ext. 207

🖨 Contact person's Fax phone number:
(301) 402-4080

✉ Mailing address: National
Coordination Office for High
Performance Computing and
Communications, B1N30 Building
38A, 8600 Rockville Pike, Bethesda,
Maryland 20894

DESCRIPTION

The menu on the Home Page and select sub-menus are as follows:

- HPCC FY 1995 Implementation Plan
- High Performance Computing and Communications: Technology for the National Information Infrastructure (FY 1995 Blue Book)
- High Performance Computing and Communications: Toward a National Information Infrastructure" (FY 1994 Blue Book)
  - NCO Fact Sheets
  - Reports, Periodicals, and Announcements
    - Reports produced by the NCO
    - Reports produced by HPCC agencies
    - Periodicals
    - Conference announcements
  - Legislation and Testimony
    - Laws
    - Bills
    - Testimony at Congressional hearings
  - Grants and Research Contracts
    - Announcements
    - Awards
  - White House Statements/Policy Papers
  - Information Servers (these are servers at some of the 12 agencies that participate in the HPCC Program: ARPA, NSF, DOE, NASA, NIH, NIST, NSA, NOAA, EPA, ED, and the recently added AHCPR and VA)
  - Related Information (these are servers at other organizations involved in high performance computing and communications)

ANNOTATION

The information available from National Coordination Office for High Performance Computing and Communications is content rich and nicely organized. I wish that it provided more information about its work in lay terms. Personally, I would like to know more about massive parallel processor computers and what is being done with them and I would like to see examples, perhaps in real time, online. Aside from my wants, this is an impressive server and if you are interested in the future of computing and the Internet, you will enjoy what you find here.

OFFICE OF ADMINISTRATION

ANNOTATION

See White House listing.

Chapter 9

THE JUDICIAL BRANCH

ANNOTATION

No online services available. However, the Supreme Court provides information electronically through Hermes. The following is a list of Hermes subscribers supplied by the Supreme Court:

Department of the Air Force

James H. Unterspan, Air Force Legal Services Agency, Air Force Legal Information Services, Maxwell Air Force Base, AL 36112

Voice: 205-953-3008; Fax: 205-953-7159

Associated Press

Mr. Geoff Haynes, Assistant to the Managing Editor, or Anne Stainback, Service Desk Supervisor, Associated Press, New York, NY 10020

Voice: 212-621-1615 or 212-621-1597; Fax: 212-621-7520

Bureau of National Affairs, Inc.

Mr. Sanford M. Morse, 1231 25th Street, NW, Washington, DC 20037

Voice: 202-452-4275 or 202-452-4200; Fax: 202-728-5203

Case Western Reserve University

Mr. Raymond K. Neff, 10900 Euclid Avenue, Cleveland, OH 44106-7019

Voice: 216-368-1025; Fax: 216-368-4693

Commerce Clearing House, Inc.

Mr. William Hurst or Mr. Eric Pamer, 601 Thirteenth Street, NW, Suite 700 South, Washington, DC 20005

Voice: 202-508-6751; Fax: 202-737-5672

Continental Micro Publishing Inc.

Mr. George M. Santamarina, 7175 SW. 8th Street, Suite 204, Miami, FL 33144

Voice: 305-261-4737; Fax: 505-262-7566

Federal News Service

Mr. C. W. Randell or Roy B. Kelly, 620 National Press Building, NW., Washington, DC 20045

Voice: 202-347-1400; Fax: 202-393-4733

U.S. Government Printing Office

Ms. Judy Russell, Director, Library Program Service STOP (SL), Washington, DC 20401

Voice: 202-512-1114; Fax: 202-512-1432

The Hannah System

Rotunda, Inc., Dr. Emerson D. Gilbert, 16 E. Broad Street, Suite 200, Columbus, OH 43215

Voice: 614-228-3113; Fax: 614-228-5897

Information Broadcasting Company, Inc.

Ms. JoMarie Ebert, 2035 N. Lincoln Street, Arlington, VA 22207-3727

Voice: 703-276-8600; Fax: 703-276-8603

InfoSynthesis, Inc.

Mr. Clayton Smalley, 10301 University Avenue., NE, Suite 105, Minneapolis, MN 55434

Voice: 612-784-7036; Fax: 612-780-3157 (contact before transmitting Fax)

Daily Journal Corp./ Los Angeles Daily Journal

Mr. Peter Belsito, Legal Publications, 915 East First Street, Los Angeles, CA 90012

Voice: 213-229-5354. Fax 213-617-1029

Matthew Bender & Co., Inc.

Laurie Kaplan, 11 Penn Plaza. New York, NY 10001

Voice: 212-967-7707; Fax: 212-244-3188

Mead Data Central

Ms. Marcia C. Baugh, 9393 Springboro Pike, P.O. Box 933, Dayton, OH 45401

Voice: 513-865-7993 or 513-865-6800; Fax: 513-865-7943

National Association of Attorneys General

Ms. Eleni Constantine, Hall of the States, 444 North Capitol Street, Washington, DC 20001

Voice: 202-434-8010; Fax:202-434-8008

National Clearinghouse for Legal Services, Inc.

Ms. Illze Hirsch, 407 South Dearborn, #400 Chicago, IL 60605

Voice: 312-263-3830; Fax: 312-263-3846

The New York Times

Steve E. Brier or Judy Wilner, 229 West 43rd Street, New York, NY 10036

Voice: 212-556-1582 or 212-556-7563; Fax: 212-556-3690

SEARCH

Mr. Gary Cooper, 7311 Greenhaven Drive, Suite 145, Sacramento, CA 95831

Voice: 916-392-2550; Fax: 916-392-8440

Shepard's McGraw-Hill

Mr. Brian Hall, 555 Middle Creek Parkway, P.O. Box 35300, Colorado Springs, CO 80935-3530

Voice: 719-488-3000; Fax: 719-481-7445

Timeline Publishing Co.

Mr. Joe W. Acton, P .0. Box 1435, Bellview, WA 98009

Voice: 206-462-7714 or 800-444-7714; Fax: 206-462-0411

Thomson Publishing Co.

Mr. Sheldon Shapiro—Administrative U.S. Supreme Court Reports, Lawyers Cooperative Publishing, Aqueduct Building, Rochester, NY 14694

Voice: 716-546-5530 ext. 3338; Fax: 716-258-3718

Technical Help Desk: 716-671-7780 ext. 4400; Fax: 716-671-1017

Harry Weidman 716-327-6330

Pauline Levarino 716-327-6217; Fax: 716-327-6237

West Publishing Company

Mr. Jerrol M. Tostrud, 610 Opperman Drive, Eagan, MN 55123

Voice: 612-687-7000; Fax: 612-687-5637

UNITED STATES DISTRICT COURTS

ANNOTATION

See Administrative Office of the United States Courts.

UNITED STATES COURT OF VETERANS APPEALS

The Court of Veterans Appeals BBS

💻)   Online service number(s): 202-501-5836, 202-501-5837, 202-501-5838

👥   Contact person & title: Antoine Fagan, Sysop

☎   Contact person's voice phone number: 202-501-5970 ext. 1280

🖨   Contact person's Fax phone number: 202-501-5848

✉   Mailing address: The Court of Veterans Appeals, 625 Indiana Avenue, NW, Suite 900, Washington, DC 20004-2950

DESCRIPTION

"The Court of Veterans Appeals BBS is an electronic bulletin board which makes available up-to-date precedential opinions by the court. Opinions are placed on the BBS as they are released each day in WordPerfect and Text form and will remain on the BBS for 90 days. The opinions on the BBS may not be viewed on your video screen but are available for downloading for later viewing at the user's convenience. At the present time, no fee is charged to use the BBS."

ANNOTATION

The information available from the Court of Veterans Appeals will interest judges, lawyers, defendants, and journalists.

Appeals Court Electronic Services

⌨N   Acronym for online service: ACES

Courts of Appeals	Clerk's Office	Computer (pre-registration not required)[1]
First Circuit (EDOS & Dockets)	(617) 223-9057	(617) 223-4640/41/42
Second Circuit (EDOS)	(212) 791-0103	(212) 385-6003
Third Circuit (EDOS & Dockets)	(215) 597-2995	(215) 597-1871
Fourth Circuit (ACES)	(804) 771-2213	(804) 771-2028, 2063
Fifth Circuit (EDOS)	(504) 589-6514	(504) 589-6850/51/52
Sixth Circuit (CITE)	(513) 684-2953	(513) 684-2842
Seventh Circuit (EDOS/Dockets)	(312) 435-5850	(312) 435-5560
Eighth Circuit (EDOS)	(314) 539-3609	(314) 539-3576/78
Ninth Circuit (ACES)	(415) 744-9800	(415) 744-9020
Tenth Circuit (EDOS & Dockets)	(303) 844-3157	(303) 844-3222
Eleventh Circuit (EDOS)	(404) 331-6187	(404) 730-9600
D.C. Circuit (EDOS)	(202) 273-0315	(202) 219-9589–9600, 273-0269
Federal Circuit	(202) 633-6550	(202) 786-6584; 633-9608

[1]In several circuits, you may be prompted for a password and/or identification; respond by typing (in lower-case letters) "bbs."

🏛 Government agency acronym: AO

👥 Contact person & title: J. Michael Greenwood, Public Access Project Director

☎ Contact person's voice phone number: 202-273-2748 (or 2730)

✉ Mailing address: Administrative Office of the United States Courts, Technology Enhancement Office, Washington, DC 20544

DESCRIPTION

"ACES (Appellate Court Electronic Services) (also known as Electronic Dissemination of Opinions System (EDOS)): ACES/EDOS is an electronic bulletin board for the rapid dissemination of appellate court information and decisions. This service allows public users to view and electronically transfer published slip opinions, court oral argument calendars, court rules, notices and reports, and press releases. Developed in 1989, ACES/EDOS is now available in all Federal circuit courts. In addition, a few district and bankruptcy courts are beginning to offer similar electronic access to their published court orders, opinions, and rules."

ANNOTATION

This online service is obviously designed to serve the legal community.

Bankruptcy Voice Case Information System

⌐N   Acronym for online service: VCIS

District/Bankruptcy Courts	General Info.	Modem
Idaho (FED NET)		(208) 334-9476
New Hampshire	(603) 225-1423	(603) 225-1544
Pennsylvania-Eastern	(215) 597-5710	(215) 597-5384;0646

Bankruptcy Courts	To Register for Access	Modem
Alabama-Southern*	(800) 676-6856	(205)-441-5638
Alaska*	(800) 676-6856	(907) 271-2695/96/97/98/99
Arkansas (East & West)*	(800) 676-6856	(501) 324-6079
California-Central		
Santa Ana*	(800) 676-6856	(714) 836-2281
Santa Barbara*	(800) 676-6856	(805) 899-7756
San Bernadino*	(800) 676-6856	(714) 383-5560
California-Eastern*	(800) 676-6856	(916) 551-1498
California-Northern*	(800) 676-6856	(415) 705-3148
California-Southern*	(800) 676-6856	(800) 870-9972
California-Southern*	(619) 557-6875	
Colorado*	(800) 676-6856	(303) 844-0263
Connecticut*	(800) 676-6856	(203) 240-3570/71/72
District of Columbia*	(800) 676-6856	(202) 273-0630,42,43,44
Florida-Southern*	(800) 676-6856	(305) 536-7492/3/4/5/6
Georgia-Northern *	(800) 676-6856	(404) 730-3264
Georgia-Middle*	(800) 676-6856	(912) 752-3551
Idaho	(208) 334-9342	(208) 334-9895
Illinois-Central*	(800) 676-6856	(217) 492-4260
Illinois-Southern*	(800) 676-6856	(618) 482-9114/5/6
Indiana-Northern*	(800) 676-6856	(219) 236-8199
Iowa-Northern*	(800) 676-6856	(319) 362-1824

Iowa-Southern*	(800) 676-6856	(800) 597-5917
Kansas *	(800) 676-6856	(800) 613-7052
Kansas *	(316) 269-6258	
Kentucky-Eastern*	(800) 676-6856	(800) 497-2777
Kentucky-Eastern*	(606) 233-2777	
Kentucky-Western*	(800) 676-6856	(502) 625-7388
Louisiana-Eastern*	(800) 676-6856	(504) 589-6761
Louisiana-Middle	(504) 389-0212	(504) 382-2176
Louisiana-Western*	(800) 676-6856	(318) 676-4235
Maine*	(800) 676-6856	(207) 780-3268/9
Maryland*	(800) 676-6856	(800) 927-0474
Maryland*	(301) 227-6866/7/8/9	
Massachusetts*	(800) 676-6856	(617) 565-6021/2/3,- 7593/4
Michigan-Eastern*	(800) 676-6856	(313) 961-4934
Michigan-Western*	(800) 676-6856	(616) 732-2765
Minnesota*	(800) 676-6856	(612) 290-4065
Mississippi-Northern*	(800) 676-6856	(601) 369-9805,9854/56/62
Missouri-Eastern*	(800) 676-6856	(314) 425-6935
Missouri-Western*	(800) 676-6856	(816) 426-6033
Nebraska*	(800) 676-6856	(800) 788-0656
Nebraska*	(402) 221-4882	
Nevada*	(800) 676-6856	(702) 388-6920
New Hampshire*	(800) 676-6856	(603) 666-7923
New Jersey*	(800) 676-6856	(201) 645-3555
New Mexico*	(800) 676-6856	(505) 766-5566
New York-Eastern*	(800) 676-6856	(718) 488-7012
New York-Northern*	(800) 676-6856	(518) 472-2643
New York-Southern*	(800) 676-6856	(212) 668-2896/7/8/9/5610
New York-Western*	(800) 676-6856	(716) 846-3152/3/4/5
North Carolina-Western*	(800) 676-6856	(704) 344-6121/2/3/4
North Carolina-Middle*	(800) 676-6856	(919) 333-5389
North Dakota*	(800) 676-6856	(701) 239-5265
Ohio-Northern*	(800) 676-6856	(800) 579-5735
Ohio-Northern*	(216) 489-4779	

Ohio-Southern*	(800) 676-6856	(513) 225-7561 or (800) 793-7003
Oklahoma-Eastern*	(800) 676-6856	(918) 756-4812
Oklahoma-Western*	(800) 676-6856	(405) 231-5064/5
Oregon*	(800) 676-6856	(503) 326-5650
Pennsylvania-Eastern*	(215) 597-8266	(215) 597-3501
Pennsylvania-Western*	(800) 676-6856	(412) 355-2588
Rhode Island*	(800) 676-6856	(401) 528-4062
South Carolina*	(800) 676-6856	(803) 765-5965
South Dakota*	(800) 676-6856	(605) 330-4342
Tennessee-Eastern*	(800) 676-6856	(615) 752-5131/36/37
Tennessee-Western*	(800) 676-6856	(901) 544-4336/7/8/9/40
Texas-Eastern*	(800) 676-6856	(903) 535-5015
Texas-Northern*	(800) 676-6856	(214) 767-8091
Texas-Southern*	(800) 676-6856	(800) 998-9037 or (713) 250-5000
Texas-Western*	(800) 676-6856	(210) 229-6262
Utah*	(800) 676-6856	(801) 524-5760
Vermont*	(800) 676-6856	(802) 747-7633
Virginia-Eastern*	(800) 676-6856	(800) 758-7050
Washington-Western*	(800) 676-6856	(206) 553-0060/1/2/3/4
West Virginia-Northern*	(800) 676-6856	(304) 233-2871/2953
West Virginia-Southern*	(800) 676-6856	(304) 347-5554
Wisconsin-Eastern*	(800) 676-6856	(414) 297-1400
Wisconsin-Western*	(800) 676-6856	(608) 264-5630
Wyoming*	(800) 676-6856	(307) 772-2037/38

* Access fee: $1.00 per minute of connect time; no charge for registration
** Fee as of November 1994

The following services are similar to PACER but were developed locally:

Bankruptcy Courts	To Register for Access	Modem
Alabama-Middle (Montgomery)**	(800) 676-6856	To be announced[s]
Alabama-Northern (Birmingham)	(205) 731-0850	
Alabama-Northern (Anniston)	(205) 236-6421	(205) 238-0456[s]
Alabama-Northern (Decatur)	(205) 353-2817	(205) 355-2349[s]

Alabama-Northern (Tuscaloosa)	(205) 752-0426	(205) 758-1309[S]
Arizona (Phoenix) (NIBS-BRASS)*	(800) 676-6856	(602) 514-7379[S]
Arizona (Tucson) (NIBS-BRASS)*	(800) 676-6856	(602) 670-6332[S]
Arizona (Yuma) (NIBS-BRASS)*	(800) 676-6856	(602) 783-9535[S]
Delaware (NIBS-BRASS)*	(800) 676-6856	(302) 573-6243[S]
Florida-Middle (Jacksonville) (NIBS)	(904) 358-1952 (Ed Jackson, Bar Assn.)[R]	
Florida-Middle (Orlando) (NIBS)	(407) 843-4421 (Debby Opelt, Bar Assn.)[R]	
Florida-Middle (Tampa) (NIBS)	(813) 222-5020 (Janet Parsons, Bar Assn.)[R]	
Georgia-Southern (Savannah)	(912) 652-4100	(912) 652-4465[S]
Georgia-Southern (Augusta)	(706) 724-2421	(706) 722-9776[S]
Hawaii (NIBS-BRASS)	(808) 541-1791	(808) 541-1392[S]
Illinois-Northern (Chicago)*	(800) 676-6856	(312) 408-5101[S]
Illinois-Northern (Rockford)*	(800) 676-6856	(815) 987-4489,90[S]
Indiana-Southern (NIBS On-Line)	(317) 226-6710	(317) 226-5146[C]
Montana (NIBS On-Line)	(406) 496-3339 x16	(406) 496-3332,3[S]
North Carolina-Eastern (NIBS)	(919) 237-0440	Annual $500 Fee
Oklahoma-Northern (NIBS On-Line)	(918) 581-7181	(918) 581-7713[R]
Puerto Rico (BRICS-BRASS)*	(809) 766-5073	(809) 766-6579/54/5871
Tennessee-Middle (NIBS On-Line)	(615) 736-5577	(615) 254-5290
Virginia-Eastern (Richmond)*	(800) 676-6856	(804) 771-2575[S]
Virginia-Eastern (Alexandria)*	(800) 676-6856	(703) 557-6272[S]
Virginia-Eastern (Newport News)*	(800) 676-6856	(804) 595-1365[S]
Virginia-Eastern (Norfolk)*	(800) 676-6856	(804) 441-3663[S]
Virginia-Western (Roanoke) (CHIP)	(703) 857-2391	(703) 857-2319[S]
Virginia-Western (Lynchburg) (CHIP)	(703) 857-2391	(804) 528-9003[S]
Washington-Eastern (NIBS-PAS)	(509) 353-2404	(509) 353-3286[R]

* Access fee: $1.00 per minute of connect time. No charge for registration
** Fee as of November 1994
Codes
[R] This court requires or strongly recommends that *PC Anywhere Version 4* software or its equivalent be installed on the public user's computer system.
[S] This court suggests *PC Anywhere Version 4* telecommunications software, but can accommodate most public user telecommunication packages.
[C] This court requires that *Carbon Copy Plus* telecommunications software be installed on the public user's computer system.

VCIS: Voice Case Information System

Bankruptcy Courts	Modem
Alabama-Southern	(205) 441-5637
Alaska	(907) 271-2658
Arizona (Phoenix) NAVIS	(602) 514-7321
Arizona (Tucson) NAVIS	(602) 670-6304
Arkansas-Eastern & Western	(501) 324-5770
California-Central (Santa Ana)	(714) 836-2278
California-Central (Santa Barbara)	(805) 899-7755
California-Central (San Bernardino)	(714) 383-5552
California-Eastern	(916) 551-2989 or (800) 736-0158
California-Southern	(619) 557-6521
Colorado	(303) 844-0267
Connecticut	(203) 240-3345 or (800) 800-5113
District of Columbia	(202) 273-0048
Florida-Southern	(305) 536-5979 or (800) 473-0226
Georgia-Middle	(912) 752-8183
Georgia-Northern	(404) 730-2866/7
Idaho	(208) 334-9386
Illinois-Central	(217) 492-4550 or (800) 827-9005
Illinois-Southern	(618) 482-9365 or (800) 726-5622
Indiana-Northern	(219) 236-8814
Iowa-Northern	(319) 362-9906
Iowa-Southern	(515) 284-6427
Kansas	(316) 269-6668 or (800) 827-9028
Kentucky-Eastern	(606) 233-2657 or (800) 998-2650
Kentucky-Western	(502) 625-7391
Louisiana-Eastern	(504) 589-3951
Louisiana-Middle	(504) 382-2175
Louisiana-Western	(318) 676-4234 or (800) 326-4026
Maine	(207) 780-3755
Maryland	(410) 962-0733
Massachusetts	(617) 565-6025/6
Michigan-Eastern	(313) 961-4940
Michigan-Western	(616) 456-2075
Minnesota	(612) 290-4070 or (800) 959-9002
Mississippi-Northern	(601) 369-8147
Missouri-Eastern	(314) 425-4054
Missouri-Western	(816) 842-7985
Montana	(406) 496-3335
Nebraska	(402) 221-3757 or (800) 829-0112
New Hampshire	(603) 666-7424
New Jersey	(201) 645-6045

New York-Eastern	(718) 852-5726
New York-Northern	(800) 206-1952
New York-Western	(716) 846-5311 or (800) 776-9578
North Carolina-Middle	(919) 333-5532
North Carolina-Western	(704) 344-6311
North Dakota	(701) 239-5641
Ohio-Northern	(216) 489-4731
Ohio-Northern	(216) 489-4771
Ohio-Southern (Dayton, Cincinnati)	(513) 225-2544 or (800) 726-1004
Ohio-Southern (Columbus)	(513) 225-2562 or (800) 726-1006
Oklahoma-Eastern	(918) 756-8617
Oklahoma-Western	(405) 231-4768
Oregon	(503) 326-2249 or (800) 726-2227
Pennsylvania-Eastern	(215) 597-2244
Pennsylvania-Western	(412) 355-3210
Rhode Island	(401) 528-4476
South Carolina	(803) 765-5211 or (800) 669-8767
South Dakota	(605) 330-4559
Tennessee-Eastern	(615) 752-5272 or (800) 767-1512
Tennessee-Western	(901) 544-4325
Texas-Eastern	(214) 592-6119
Texas-Southern	(713) 250-5049 or (800) 745-4459
Texas-Western	(210) 229-4023
Utah	(801) 524-3107 or (800) 733-6740
Vermont	(802) 747-7627
Virginia-Eastern	(804) 771-2736 or (800) 326-5879
Washington-Western	(206) 442-8543, 6504
West Virginia-Northern	(304) 233-7318
West Virginia-Southern	(304) 347-5337
Wisconsin-Eastern	(414) 297-3582
Wisconsin-Western	(800) 743-8247

Contact person & title: J. Michael Greenwood, Public Access Project Director

Contact person's voice phone number: 202-273-2748 (or 2730)

Mailing address: Administrative Office of the United States Courts, Technology Enhancement Office, Washington, DC 20544

DESCRIPTION

"VCIS (Bankruptcy Voice Case Information System): VCIS uses an automated voice response system to read case information directly from the court's database in response to Touch-Tone telephone inquiries. First offered in a few bankruptcy courts in 1989, the service is now operating in approximately 75 bankruptcy courts. Usage of VCIS is currently free and is likely to remain so."

ANNOTATION

This online service is designed to serve the legal community.

Electronic Filing

⌐N   Acronym for online service: ELF

ELF: ELECTRONIC FILING

District Courts	To Register for Access	Modem
Pennsylvania-Eastern	(215) 597-5861	(215) 597-3773
Texas-Western	(512) 229-4164	(210) 229-6256

👥 Contact person & title: J. Michael Greenwood, Public Access Project Director

☎ Contact person's voice phone number: 202-273-2748 (or 2730)

✉ Mailing address: Administrative Office of the United States Courts, Technology Enhancement Office, Washington, DC 20544

DESCRIPTION

"ELF (Electronic Filing): ELF is a document submission service that allows attorneys to use their computer to electronically file documents with the court. Either an ASCII text file or a WordPerfect version of a document can be submitted electronically within specified formats; for example, WordPerfect formatted documents must use Courier type font. The system allows users to transmit documents using XMODEM (Checksum), XMODEM (CRC), or YMODEM communications protocols. The system is presently available in two district courts (Eastern District of Pennsylvania and the Western District of Texas). Each district that uses the ELF system may impose different restrictions on the kinds of documents that may be submitted electronically. Law firms and agencies desiring to use the system *must* file an application with the appropriate Clerk of Court."

ANNOTATION

This online service is designed to serve the legal community.

PACER Service Center Electronic Bulletin Board

⌐) Online service number(s): 800-214-0847 (available to existing PACER/NIBS registrants)

🏛 Government agency acronym: OA

👥 Contact person & title: J. Michael Greenwood, Public Access Project Director

☎ Contact person's voice phone number: 202-273-2748 (or 2730)

✉ Mailing address: Administrative Office of the United States Courts, Technology Enhancement Office, Washington, DC 20544

DESCRIPTION

"PACER Service Center Electronic Bulletin Board has been recently established by the Federal court's centralized registration and billing service in San Antonio, Texas. This new service (800-214-0847) available at no charge allows *existing* PACER/NIBS registrants to dial in 24 hours a day, 7 days a week (your PC software should be set for 8 bits, no parity, 1 stop bit and RTS/CTS or NONE for flow control using 2400-baud modems or faster; 9600 baud modems must be V.32 compatible). The service: (a) provides an updated listing of courts serviced by the service center, (b) allows users to automatically register for additional courts and change passwords, (c) review user's billing history for all courts nationwide, (d) provides user manuals and status of each court's PACER system (e.g., courts with computer disruptions or other technical problems), and (e) allows users to leave messages and comments for service center personnel."

This online service is designed to serve the legal community.

Public Access to Court Electronic Records

🖵ᴺ   Acronym for online service: PACER

PACER: PUBLIC ACCESS TO COURT ELECTRONIC RECORDS

Courts of Appeals	To Register for Access	Modem
Second Circuit	(212) 791-8910	(212) 385-6004
Fourth Circuit	(804) 771-2213	(804) 771-8084
Eighth Circuit	(314) 539-3652	(314) 539-3584

The following services are similar to PACER, but were developed locally. Several of these courts offer their dockets only during regular court office hours.

First Circuit (Dockets)	(617) 223-4640/41/42
Third Circuit (Dockets)	(215) 597-1871
Sixth Circuit (CITE)	(513) 684-2842
Seventh Circuit (Dockets)	(312) 435-5560
Tenth Circuit (Dockets)	(303) 844-3222

U.S. District Courts

PACER: Public Access to Court Electronic Records

District Courts	To Register	Modem	Dockets
Alabama-Northern	(205) 731-2002	(205) 731-3502	Civil only
Arizona*	(800) 676-6856	(602) 514-7113	Civil &Criminal
Arkansas-Eastern*	(800) 676-6856	(501) 324-6190	Civil only
Arkansas-Western	(501) 783-6833	(501) 783-3538	Civil only
California-Central*	(800) 676-6856	(213) 894-3625	Civil & Criminal
California-Southern*	(800) 676-6856	(619) 557-7138	Civil & Criminal
Colorado	(800) 676-6856	(303) 844-3454	Civil only
Connecticut*	(800) 676-6856	(203) 773-2451	Civil &Criminal
Delaware*	(800) 676-6856	(302) 573-6651	Civil &Criminal

District of Columbia*	(800) 676-6856	(202) 273-0606	Civil & Criminal
Florida-Middle*	(800) 676-6856	(904) 232-2566	Civil only
Florida-Southern*	(800) 676-6856	(305) 536-7265	Civil & Criminal
Georgia-Northern*	(800) 676-6856	(404) 730-9668	Civil &Criminal
Georgia-Southern*	(800) 676-6856	(912) 652-4601	Civil &Criminal
Idaho	(208) 334-9097	(208) 334-9590	Civil &Criminal
Illinois-Central*	(800) 676-6856	(217) 492-4997	Civil only
Illinois-Northern*	(800) 676-6856	(312) 408-7777	Civil &Criminal
Illinois-Southern*	(800) 676-6856	(618) 482-9430	Civil only
Iowa-Southern*	(800) 676-6856	(515) 284-6475	Civil &Criminal
Kansas	(316) 269-6491	(316) 269-6224	Civil only
Kentucky-Eastern*	(800) 676-6856	(606) 233-2787	Civil &Criminal
Louisiana-Eastern*	(800) 676-6856	(504) 589-6714	Civil &Criminal
Louisiana-Western*	(800) 676-6856	(318) 676-3957	Civil &Criminal
Maryland*	(800) 676-6856	(410) 962-1812	Civil only
Massachusetts*	(800) 676-6856	(617) 223-4294	Civil &Criminal
Michigan-Western*	(800) 676-6856	(616) 732-2765	Civil &Criminal
Minnesota*	(800) 676-6856	(612) 290-4167	Civil &Criminal
Mississippi-Northern*	(800) 676-6856	(601) 236-4706	Civil &Criminal
Missouri-Western*	(800) 676-6856	(816) 426-6033	Civil only
Nebraska*	(800) 676-6856	(402) 221-4797	Civil only
New Hampshire*	(800) 676-6856	(603) 226-7737	Civil &Criminal
New Jersey*	(800) 676-6856	(609) 989-0590	Civil only
New Mexico*	(800) 676-6856	(505) 766-1911	Civil only
New York-Eastern*	(800) 676-6856	(718) 330-7200	Civil &Criminal
New York-Northern*	(800) 676-6856	(315) 423-6551	Civil &Criminal
New York-Southern*	(800) 676-6856	(212) 791-8050	Civil &Criminal
New York-Western	(716) 846-4211	(716) 846-3117	Civil only
North Carolina-Eastern	(919) 856-4370	(919) 856-4768	Civil only
North Carolina-Middle	(910) 333-5071	(910) 333-5788	Civil &Criminal
Ohio-Northern*	(800) 676-6856	(216) 522-3669	Civil &Criminal
Ohio-Southern*	(800) 676-6856	(614) 469-6990	Civil &Criminal
Oklahoma-Northern*	(800) 676-6856	(918) 581-6903	Civil only
Oklahoma-Western*	(800) 676-6856	(405) 231-4531	Civil &Criminal
Oregon*	(800) 676-6856	(503) 326-5924	Civil &Criminal
Pennsylvania-Eastern*	(215) 597-5861	(215) 597-0258	Civil &Criminal
Puerto Rico*	(800) 676-6856	(809) 766-5774	Civil only
Rhode Island*	(800) 676-6856	(401) 528-5145	Civil &Criminal
South Carolina*	(800) 676-6856	(803) 765-5871	Civil &Criminal
Texas-Eastern*	(800) 676-6856	(903) 531-9210	Civil &Criminal
Texas-Northern*	(800) 676-6856	(214) 767-8918-20	Civil &Criminal
Texas-Northern*	(800) 676-6856	(800) 684-2393	Civil &Criminal
Texas-Southern*	(800) 676-6856	(713) 250-5000	Civil &Criminal
Texas-Southern*	(800) 676-6856	(800)998-9037	Civil &Criminal
Texas-Western*	(800) 676-6856	(210) 229-5241	Civil &Criminal
Utah*	(800) 676-6856	(801) 524-4221	Civil &Criminal

Log on: Call Martin Marietta Corporation at 301-306-8060 for subscription information.

🏛 Government agency acronym: USDA

👥 Contact person & title: Russel T. Forte, CID Service Coordinator

💻 Contact person's e-mail address: !A13RFORTE (On FTS2000)

☎ Contact person's voice phone number: 202-720-5505

🖨 Contact person's Fax phone number: 202-690-1131

✉ Mailing address: United States Department of Agriculture, Office of Public Affairs, Room 536-A, Washington, DC 20250-1301

DESCRIPTION

"The Computerized Information Delivery Services (CIDS) is an integrated system of agricultural current information, specialized software and data storage, and a national telecommunications network providing access to the host computer system on which CIDS resides.

The principal component of the CIDS system is the comprehensive database of agricultural statistical and narrative data issued by several agencies of the U.S. Department of Agriculture.

Contributing agencies include:
- Agricultural Cooperative Service (ACS)
- Agricultural Marketing Service (AMS)
- Agricultural Research Service (ARS)
- Agricultural Stabilization & Conservation Service (ASCS)
- Economic Research Service (ERS)
- Extension Service (ES)
- Foreign Agricultural Service (FAS)
- National Agricultural Library (NAL)
- National Agricultural Statistics Service (NASS)
- Office of Public Affairs (OPA)
- Soil Conservation Service (SCS)
- World Agricultural Outlook Board WAOB"

ANNOTATION

CIDS is not inexpensive to use. The monthly minimum rate is $75. The hourly rate for 1,200/2,400 bps is $12 and data retrieval is charged at 95 cents for 100 lines and 4 cents for menu lines. Russel Forte says, "The computer is available with a local phone call from anywhere in the world. We use the CompuServe packet-switching network. If subscribers don't have a node locally, Martin Marietta will give them an 800 number to use." There is a huge quantity of agricultural data available through CIDS. If you feel tempted to explore CIDS, contact Russel Forte to obtain more in-depth information and instructions for subscribing.

Economic Research Service/National Agricultural Statistics Service BBS

🔊 Parent organization: Economic Research Service

🖥 Acronym for online service: Call-ERS/NASS

💻 Online service number(s): 800-821-6229, 202-219-0377, 202-219-0378, FedWorld BBS 703-321-8020

🌐 Internet address(es): telnet to fedworld.gov then gateway to Call-

ERS/NASS. Gopher usda.mannlib.cornell.edu. telnet usda.mannlib.cornell.edu and login as usda (no password is needed). Ftp usda.mannlib.cornell.edu then login as "anonymous" with your ID name or e-mail address as the password.

🏛 Government agency acronym: USDA

👥 Contact person & title: Jim Horsfield, SYSOP

💻 Contact person's e-mail address: jimh@ers.bitnet

☎ Contact person's voice phone number: 202-219-0012

🖨 Contact person's Fax phone number: 202-219-0044

✉ Mailing address: Department of Agriculture, Economic Research Service, 1301 New York Avenue, NW, Washington, DC 20005-4788

DESCRIPTION

"Call-ERS/NASS is the official bulletin board of the Economic Research Service (ERS) and the National Agricultural Statistics Service (NASS). It is maintained for cooperating users of ERS and NASS information and data products and services. Through Call-ERS/NASS you can browse and download ERS Situation & Outlook reports and summaries, get an update to the FINDERS advisory system, download samples of our data products, read our bulletin of 'What new from ERS', and list our latest catalog of data products. NASS report subscribers can get the latest copies of the Broiler Hatchery, Crop Progress, Agricultural Prices and Crop Production Reports."

ANNOTATION

Are you looking for data about the production of oil crops, rice, fruit trees, aquaculture, and other similar types of agricultural production? If you said yes, this is the place to be. Some of the information available from Call-ERS/NASS is by paid subscription. Other data is available free for downloading.

ERS-NASS also maintains an automated Fax system named AutoFAX at 202-219-1107. Call and request document ID number 0411 to obtain more information and a directory of files available.

Nutrient Data Bank Bulletin Board

🖥 Acronym for online service: NDB

🖥 Online service number(s): 301-436-5078, FedWorld BBS 703-321-8020

🌐 Internet address(es): telnet fedworld.gov, telnet info.umd.edu

🏛 Government agency acronym: USDA

👥 Contact person & title: David Haytowitz, SYSOP

💻 Contact person's e-mail address: info-12@info.umd.edu

☎ Contact person's voice phone number: 301-436-8491

🖨 Contact person's Fax phone number: 301-436-5643

✉ Mailing address: Nutrient Data Bank Bulletin Board, U.S. Department of Agriculture, Human Nutrition Information Service, Nutrition Monitoring Division, 6505 Belcrest Rd., Room 316, Hyattsville, MD 20782

"The NDB Bulletin Board provides up-to-date information about USDA-HNIS food composition data release, publications, and the Nutrient Data Bank." "The NDB Bulletin Board provides you with three types of services: reading bulletins, downloading files, and sending messages to us. Functions available on other computer bulletin board services such as uploading files or sending messages to other users are not available. BULLETINS will provide you with general news, information about the latest USDA nutrient data releases, Nutrient Data Bank Conference announcements, and instructions on how to use the bulletin board."

ANNOTATION

Do you want to know the nutritional content in thousands of foods; or maybe you're considering a dietary analysis program? If so, this may be the BBS you have been looking for. The file names and descriptions were not especially informative, but I'm not a nutritionist.

Rutgers Cooperative Extension Bulletin Board System

☎ Parent organization: Rutgers Cooperative Extension

💻 Acronym for online service: RCEBBS

💻) Online service number(s): 201-383-8041, 800-722-0335 (New Jersey only)

👥 Contact person & title: Bruce Barbour, County Agricultural Agent

💻 Contact person's e-mail address: barbour@aesop.rutgers.edu

☎ Contact person's voice phone number: 908-932-9307

🖨 Contact person's Fax phone number: 908-932-6633

✉ Mailing address: P.O. Box 231, Cook College, Martin Hall, Room 111, New Brunswick, NJ 08903-0231

DESCRIPTION

"This service exists for practical education and self-improvement in the numerous subject matter areas addressed by Rutgers University Cooperative Extension."

"Features:

- Daily agricultural weather forecast, which becomes, in winter, a weekly summary
- The farmer's market line, which lists New Jersey agricultural products of all kinds
- Ag A.M., a national summary of farm-related news from the USDA
- The financial tip of the week by an RCE home economist and certified financial planner
- Educational calendar of events
- The horticultural engineering report
- The Rutgers fruit and vegetable IPM newsletter
- The insect and disease newsletter
- Food technology update
- Census files containing demographic, economic, and agricultural information
- Summaries of NJ regulations and laws affecting agriculture
- Recent commodity prices from major wholesale markets
- RCE fact sheets and bulletins

History:

The Rutgers Cooperative Extension Bulletin Board Service began operation in 1987. Its goal was to increase access to the wealth of practical information contained in RCE fact sheets, bulletins, newsletters, and handbooks and to create new ways for the public to interact with RCE professionals. From the start, the service was popular, rapidly growing to a user base of more than 2,000 and handling 10,000 to 15,000 calls per year. A major reason for the popularity was the convenience offered by the 7-day-per-week, 24-hour-per day operation and the economy of a toll-free line. As use grew larger, so did the service. From an original core of fact sheets and bulletins, the service grew to offer over 2 gigabytes of text, programs, and graphics."

📇 E-mail addresses:
gwncg@ncg.scs.ag.gov

🏛 Government agency acronym: SCS (NRCS in the near future)

👥 Contact person & title: Emil H. Horvath, NRDB Branch Leader

💻 Contact person's e-mail address: ehorvath@ncg.scs.ag.gov

☎ Contact person's voice phone number: 817-334-5292 x3028

📠 Contact person's Fax phone number: 817-334-5469

✉ Mailing address: National Cartography and GIS Center (GIS) P.O. Box 6567, Bldg. 23, 501 Felix, Bldg. 23, Fort Worth, TX 76115

ANNOTATION

If you explore the RCE BBS from outside New Jersey you will become jealous of New Jersey residents having access to such a wonderful resource. However, you may want to capture your session and send to your local agricultural extension office as an example of how they should be offering information. I'm not alone in my praise for the RCE BBS. Numerous articles have been written about the BBS and its SYSOP Bruce Barbour. Barbour's vision of disseminating agricultural information via modem was, and is, brilliant. I wish New York had a similar service.

Soil Conservation Service, National Cartography and GIS Center (GIS) Internet / Mosaic Data Catalog Pages

🌐 Internet address(es):
http://www.ncg.scs.ag.gov/nrdb.html

DESCRIPTION

"The USDA Soil Conservation Service has been responsible for gathering on-site technical information about natural resources, and especially soil resources, on private agricultural lands in the US for the past 52 years.

Much of these data are available through County Soil Survey reports at county SCS offices, but recently much of the soil survey data have been digitized at various levels (NATSGO: national soil survey database, STATSGO: state soil survey database, and SSURGO: county soil survey database). Other data sets, such as the National Resources Inventory (NRI), which are site-specific technical data collected every five years on-site for some 300,000 locations on US agricultural land, are now also available to the public for the last three inventories: 1982, 1987, and 1992.

Other data sets are available, and more are being added to the catalog periodically. The information listed is primarily intended to be used within GIS systems and database management systems software."

The opening graphic is beautiful and huge, so if you are using a ppp connection you may want to turn off the graphics when using this server.

The National Biological Impact Assessment Program Bulletin Board

💻 Acronym for online service: NBIAP

💻) Online service number(s): Registration BBS 703-231-3858, BBS 800-624-2733

Log on: Standard BBS for registration BBS. For ftp use anonymous as user id and your e-mail address as your password.

🌐 Internet address(es): ftp.vt.edu cd pub/biotechnology/ (directory).

🏛 Government agency acronym: USDA

👥 Contact person & title: Doug King, SYSOP

☎ Contact person's voice phone number: 703-231-3747

✉ Mailing address: The National Biological Impact Assessment Program Bulletin Board, Virginia Polytechnic Institute, 120 Engle Hall, Blacksburg, VA 24061

DESCRIPTION

The NBIAP BBS disseminates information about the following areas:

- USDA Regulations, Notices and Policies
- Other Agency Regulations, Notices and Policies—EPA, FDA, NIH, etc.
- Resource and Information Lists
- Permit Application/Termination Report
- Grant Programs, Invitations for Proposals
- Current And Past News Reports
- University of Wisconsin Listserver News Items
- HOT TOPICS—Bovine Somatotropin (BSt, BGH, Bovine Growth Hormone)

ANNOTATION

On one of the days that I explored the NBIAP BBS a local newspaper reporter published a story on bovine somatotropin, or BST, a bovine growth hormone given to dairy cows. I found several informative files about BST on the BBS, so I selected the one that I thought the reporter would find interesting and downloaded it. I opened the file as a wordprocessing document and then Faxed it to the reporter along with the telephone number of the BBS. This is one example of the many useful ways government information can be disseminated by electronic means.

DEPARTMENT OF COMMERCE

Census—BEA Electronic Forum

💻 Acronym for online service: BEA BBS

💻) Online service number(s): 301-763-7554, FedWorld BBS 703-321-8020

🌐 Internet address(es): telnet fedworld.gov

🏛 Government agency acronym: BEA

👥 Contact person & title: Nancy Smith

☎ Contact person's voice phone number: 301-763-1580

✉ Mailing address: Bureau of the Census, Data User Services, Washington, DC 20233

DESCRIPTION

"The CENSUS-BEA ELECTRONIC FORUM, referred to in this guide as the FORUM, is a personal computer-based electronic bulletin board (EBB) operated by the U.S. Department of Commerce's Bureau of the Census in Upper Marlboro, MD. This service is provided free of charge.

Users of the FORUM can access files that contain official press releases, telephone contact lists, training and publication schedules, excerpts of some data files, and CD-ROM software.

Our users have the option of joining one of the Special Interest Groups (SIGs) and asking questions of the subject specialist listed there."

ANNOTATION

Do file descriptions like "Demographic and Economic Data for Disaster Counties," "Children Living with Married Couples Live in Better Conditions," "New Racial and Ethnic Information May Debunk Stereotypes," and "Census Bureau Finds" interest you? If they do, you won't be disappointed in the BEA BBS. Not every file found here is so readily understandable. Many of the files are oriented toward serious census data users. The public domain CD-ROM reader software may be valuable to users who obtain census data on CD-ROM disks. Perusing the Presidential Announcements section I found the entire GATT Uruguay Round Final Report, the Health Security Plan Report and Legislative Proposal, and The National Information Infrastructure Proposal.

Census Vacancy BBS

🖥N Acronym for online service: CV BBS

🖥) Online service number(s): 301-763-4574, 800-451-6128

🏛 Government agency acronym: BOC

👥 Contact person & title: Nevins A. Frankel, Chief, Office Automation Branch

💻 Contact person's e-mail address: nfrankel@info.census.gov

☎ Contact person's voice phone number: 301-763-4950

📠 Contact person's Fax phone number: 301-763-2091

✉ Mailing address: Bureau of the Census, Room 3102, Federal Building, Suitland, MD 20233

DESCRIPTION

"The purpose of this board is to display Census Bureau vacancies from entry level to senior management. The Census Bureau offers a unique opportunity to be at the leading edge of statistical research and computer science technology in an historically state-of-the-art Federal Agency. If you would like to talk to a personnel representative, please call College Relations on: 763-5780. TTY (301) 763-4944."

ANNOTATION

If you aren't looking for a job with the Bureau of the Census there isn't much reason to log onto this BBS. However, if you are looking for work, it is worth the call to see if there is a position posted that you are qualified for.

Climate BBS

⌨ Acronym for online service: NWS CLIMON

💻) Online service number(s): 301-899-0827 1,200 bps, 301-899-1173 2,400 bps, 301-899-1174 2,400 bps with error correction, FedWorld BBS 703-321-8020

Log on: Use username "sample" and password "sample."

🌐 Internet address(es): telnet climon.wwb.noaa.gov or telnet fedworld.gov.

🏛 Government agency acronym: NOAA

👥 Contact person & title: Joanna M. Dionne, Physical Scientist

☎ Contact person's voice phone number: 301-763-4670

✉ Mailing address: Climate Analysis Center, 5200 Auth Road, Room 800, Camp Springs, MD 20746

DESCRIPTION

"As reported in the Federal Register Vol. 56, No. 139, Friday, July 19, 1991, 'The National Oceanic and Atmospheric Administration (NOAA) announces a new schedule of fees for the sale to the public of a variety of environmental data, information and products. NOAA will waive these fees as necessary to continue to participate in international data sharing arrangements and will continue to provide its data and information, at cost of reproduction and transmission, to other governmental entities and to universities and non-profit organizations for non-commercial use.

Commercial users of the Climate Dial-up service have been charged a fee for the number of calls placed per year...'"

ANNOTATION

This is a fee-based service. If you have a need for climate data, call Ms. Dionne for additional information on the fee schedule. To sample the system, the best method is to telnet directly to the BBS. The second recommended choice is to call the dial-up BBS. The last and least recommended path is through the FedWorld BBS.

Economic Bulletin Board

👥 Parent organization: Economics and Statistics Administration

⌨ Acronym for online service: EBB

💻) Online service number(s): 202-482-3870 300–2,400 bps, 202-482-2167 and 202-482-2548 300-9600 bps. FedWorld BBS 703-321-8020.

🌐 Internet address(es): telnet ebb.stat-usa.gov and telnet fedworld.gov

🏛 Government agency acronym: DOC

👥 Contact person & title: Paul Christy, EBB Manager

☎ Contact person's voice phone number: 202-482-1986

✉ Mailing address: U.S. Department of Commerce, Economics and Statistics Administration, Office of Business Analysis, HCHB, Room 4885, Washington, DC 20230

DESCRIPTION

The following is a partial description of the Federal agencies and files found on the EBB.

Agency for International Development Procurement Information Service (PAIS)

Congressional Budget Office Summary from CBO's Economic and Budget Outlook

Federal Reserve Board

- Aggregate Reserves (H.3)
- Atlanta Manufacturing Survey
- Bank Credit (H.8)
- Consumer Credit Report (G.19)
- FRB Monthly Foreign Exchange Rates (G.5)
- Factors Affecting Reserves (H.4.1)
- Flow of Funds (Z.7)
- Foreign Exchange Rates (G.5 and H.10)
- Historical Money Stock (H.6)
- Implied Volatility Rates for Foreign Exchange Options
- Industrial Production and Capacity Utilization (G.17)
- Money Stock Data (H.6)
- Noon EST Foreign Exchange Rates
- Selected Interest Rates (H.15)
- Treasury Quotations
- Various public statements
- 10:00 a.m. EST Foreign exchange rates

Office of the U.S. Trade Representative

- Various releases, agreements, and public statements

U.S. Department of Agriculture, Foreign Agricultural Service

- USDA Trade Leads

U.S. Department of Commerce, Bureau of Economic Analysis

- Business Conditions Indicators
- Capital Expenditures by Majority-Owned Foreign Affiliates Of U.S. Firms
- Current Business Statistics by Industry
- FDI Employment by State and Industry
- Gross State Product by State and Region
- Gross Domestic Product
- Leading, Lagging, Coincident Indexes
- Merchandise Trade, Balance of Payments Basis
- Metropolitan Area Projections
- Metropolitan Personal Income
- National Income and Product Account (NIPA) data, annual from 1929 forward
- National Income and Product Account (NIPA) Data, Quarterly from 1946 for ward
- Net International Investment Position in the U.S.
- Per Capita Income
- Personal Income and Earnings by State and Region
- Personal Income and Outlays
- Personal Income and Wages by State and Region
- Personal Income by County
- Population projections
- State Disposable Per Capita Income
- State Disposable Total Personal Income
- State Per Capita Personal Income
- State Economic And Population Projections
- Survey of Current Business (Various Articles and Tables)
- The Business Situation

- Total Personal Income
- U.S. Direct Foreign Investment Abroad
- U.S. Direct Investment Abroad
- U.S. International Transactions
- U.S. International Sales and Purchases of Private Services
- Various Press Releases
- Wages and Salaries by Industry by State and Region

U.S. Department of Commerce,
Bureau of Export Administration

- Associations, Institutes, and Think Tanks
- Consultants
- Defense Conversion Subcommittee Reports and leads
- Defense Enterprise Investment
- Russian and NIS Government contacts
- U.S. Government contacts

U.S. Department of Commerce,
Bureau of the Census

- Advance Retail Sales
- Benchmark Data
- Census Construction Review
- Quarterly Financial Report
- Durable Goods Shipments
- Housing Vacancies
- Housing Units Completed
- Housing Starts
- Imports and Exports by Country
- Imports and Exports by District
- Manufacturing and Trade
- Merchandise Trade
- Monthly Wholesale Sales

- New Construction
- New Home Sales
- Plant and Equipment
- Revised Monthly Retail Sales
- Shipments, Inventories, and Orders
- State Housing Permits
- U.S. Exports by 10-digit HS Number (No Country Detail)
- Various Industry Reports
- Various Press Releases

U.S. Department of Commerce,
Economics and Statistics Administration

- Economic Indicators
- Financial Ratios for Manufacturing Corporations
- Summaries of Various Economic Indicators

U.S. Department of Commerce,
International Trade Administration

- BISNIS Search for Partners Newsletter
- Eastern Europe Looks for Partners
- Environmental Technologies Exports
- Export Contacts by State
- Government Tender Trade Opportunities (TOP)
- HS Codes and Short Description
- Industry Sector Analysis (ISA) reports
- International Marketing Insight (IMI) reports
- Key Dollar Exchange Rates
- Private Sector Trade Opportunities (TOP)
- SIC Codes Correlated to HS Codes
- Textile and Apparel Imports

- Textile Summary of Agreements
- Textile Quotas Filled
- TPCC Trade Promotion Calendar data
- U.S. Foreign Trade Update
- U.S. Industrial Outlook 1993—Highlights

U.S. Department of Energy

- Comprehensive Oil and Gas Information Source (COGIS)
- Coal Overview
- Consumption of Energy by Source
- Crude Oil Price Summary
- Crude Oil and Petroleum Products Overview
- Energy Prices
- Energy Overview
- Forecast Components for U.S. Crude Oil
- Macroeconomic and Weather Assumptions
- Natural Gas Supply and Disposition
- Net Generation of Electricity by source
- Net Imports of Energy by Source
- Production of Energy by Source
- Supply, Demand, and Outlook by Type of Resource

U.S. Department of Labor, Bureau of Labor Statistics

- Average Wage and Compensation
- Real Earnings
- Consumer Price Index, Urban Wage Earners
- Consumer Price Index, Urban Consumers
- Earnings of Production Workers

- Earnings of Production/Nonagricultural
- Employment Situation
- Employment Cost Index
- Employment and Unemployment by State
- Establishment Employment Statistics
- Export/Import Price Indexes
- Household Employment Statistics
- Local Area Employment/Unemployment by Industry
- Major Collective Bargaining Settlements
- Producer Price Index
- Productivity and Cost
- Revised Seasonally Adjusted Average
- Various Releases and Public Statements

U.S. Department of Treasury, Bureau of Public Debt

- Cash Management Bill Auction Results
- Holdings of Treasury Securities in STRIP'ed format (STRIPS)
- Monthly Statement of Public Debt
- Note and T-bill Auction Results
- Savings Bond Current Redemption Values

U.S. Department of Treasury, Financial Management Services

- Daily Treasury Statement

U.S. Department of Treasury, Office of Foreign Assets Control

- Information of Transactions Control Restrictions
- U.S. Embargo Synopses

U.S. Department of Treasury,
Office of Market Finance

- Savings and Loan Bond Rates
- State and Local Government Bond Rates
- Treasury Yield Curve

U.S. Department of Treasury,
Savings Bond Division

- Treasury Savings Bond Rates
- Treasury Savings Bond Sales

The White House

- National Performance Review
- North American Free Trade Agreement
- President's Economic Plan
- FY95 U.S. Government Budget"

ANNOTATION

EBB is both free and fee-based. You can log on using "GUEST" as your password and you will have access to some of the data found on EBB. To obtain full access you will have to pay a $45 annual fee and 20 cents per minute from 8 A.M. to Noon; 15 cents per minute from Noon to 6 P.M.; and 5 cents per minute from 6 P.M. to 8 A.M. and for weekend time. All hours listed are EST. Check with EBB to see if these rates are still in effect. Paul Christy points out that the "annual fee includes $20 credit toward connect time charges."

Some of the information on the EBB is also available online from other sources for free. Before signing up for a fee-based online service, investigate whether you can obtain what you are looking for free from other sources. For example, try using an Internet search tool to look for the keywords associ-

ated with the data you are looking for. Sometimes you will get lucky and find a free source of the data. This is especially true for documents like trade agreements and White House Statements.

National Technical Information Service

FedWorld Online System

💻 Acronym for online service: Fedworld

💻) Online service number(s): FedWorld BBS 703-321-8020

🌐 Internet address(es): telnet Fedworld.gov, Gopher fedworld.gov

🏛 Government agency acronym: DOC

👥 Contact person & title: Bob Bunge, Business Manager

💻 Contact person's e-mail address: rbunge@access.digex.net

☎ Contact person's voice phone number: 703-487-4608

📠 Contact person's Fax phone number: 703-487-4009

✉ Mailing address: U.S. Department of Commerce, Technology Administration, National Technical Information Service, 5285 Port Royal Road, Springfield, VA 22161

DESCRIPTION

What is NTIS FedWorld? Each year, the U.S. Federal Government spends more than $70 billion on scientific and technical research. The National Technical Information Service (NTIS) is tasked by Congress to help disseminate the vast amount of scientific and technical information along with other, non-technical information. As a central point of connectivity, NTIS

FedWorld offers access to thousands of files across a wide range of subject areas. You can find information ranging from Environmental Protection to Small Business. If you are interested in any of the thousands of NTIS products, download the NTIS Products and Services Catalog—P&SCAT.TXT, located in the NTIS Library of files.

FedWorld Features include: FedWorld Gateway, a gateway connection to other Govt. systems worldwide; online database, CALS, NTIS, Patent abstracts and more; Locator Access Retrieval System, Boolean searches on wide area subjects; International Federal jobs opportunities; White House press releases and documents; Private mail; Public mail conferences; online ordering of documents; Registry of users; and much much more.

The following is the FedWorld list of electronic bulletin boards that can be reached through FedWorld. (There is no number 1 and the following numbers change. Use FedWorld's current list for accurate number listings):

2:ALF (USDA) National Agricultural Library BBS

3:ALIX (LC) Automated Library Information eXchange

4:BOM-BBN (DOI) Bureau of Mines-Bulletin Board Network

5:ISM-SIS (IRS) ISM Support Info System

6:CIC-BBS (GSA) Consumer Information Center

7:CLU-IN (EPA) Superfund Data and Information

8:CPO-BBS (Census) Lists Open Jobs at the Census Dept

9:CRS-BBS (DOJ) Americans with Disabilities Act Information

10:Computer Security (NIST) Computer Sys Lab Computer Security BBS

11:DCBBS (DC Govt) DC Government Information

12:DMIE (NIST/CSL) NIST/CSL Data Management Information

13:EBB (DOC) Economic Data and Information

14:ELISA System (DOD) DoD Export License Tracking System

15:GSA/IRM BBS (GSA) Information Resources Management Issues

16:EPUB (DOE) Energy Information and Data

17:FDA's BBS (FDA) and Policies

18:FDA/DMMS (FDA) PMA, IDE, 510k & Guidance Documents

19:FERC-CIPS (DOE) Fed Energy Regulatory Commission

20:FEBBS (FHWA) FHWA Information and Data

22:FEDERAL BBS (GPO) GPO and Govt Data (Fee-Based)

23:OSS-BBS (GSA) GSA Online Schedules System

24:Eximbank BBS (EXIMBANK) Export/Import Bank data

25:JAG-NET (USN) Navy Judge Advocate General

26:Labor News (DOL) Dept. of Labor Information and Files

27:Megawatt 1 (DOE) Information on Energy and DoE

28:NADAP (USN) Navy Drug and Alcohol Abuse Prevention

29:NAVTASC (USN) NAVCOMTELSTA Washington DC

30:EHSC-DDS Army Engineering & Housing

31:NDB-BBS(USDA) Human Nutrition Information Service

32:NSSDC\NASA\Goddard:The NASA NODIS Locator System.

33:1040 BBS (IRS) Electronic Tax Filing Information

34:SBB-BB (Treasury) Surety Bond Branch, Circular 570

35:OIS (Bureau of Prisons) US Bureau of Prison Employees

36:SBIR-BBS (NASA) NASA Small Business Innovation Research

37:WTIE-BBS (EPA) Wastewater Treatment Information Exchange

38:QED-BBS (USGS) Quick Epicenter Determ and EQ data

39:SALEMDUG-BBS (FEMA) State and Local FEMA User Groups

40:SBA On Line (SBA) SBA Information & Data (Full Service)

41:GAO WATCHDOG (GAO) Identify Waste Fraud and Abuse

42:SBAI-BBS (SBA) Small Business Administration Internal BBS

43:Sample Weather Data (NWS):Sample data from Fee Based System

44:OPM Mainstreet (OPM) OPM—Job information, Personnel Guidance

45:TELENEWS (DOE) Data and on Fossil fuels

46:USA-GPCS BBS (USA) Army Information System Software

47:USCS-BBS (USCS) Customs and Exchange Rate Data & Information

48:USGS-BBS (USGS) Geological Survey BBS/CD-ROM Information

49:NLPBB (USN) CNO's Navy Leadership Policy BB

50:FMS-BBS (Treasury) Inventory Management Data & Programs

51:OASH-BBS (HHS) Health & AIDS Information & Reports

52:FEDIX :Links Fed Data to Higher Education

53:DASC-ZE (DLA) PC Information and Files

54:GPSIC (USCG) GPS, Loran & Omega Information/Status

55:NGCR-BBS (USN) Next Generation Computer Resources Standards

56:PPIC-BBS (EPA) Pollu. Preven, Clean Product, Ozone

57:Gulfline (EPA&NOAA) Gulf Coast Pollution Information

58:FAA Safety Exchange (FAA):Small Plane Safety Reports &)

59:NTIS QuikSERVICE (NTIS) Order NTIS Documents Online

61:STIS (NSF) Science & Technology Information System

62:MI-BBS (DOE) DoE Minority Impact Bulletin Board

63:TECH SPECS (NRC) Technical Specifications Improvement Pr

64:Census-BEA (Census) Census BEA Electronic Forum

65:IHS-BBS (HHS) Indian Health Service BBS

66:NOAA-ESDD (NOAA) NOAA Environmental Services Data Direct

67:Offshore-BBS (DOI) Off Shore Oil & Gas Data

68:TQM-BBS (T. Glenn) Total Quality Management

69:NIDR Online (NIH) Nat. Institute of Dental Research

70:NIHGL (NIH) Nat. Institute of Health Grant Line BBS

71:PayPerNet #1 (OPM) Federal. Pay & Performance Management BBS

73:CASUCOM (GSA) Interagency Shared Services/Resources

74:ATTIC (EPA) Alternative Treatment Tech Information Center

75:NCJRS-BBS (DOJ) National Criminal Justice Reference Sy

76:DRIPSS (EPA) Drinking Water Information Processing Support

77:PIM BBS (EPA) Pesticide Information Network

78:SWICH BBS (EPA&SWANA) Solid Waste Management

79:NPS-BBS (EPA) Nonpoint Source Program BBS

80:OEA BBS (DOI) Interior's Off. of Environment. Affairs

81:Metro-Net (USA) Army Morale, Welfare, and Recreation

82:CABB (Dof State) Passport Information/ Travel Alerts

83:BUPERS Access (USN) Navy Personnel Information

84:FCC-State Link (FCC) FCC Daily Digest & Carrier Stats/Report

85:HUD-N&E BB (HUD) HUD News & Events BB. Press Releases

87:FREND #1 (NARA) Fed. Register Electronic News Delivery

88:FREND #2 (NARA) Fed. Register Electronic News Delivery

89:NHS-BBS (HHS) National Head Start BBS

90:WSCA-BBS (DOL) Board of Wage & Service Contract Appeal

91:TEBBS (OGE) Office of Government Ethics BBS

92:HSETC MD (USN) Naval Health Sci. Edu. & Training Command

93:PPCUG/RDAMIS (DOD) Pentagon Users Group BBS

94:ORDBBS (EPA) EPA Office of Research & Development BB

95:CBEE (USCG) Coast Guard Online Magazine & News

96:ATD BBS (FAA) Air Transport Div. BBS

97:ATOS-BBS (FAA) Air Traffic Operations Service BBS

98:AEE BBS (FAA) FAA Office of Environment & Energy

99:OCA BBS (PRC) Postal Rate Commission/Consumer Advocat

100:GEMI (GSA) GSA Electronic Management Information

101:Airports BBS #1 (FAA) Airport Operators and Designers

102:EnviroNET (NASA) Space Environment Information Service

103:FAA HQ BBS (FAA) FAA Headquarters BBS

104:IRS-SOI (IRS) Public Taxpayer Statistical Information

105:ARA-BBS (FAA) Aviation Rulemaking Advisory BBS

106:IIAC BBS (USA) Integration & Analysis Center BBS

108:ACF-BBS (HHS) Administration for Children and Families

109:NTIA-BBS (DOC) Radio Frequency Management Issues

110:ED Board (DOEdu) Dept. of Education Grant & Contract Information

111:BHPr-BBS (HHS) Medical & Health
Services Information

112:Marine Data BBS (NOAA) Marine
Databases & Files

113:Call-ERS BBS (USDA) Agriculture
Economic Research Information

114:Call ERS (USDA) Economic Research
Line Service Line 2

115:ABLE INFORM (DOEdu) Disability &
Rehabilitation Data & Information

116:PTO-BBS (PTO) Patent and Trademark
Office BBS

117:PerManNet (Dof State) US Agency for
International Development

118:Quick Facts! (NIAAA/HHS) Alcohol
Abuse & Alcoholism Information

119:IITF-BBS (NTIA) Information
Infrastructure Task Force BBS

123:IBNS/OMPAT BBS (DOD) Military
Performance Assessment

124:EDOS (DC Crt Appeals) US Court of
Appeals, District of Columbia

125:RSA-BBS (RSA) Rehabilitation Services
Administration

126:FRESBB (GSA) Federal Real Estate Sales
Bulletin Board

127:NIH Information Center (NIH) NIH
Information, Files and Publications

128:NCUA BBS (NCUA) National Credit
Union Administration

130:OECI-BBS (DOC&DOD) Defense
Conversion Information

132:AVADS-BBS (DOI) Dept. of Interior Job
Announcements

133:NRCDR-BB (NRC) NRC
Decommissioning Rulemaking BBS

Massive is the best word to describe
FedWorld. With more than 130 electronic
bulletin boards to choose from, FedWorld
is the largest single means of accessing U.S.
Government information online. You can
connect with FedWorld directly by phone
or through the Internet. Their Internet connection is often slower than their direct dial
connection. If speed is important you may
want to bypass FedWorld and call the
listed bulletin boards directly.

I found that using FedWorld's Internet
connection to connect to BBSs was
extremely slow and sluggish. File transfers
were often impossible using this method.
Also, I found that ZMODEM file transfer
protocol did not work. KERMIT file transfer protocol, which is much slower, did
work, sometimes. FedWorld still needs to
solve lots of problems. For example, there is
no uniformity between the BBBS. Each government agency uses its own software con-
figuration and the configurations vary
widely. Its Internet connection can be slow,
sluggish, or just not available, depending
on the time of day of the connection.
During the course of compiling this book
FedWorld's performance improved significantly. Although FedWorld has done a
great job making information accessible,
accessing and using it can still be a daunting and confusing experience for a novice
user.

Information Infrastructure Task Force Gopher

🖥 Acronym for online service: NTIAU-NIX1

🖥) Online service number(s): 202-501-1920

🌐 Internet address(es): gopher@iitf.doc.gov

🏛 Government agency acronym: USDC / NTIA

👥 Contact person & title: Charles Franz

💻 Contact person's e-mail address: cfranz@ntia.doc.gov

☎ Contact person's voice phone number: 202-482-1835

📠 Contact person's Fax phone number: 202-482-0979

✉ Mailing address: U.S. Department of Commerce / NTIA, 14th & Constitution Ave., NW, Room 4888, Washington, DC 20230

DESCRIPTION

"NTIA is responsible for developing and implementing regulations regarding the Federal Government's management and use of the radio frequency spectrum."

ANNOTATION

The IITF Gopher is not a BBS. It is not possible to send or receive e-mail or messages here. The IITF Gopher is a file distribution system. That means that you can log on, without a password, and read or download text files related to the Information Infrastructure Task Force. The Frequently Asked Questions (FAQ) is worth reading for anyone interested in the Information Superhighway. Other files available include press releases, policy statements, minutes of meetings and much more.

Marine Data Bulletin Board System

📡 Parent organization: United States Coast & Geodetic Survey

🖥 Acronym for online service: MDBBS

🖥) Online service number(s): 301-713-4573, FedWorld 703-321-8020

🌐 Internet address(es): telnet fedworld.gov then gateway to Marine Data BBS

💻 E-mail addresses: rbecker@banyan.doc.gov

🏛 Government agency acronym: NOAA

👥 Contact person & title: Ruby Becker, SYSOP

☎ Contact person's voice phone number: 301-713-2653

📠 Contact person's Fax phone number: 301-713-4581

✉ Mailing address: Nautical Charting Research & Development Lab, NOAA, National Ocean Service, N/CG211, 1315 East-West Highway, Room 4746, Silver Spring, MD 20910-3233

DESCRIPTION

"The Marine Data Bulletin Board System is a free public service of the National Oceanic and Atmospheric Administration (NOAA), National Ocean Service, Coast and Geodetic Survey. The bulletin board provides access to existing digital nautical charting data.

The Coast and Geodetic Survey performs hydrographic surveys of the coastal waters of the United States and its territories and possessions. The data collected in these surveys are used in the preparation of nautical charts and for other purposes. The Marine Data BBS makes these data available to the public at no cost.

Accessible databases include: NOAA Wrecks and Obstructions, Nautical Chart Locator, Hydrographic Surveys Index, Sediments, NADCON Datum Conversion, Aerial Photographs Index, Chart Sales Agents, Tide Gauge Locations, and others. Additional databases will be added as they become available. The BBS also serves to gather information on the demand for and uses of these databases.

The system is menu-driven, easy to use, and provides help with every screen. Callers can search the databases, view the results of the search, and then, if desired, download the results as compressed text files.

The BBS also contains special bulletin files. These may be read on-line or downloaded. Bulletin topics include: NOAA products and services, NOAA points of contact, monthly announcements of new editions of nautical charts, and announcements of special conferences and events."

ANNOTATION

Sea captains, boaters, and other mariners, the Marine Data Bulletin Board is the BBS you need to know about. The files available on the MD-BBS are mostly pointers to other NOAA services, but this is still an excellent resource. Be sure to download the file B1.ZIP. It will tell you nearly everything you need to know about obtaining NOAA products and services. The only person you can exchange messages with is the SYSOP, but the SYSOP is quick to respond to questions.

National Computer Systems Laboratory Computer Security BBS

⌨) Online service number(s) 301-948-5717, 2400 bps 301-948-5140, 9600 bps

🌐 Internet address(es): telnet to cs-bbs.ncsl.nist.gov (129.6.54.30) download files available via anonymous ftp from csrc.ncsl.nist.gov (129.6.54.11)

🏛 Government agency acronym: NIST

👥 Contact person & title: Marianne Swanson

☎ Contact person's voice phone number: 301-975-3359

🖨 Contact person's Fax phone number: 301-948-0279

✉ Mailing address: National Computer Systems Laboratory Computer Security BBS, National Institute of Standards and Technology, Technology Building, Room A-215, Gaithersburg, MD 20899

DESCRIPTION

"This Bulletin Board is maintained by the Computer Systems Laboratory and is intended to encourage the sharing of information that will help users and managers better protect their data and systems."

ANNOTATION

Computer viruses, encryption schemes, anti-viral software reviews, journals, newsletters, bibliographies, and more are available from the NIST BBS. Whether you are just curious or a serious researcher interested in computer security, this BBS offers an extensive collection of files worthy of your attention. Pay attention to the message on the bulletin menu or you may find yourself wasting time repeating commands.

National Geophysical Data Center

Acronym for online service: NGDC BBS

Online service number(s): 303-497-7319

Log on: The BBS does not use a standard log on sequence, but the menus are easy to follow. For the Internet connection respond to login with "online" and password with "onlln3"

Internet address(es): telnet meridian.ngdc.noaa.gov, WWW-http://web.ngdc.noaa.gov.html, ftp.ngdc.noaa.gov, Gopher gopher@boombox.micro.umn.edu.

E-mail addresses: info@ngdc.noaa.gov

Contact person & title: Eric Kihn

Contact person's voice phone number: 303-497-6346

Contact person's Fax phone number: 303-497-6513

Mailing address: National Geophysical Data Center, 325 Broadway, Boulder, CO 80303-3328

DESCRIPTION

"This system was designed to allow the user to retrieve, browse, and use NGDC data holdings from a remote site.

NGDC maintains an archive of all data recorded on DMSP satellites as relayed to NGDC by Air Force Global Weather Central. Data from March 1992 to March 1994, are con-

sidered to be experimental. After March 1994, the system should be fully operational.

NGDC archives contain data that are post processed, reconstructed, positioned, and geolocated using the same software. NGDC and the National Snow and Ice Data Center will provide a broad range of user services within two weeks of observation. Copies of the 8 mm archive tapes are provided by NGDC. Digital data, for selected areas during specific times, and publication quality prints of selected images are provided by both NGDC and NSIDC, with NSIDC providing special services to the snow and ice community."

ANNOTATION

Describing how to access NGDC requires additional instruction because of the options available. The following was captured from NGDC:

"On-line Access to Sample Data, Imagery and Information from the Defense Meteorological Satellite Program (DMSP) Data Archive at the National Geophysical Data Center (NGDC).

DMSP is a two satellite constellation of near-polar orbiting, sun-synchronous satellites moni-toring meteorological, oceanographic and solar-terrestrial physics environments. DMSP sample data and information may be accessed on-line through the following:

1) Anonymous FTP
   First ftp ftp.ngdc.noaa.gov. Login as anonymous with your e-mail address as your password. Change directory (cd) to DMSP. You will find an ASCII file containing an overview of the program at NGDC (program-overview.txt) and a file describing the general directory structure of the DMSP section (dmsp.readme). Sample images and/or plots along with sensor descriptions can be found within the SENSORS subdirectory.

2) Bulletin Board System
   Telephone: (303) 497-7319

The modem settings are: standard preferred terminal emulation's are VT100 or VT102- 8 data bits, no parity, 1 stop bit modem speeds are 300–14,400 bps, auto baud detection, V.32 Enter the DMSP subdirectory. Sample imagery and/or plots along with documentation describing the program and satellite sensors can be found here.

3) GOPHER

The NGDC Gopher is at gopher. ngdc.noaa.gov. Change directory to the NGDC Public Data and Access Tools. Change directory again to Defense Meteorological Satellite Program (DMSP) Archive. Sample imagery and/or plots along with documentation describing the program and satellite sensors can be found here.

4) MOSAIC

The DMSP Mosaic page is located at http://web.ngdc.noaa.gov/dmsp/dmsp.html. Sample imagery and/or plots along with documentation describing the program and satellite sensors can be found here."

Capturing screens continuously doesn't work while using the NGDC BBS. The reason for this is that it uses a sophisticated graphical arrangement for navigating its structure.

National Telecommunications & Information Administration BBS

🖳N   Acronym for online service: NTIA BBS

🖳)   Online service number(s): 202-482-1199, FedWorld BBS, 703-321-8020

🌐   Internet address(es): telnet ntiabbs.ntia.doc.gov or telnet fedworld.gov then gateway to NTIA BBS

🏛   Government agency acronym: DOC

👥   Contact person & title: Roger Clark, SYSOP

💻   Contact person's e-mail address: rclark@ntia.doc.gov

☎   Contact person's voice phone number: 202-487-1407

📠   Contact person's Fax phone number: 202-482-4396

✉   Mailing address: U.S. Department of Commerce, National Telecommunications & Information Administration, Herbert C. Hoover Building (HCHB), 14th and Constitution Avenue, Washington, DC 20230

DESCRIPTION

The following is a listing of the opening menu:

- Who is NTIA?
- Openness Program Information
- National Information Infrastructure Initiatives
- TeleView— Testimony/Notices/Comments
- Spectrum Management Activities
- International Activities
- NTIA Grant Programs— TIIAP/PTFP/NECET
- Press Releases and Public Notices
- Legislation— Existing/Pending/Initiatives
- TeleConnect—Gateway Services
- White House Documents
- Definitions of Key Terms
- What's New—List of New Files
- World Cup '94 Information

The NTIA BBS is a good place to visit if your interests lean toward telecommunications and information. The online employee telephone book is huge and takes forever to scroll off your screen.

The NTIA message area is active and a good place to visit if you need information or wish to share information about telecommunication issues.

NOAA Environmental Information Services

💻) Online service number(s): (202) 606-4666, at "xyplex>" prompt type "c esdim1", login as "lynx" or "Gopher"

Log on: "lynx" or "gopher"

🌐 Internet address(es): WWW http://www.esdim.noaa.gov, Gopher gopher.esdim.noaa.gov, telnet esdim.noaa.gov, gopher.esdim.noaa.gov

💻← E-mail addresses: help@esdim.noaa.gov

🏛 Government agency acronym: NOAA

👥 Contact person & title: Anne O'Donnell

💻← Contact person's e-mail address: odonnell@esdim.noaa.gov

☎ Contact person's voice phone number: (202) 606-5012

🖨 Contact person's Fax phone number: (202) 606-0509

✉ Mailing address: NOAA Environmental Information Services, 1825 Connecticut Ave., NW, Rm. 506, Washington, DC 20235

"The NOAA Environmental Information Services provides access to data and information available from NOAA through the World Wide Web and Gopher. Users without Gopher or World Wide Web clients can access these services through telnet and dial-up services. Connections to many NOAA systems, including other Gophers and home pages are available from this service. Users can also search for data and information through the NOAA Data Set Catalog which provides pointers to data sets available from NOAA."

Great graphics, excellent design, and useful content are what you can expect from the NOAA Environmental Information Services WWW server. This server is large enough and interesting enough to explore for hours.

NOAA Home Page

🌐 Internet address(es): http://www.noaa.gov

💻← E-mail addresses: noaa-www@www.noaa.gov

🏛 Government agency acronym: NOAA

👥 Contact person & title: Anne O'Donnell

💻← Contact person's e-mail address: odonnell@esdim.noaa.gov

☎ Contact person's voice phone number: (202) 606-5012

🖨 Contact person's Fax phone number: (202) 606-0509

✉ Mailing address: NOAA Environmental Information Services, 1825 Connecticut Ave., NW, Rm. 506, Washington, DC 20235

"The NOAA Home Page is the official entry point for Internet users to a variety of NOAA data, products, and information. The NOAA home page gives users several views of the agency. One view centers on the various environmental research programs and strategic areas for which NOAA is responsible. Other views include an interactive map showing the locations of various NOAA facilities, an interactive organizational chart, and a list of the various NOAA offices with links to information about the offices and connections to home pages. From the NOAA home page, one can learn about NOAA's mission, locate NOAA personnel, find job vacancy announcements, read the latest news on topics such as the ozone hole, and connect to many other services available from NOAA offices."

ANNOTATION

You will find more great graphics, more data, and more information on the NOAA home page WWW server. Other NOAA WWW servers are accessible through this home page.

North American ISDN Users Forum

📡 Parent organization: National Institute of Standards and Technology

🖳 Acronym for online service: ISDN

🖳 Online service number(s): 301-869-7281

🌐 Internet address(es): telnet 129.6.53.11

🏛 Government agency acronym: NIST

👥 Contact person & title: Dawn Hoffman

📧 Contact person's e-mail address: dawn@isdn.ncsl.nist.gov

☎ Contact person's voice phone number: 301-975-2937

📠 Contact person's Fax phone number: 301-926-9675

✉ Mailing address: National Institute of Standards and Technology, National Computer Systems Laboratory, Advanced Systems Division, Bldg. 223, Room B364, Gaithersburg, MD 20899

DESCRIPTION

"Its intended use is purely for depositing and retrieving information concerning the North American ISDN Users Forum, & the Integrated Services Digital Network emerging technologies."

ANNOTATION

The ISDN-Forum BBS uses TEAMate BBS software which does not conform to widely used electronic bulletin board structure or commands. After following the instructions for establishing myself as a new user, I couldn't figure out how to download a manual or negotiate the menus. I accidentally logged out and couldn't get back in using the user name and password previously supplied. Due to that, I can't provide much of an annotation of the bulletin board's content.

Office of Economic Conversion Information BBS

🖳 Acronym for online service: OECI BBS

🖳 Online service number(s): 800-352-2949, FedWorld 703-321-8020

- Internet address(es): telnet ecix.doc.gov or fedworld.gov then gateway to OECI BBS

- Government agency acronym: DOC

- Contact person & title: Nathan Maryn, SYSOP

- Contact person's e-mail address: nmaryn@doc.gov

- Contact person's voice phone number: 800-345-1222

- Contact person's Fax phone number: 202-482-0995

- Mailing address: U.S. Department of Commerce, Economic Development Administration, Room 7112, 14th Street & Pennsylvania Avenue, Washington, DC 20230

DESCRIPTION

"Welcome to the Office of Economic Conversion Information's clearinghouse service. This Service is a collaborative effort of the U.S. Department of Commerce's Economic Development Administration and the U.S. Department of Defense.

This Clearinghouse is designed to serve the information needs of communities, businesses and individuals in adjusting to the effects of defense downsizing and other changing economic conditions. It provides a one-stop locator service to provide users ready access to critical information such as current economic data; status of the national defense downsizing effort; relevant legislation, policies and regulations; descriptions of Federal, State and local assistance programs; and perhaps most importantly, identification of the right contacts for further details and services.

WHAT YOU CAN FIND

The Clearinghouse is designed to provide three major groups of users—INDIVIDUALS, BUSINESSES and COMMUNITIES—with five basic kinds of information:

1. GENERAL BACKGROUND: Current news and press releases on economic conversion; bulletins and calendar of events; and a bibliography of guides and other references.

2. ECONOMIC and DEFENSE IMPACTS: Defense base closure and realignment status reports; defense budgets and projected job and industry sector impacts; civilian output trends; and national economic data.

3. TECHNOLOGY ISSUES: Application of defense technology to the civilian sector; incentives for research and development; and emerging product innovations.

4. CONTACTS and HELP GUIDES: Community and industry models of economic adjustment; available defense assets; and directories and points of national, state and local contact.

5. ADJUSTMENT PROGRAMS: Federal, State, local and private assistance programs; awarded grants; and legislation, regulations and policies.

USING THE SYSTEM

The Information Clearinghouse contains a wide variety of data and material intended to meet the information needs of many different types of users. To help you find what you need, the system will ask you to choose from menu prompts that target the category of information most responsive to your inquiry. Once you find the information you need, you will be able to retrieve the data in one or more ways depending on your method of accessing the Clearinghouse."

ANNOTATION

It is important to note that the OECI BBS is operated jointly by the U.S. Department of Commerce and the Department of Defense.

Patent and Trademark Bulletin Board

💻N Acronym for online service: PTO BBS

💻) Online service number(s): 703-305-8950, FedWorld BBS 703-321-8020

🌐 Internet address(es): telnet fedworld.gov then gateway to PTO BBS

🏛 Government agency acronym: DOC

👥 Contact person & title: Jane S. Myers, Director OEIPS

☎ Contact person's voice phone number: 703-305-5652

📠 Contact person's Fax phone number: 703-308-3280

✉ Mailing address: U.S. Patent and Trademark Office, 2121 Crystal Drive, Suite 1100C, Washington, DC 20231

DESCRIPTION

"The U.S. Patent and Trademark Office (PTO) Bulletin Board System (BBS) provides a mechanism for easy access to the weekly issue file of patent data, including Official Gazette (OG) notices, PTO news bulletins, press releases, directory information and product & services information and brochures.

The PTO BBS allows the caller to search and list weekly issue files for patent titles, abstracts and classes. Included are the weekly OG notices for Patents & Trademarks. We encourage your use of the system, but ask that you become aware of the rules and policies of this bulletin board."

ANNOTATION

The U.S. Patent and Trademark Office is a high-volume information handling facility. Making its information public through com-puter technology is logical and necessary. The PTO-BBS does a great job disseminating PTO information. However, there is so much information available from PTO that the BBS should be considered a stepping stone to the larger amounts of data available by CD-ROM, magnetic tape, and other media. The PTO-BBS is a serious no-nonsense BBS with a mission. It is a valuable resource to patent searchers, patent lawyers, inventors, and anyone else working with patents and trademarks.

Space Environment Laboratory BBS

💻N Acronym for online service: SEL

💻) Online service number(s): 303-497-5000

🌐 Internet address(es): URL http:www.sel.noaa.gov

👥 Contact person & title: For BBS Kurt Carran, SYSOP and for WWW, Vi Raben

💻 Contact person's e-mail address: Raben vhill@sel.noaa.gov

☎ Contact person's voice phone number: Carran 303-497-3188

✉ Mailing address: National Oceanic and Atmospheric Administration, Space Environment Laboratory, 325 Broadway, Boulder, CO 80303

DESCRIPTION

"This Bulletin Board is a service provided by the Space Environment Laboratory (SEL) of NOAA, U.S. Dept. of Commerce. It is a means of conveniently making available the various text message products produced by the Space Environment Service Center (SESC) which is operated by SEL. The center monitors Solar activity in collaboration with the USAF and provides advisories and forecasts of this activity and the effects on the near space environment of the Earth. Feedback from users on the utility of the board and suggestions are welcome.

NOAA's Space Environment Laboratory provides near-real-time monitoring and forecasting of the environment between the Sun and Earth. Our WWW server features Today's Space Weather with current solar imagery, plots of x-ray data from the GOES satellites, and forecasts of solar-terrestrial conditions. The WWW, Gopher, and ftp servers provide access to the most recent solar images and data as well as information for the past 30 days."

ANNOTATION

Short-wave radio enthusiasts, among others, should find the NOAA SEL BBS interesting. Sunspot activity often affects the quality of short-wave radio broadcasts. By logging onto this BBS, radio listeners can read reports and predictions of events that may affect radio listening. Science students may find the reports here an excellent source of data for experiments and simulations. Take a look at the sun images on the WWW server—they are fascinating.

DEPARTMENT OF DEFENSE

Enterprise Integration News BBS

⌨N   Acronym for online service: EI News BBS

⌨)   Online service number(s): FedWorld 703-321-8020

⊕   Internet address(es): telent fedworld.gov then gateway to EI News BBS

🏛   Government agency acronym: DOD

👥   Contact person & title: Laura A. Sheehy, Systems Analyst & Becky Ackerman, Collaborative Computing Specialist

💻   Contact person's e-mail address: Sheehy (sheehyl@cc.ims.disa.mil)

☎   Contact person's voice phone number: 703-486-3500

🖨   Contact person's Fax phone number: 703-521-7288

✉   Mailing address: Logicon Technology, 2100 Washington Blvd., Arlington, VA 22204

DESCRIPTION

"The goal of the Center for Functional Process Improvement Expertise is to assist the DoD functional community and other government agencies in reducing their annual operating costs, increasing their effectiveness, and responding in a flexible and timely manner to evolving requirements. Specifically, the Center for Functional Process Improvement Expertise is to introduce the functional community to tools and techniques that support Business Process Reengineering (BPR) and ongoing BPR Projects.

The EI News BBS is an expanded platform that includes forums on DoD reinvention and change management."

ANNOTATION

This BBS was formally the Corporate Information Management BBS or CIM BBS. You won't find games or other frivolous files here. The message sections are not large, but they are interesting to read if you are interested in business methods.

Office of Economic Conversion Information BBS

⌨N Acronym for online service: OECI BBS

💻) Online service number(s): 800-352-2924, FedWorld 703-321-8020

🌐 Internet address(es): telnet ecix.doc.gov or fedworld.gov then gateway to OECI BBS

See the Department of Commerce listing for OECI BBS. This BBS is jointly operated by the Department of Commerce and the Department of Defense.

Export License Status Advisor

⌨N Acronym for online service: ELISA

💻) Online service number(s): 703-697-6109, FedWorld BBS 703-321-8020

🌐 Internet address(es): telnet fedworld.gov and gateway to ELISA.

👥 Contact person & title: Ken Freshwater

☎ Contact person's voice phone number: 703-693-1098

📠 Contact person's Fax phone number: 703-693-5305

✉ Mailing address: Export License Status Advisor BBS, 400 Army Navy Drive, Arlington, VA 22203

ELISA provides information about the status of export license applications.

ELISA does one thing and it does that thing well. If export applications do not interest you, neither will ELISA.

Information Mission Area Bulletin Board System

👁 Parent organization: U.S. Army Integration and Analysis Center

⌨N Acronym for online service: IMA BBS

💻) Online service number(s): 703-285-6400, 703-285-6401, FedWorld 703-321-8020

🌐 Internet address(es): telnet fedworld.gov then gateway to IMA BBS.

🏛 Government agency acronym: IIAC

👥 Contact person & title: Major Mark Fichten

💻← Contact person's e-mail address: mark.fichten@pentagon-1dms.army.mil

☎ Contact person's voice phone number: 800-453-4422, 703-285-6105

📠 Contact person's Fax phone number: 703-285-6016

✉ Mailing address: Office of the Director of Information Systems for Command Control, Communications and Computers, IMA Integration and Analysis Center (IIAC), ATTN: SAIS-IIAC (Bit Division), The Pentagon, Washington, DC 20310-0107

DESCRIPTION

"…The IMA bulletin board was set up to facilitate the free flow of information between the IIAC and any Army agency or organization that can benefit from it.

The IMA BBS is an electronic repository of documents relating to the Army Information Mission Area (IMA). The Information Mission Area is composed of 6 areas: Automation, Telecommunications, Records Management, Visual Information, Publications & Printing, and Libraries.

Some of the services this bulletin board provides are:

1. The ability to download:
    a. DISC4 Point-of-Contact Lists (with phone numbers)
    b. 25 Series Publications
    d. DoD Publications
    e. IMA Newsletter, VIEWPOINT (Published by IIAC)
2. Ability to leave mail for other users of the bulletin board."

ANNOTATION

Military acronyms are lost on me and most of the files on the IMA BBS use acronyms as descriptors. The point I'm making is that I'm not going to be of much help evaluating this BBS. However I can recommend this BBS to U.S. Army personnel and to readers of military literature. They will probably understand the acronyms. One file group that attracted my attention was:

"The Army Data Dictionary is now available on the BBS in the MISC area. This package is in 5 parts totaling over 7 megabytes of ZIP files. It upzips to OVER 30 megabytes! If you need more time to download the files, call the SYSOP at (703) 285-6105.

INSTRUCTIONS: Download the files ARMY-DD.1 through ARMY-DD.5 and ASSEMBLE.BAT. Run the file ASSEMBLE.BAT by typing ASSEMBLE and follow the directions. If you have questions, please call the IMA BBS SYSOP.

We can mail you a copy of the ZIP files of the Army Data Dictionary if you send us a STAMPED, SELF-ADDRESSED disk mailer with 6 high-density 3-1/2" disks inside labeled parts 1 through 6. Please include your name and phone number so we can contact you if we have questions. Send to CPT(P) Mark Fichten / 6147 Palmcrest Court / Dale City, VA 22193.

ARMY-DD.11401393 01-27-93 Army Data Dictionary (ADD) contains the data files and viewer. Part 1 of 5 parts plus ASSEMBLE.BAT which is needed to put the parts together. This package takes over 30 megabytes of hard disk space! We will mail you these files. See the NEWS for more information. (View the BULLETINS and select News)

ARMY-DD.21401082 01-27-93 Part 2 of the Army Data Dictionary (ADD)

ARMY-DD.31401082 01-27-93 Part 3 of the Army Data Dictionary (ADD)

ARMY-DD.41401082 01-27-93 Part 4 of the Army Data Dictionary (ADD)

ARMY-DD.51400769 01-27-93 Part 5 of the Army Data Dictionary (ADD)

ASSEMBLE BAT 1532 01-27-93 Needed to assemble the 5 parts of the ADD."

If you download this file set, send me an e-mail message describing what you found and what you think of it.

U.S. Army Center for Public Data Distribution System BBS

🖳N Acronym for online service: CPW-BBS

🖳) Online service number(s): 703-355-3471

🌐 Internet address(es): telnet fedwold.gov and gateway to CPW-BBS or telnet 160.147.90.240.

🏛 Government agency acronym: USADPW

👥 Contact person & title: Jack Giefer, SYSOP

🖳← Contact person's e-mail address: gieferj@belvoir-cpw1.army.mil

☎ Contact person's voice phone number: 703-355-0073

🖷 Contact person's Fax phone number: 703-355-2189

✉ Mailing address: U.S. Army Center for Public Works, Attn.: CECPW-FM, 7701 Telegraph Road, Alexandria, VA 22310-3862

DESCRIPTION

"The Data Distribution System (DDS) primarily supports Army Directorate of Public Works activities at Army installations and especially emphasizes support for users of the Integrated Facilities System, Mini/Micro (IFS-M) and the Housing Operations Management System (HOMES). It has very little of interest to persons not in Army Facilities Maintenance and Housing. The system supports private E-mail, public forum mail, and file libraries. It automatically selects RIP, ANSI or ASCII screens to match user terminal emulations."

ANNOTATION

Does deciphering military acronyms and reading about "Master Planning for Army Installations" excite the Tom Clancy in you? If it does, the EHSC-BBS will be a fun place for you to explore. However, this BBS is primarily for U.S. Army personnel.

DEPARTMENT OF THE NAVY

Ada Technical Support Bulletin Board System

📡 Parent organization: Naval Computer & Telecommunications Area Master Station

🖳N Acronym for online service: ADABBS

🖳) Online service number: 804-444-784, 1 DSN 564-7841

🌐 Internet address(es): N/A

🖳← E-mail addresses: FidoNet 1:275/62

🏛 Government agency acronym: NCTAMS LANT

👥 Contact person & title: Gloria Blottenberger

🖳← Contact person's e-mail address: N/A

☎ Contact person's voice phone number: 804-444-4680

🖷 Contact person's Fax phone number: 804-444-2835

✉ Mailing address: Commanding Officer, N912.4, NCTAMS LANT, 9456 Fourth Avenue, Ste 200, Norfolk, VA 23511-2199

"The purpose of this BBS is to serve the Ada technical community at large. It is sponsored by the Department of Defense Ada Joint Program Office.

BBS users can ask technical questions about the Ada language and exchange technical information. There is a section for Ada News where bulletins are posted about what's happening in the Ada world. BBS users are encouraged to upload code that demonstrates Ada features and software engineering techniques. The BBS provides useful software such as AdaSage to assist Ada software engineers. Information is given regarding the procedure to obtain free copies of AdaSage. There are sections for reuse repository information, Ada complaints, and Ada product descriptions where vendors can post information regarding their Ada tools, compilers, etc.

The purpose of this BBS is to offer Ada programmers an avenue through which they can obtain answers to their questions about the Ada language. The BBS is backed by a cadre of Ada programmers experienced in the field of Management Information Systems (MIS).

The Naval Computer & Telecommunications Area Master Station Atlantic (NCTAMS LANT) operates the Ada Technical Support Bulletin Board Service (BBS). The BBS is sponsored by the Naval Computer & Telecommunications Command (NAVCOMTELCOM). The BBS is free and available to the public."

ANNOTATION

What is Ada? The ADABBS User's Guide states, "Ada, a programming language originally created by the Department of Defense for embedded systems, has gained wide acceptance as the language of choice for many types of systems both in government and commercial software development centers. Ada is a modern programming language and has features that support sound software engineering practices." If you are looking for Ada specific files and messages, this is an excellent resource.

Health Sciences Education & Training Command BBS

⌨N Acronym for online service: HSETC BBS

💻) Online service number(s): 301-295-5775, 201-295-2373, FedWorld 703-321-8020

🌐 Internet address(es): telnet fedworld.gov then gateway to HSETC BBS

👥 Contact person & title: David E. Evans, SYSOP

☎ Contact person's voice phone number: 301-295-0561

✉ Mailing address: Naval Health Sciences Education & Training Command, Code 331, Bldg. 1, room 17110, 8901 Wisconsin Avenue, Bethesda, MD 20889-5612

DESCRIPTION

"The HSETC Bulletin Board system is designed to share Navy Medical Department training information with you."

ANNOTATION

The HSETC BBS is specifically directed toward serving the needs of USN medical personnel. There are no files or messages here of interest to the general public.

Judge Advocate General's Office BBS

💻 Acronym for online service: JAGNET

🖥️ Online service number(s): 703-325-0748, 703-325-2283, 703-325-4624, 703-325-4621

🏛️ Government agency acronym: DOD

👥 Contact person & title: Ron Stokes, SYSOP

💻 Contact person's e-mail address: JAGIC

☎️ Contact person's voice phone number: 703-325-2924, 703-325-2925

✉️ Mailing address: Department of the Navy, Judge Advocate General's Office, 200 Stovall St., Alexandria, VA 22332-2400

DESCRIPTION

"The purpose of this BBS is to foster exchange of information. It was originally established for communications relating to the Navy Judge Advocate General's Management Information System (JAGMIS). We hope the BBS will be used by technical coordinators in all of the activities of the Naval Legal Service Command and participating Staff Judge Advocate's offices to pass along questions, suggestions, and other information about their experiences implementing JAGMIS and doing other work on their microcomputers.

This original purpose has been expanded to include participation and information exchange by any U.S. Navy or other DoD personnel interested in microcomputers and office automation, generally oriented towards IBM-PC compatibles and legal offices. Employees of other Federal Government agencies and private citizens are also welcome, subject to possible future time restrictions."

ANNOTATION

According to the file directory description for JAGNET there are 12 directories with a total of 71 Megabytes of files. Looking through the directories I found few files having anything to do with the Navy or the military in general. Most of the files are typical of a general purpose BBS and many were more than two years old. There is Navy and military related data is in the message section, but even these messages are of a more general type. If you have business with the Judge Advocate General's Office, this is the BBS for you. If you are just exploring BBSs with interesting names, this may not be worth your time.

Navy Drug and Alcohol Abuse Prevention BBS

💻 Acronym for online service: NADAP

🖥️ Online service number(s):703-693-3831 and FedWorld BBS 703-321-8020

🌐 Internet address(es): telnet fedworld.gov and gateway to NADAP

🏛️ Government agency acronym: DOD

👥 Contact person & title: Randy Woods, SYSOP

☎️ Contact person's voice phone number: 703-697-3076

✉️ Mailing address: Admits Proc Office, Pers 633, 2 Navy Annex, Washington, DC 20370-6330

DESCRIPTION

NADAP appears to be a communications service for Navy Drug and Alcohol Abuse Prevention.

I found nothing on NADAP concerning Navy Drug and Alcohol Abuse Prevention. There were only a couple of public messages and the file area was filled with BBS software support files. I left a message for the SYSOP, but never received a reply. It is hard to say whether this BBS was just starting up or about to close down, but there was little worth exploring.

Navy Leadership Policy Bulletin Board

🖥️N   Acronym for online service: NLPBB

🖥️)   Online service number(s): 800-582-6940, 800-582-2355, 703-695-6198, 703-695-6388, 703-697-2442, 703-697-2446 or FedWorld 703-321-8020.

🌐   Internet address(es): telnet fedworld.gov then gateway to NLPBB

🏛️   Government agency acronym: DOD

👥   Contact person & title: Henrietta Wright, SYSOP

💻←   Contact person's e-mail address: nav-palib@opnav-emh.navy.mil

☎️   Contact person's voice phone number: 703-695-5471

📠   Contact person's Fax phone number: 703-695-3478

✉️   Mailing address: Navy Office of Information, Code OI-3, Washington, DC 20350-1200

DESCRIPTION

"NLPBB is sponsored by the Chief of Naval Operations and operated by the Navy Office of Information. NLPBB is an information service designed to provide you with access to a wide variety of general-interest Navy news and information."

Unless you saw some of the black-and-white war movies from the 1950s you may not be aware that American Indian language was used to encode messages during battles. L.C. Kukral in an article entitled, "The Navajo Code Talkers," available from the NLPBB BBS says that "The Navajo code talkers took part in every assault the U.S. Marines conducted in the Pacific from 1942 to 1945." This is an example of the interesting information stored on this BBS. You may find the structure of the BBS daunting at first, but if you read the instructions carefully you will find a large information repository here. Journalists, researchers, and military buffs will find this BBS worth the call.

Navy Public Affairs Library

🖥️N   Acronym for online service: NAV-PALIB

🖥️)   Online service number(s): See NLPBB

   Log on: see below

🌐   Internet address(es): The World Wide Web (WWW) provides fast and easy access to the Navy Public Affairs Library. If your Internet system includes Mosaic, Lynx or another WWW client, you can connect directly to NAVPALIB through this URL:

http://www.ncts.navy.mil/navpalib/ .www/welcome.html

If you prefer an FTP-style interface, you can get the NAVPALIB main directory with this URL:

ftp://ftp.ncts.navy.mil/pub/navpalib

The file transfer protocol (FTP) is a standard feature on most Internet systems. To reach the NAVPALIB main directory, anonymous FTP to connect to ftp.ncts.navy.mil then change directory (cd) to pub/navpalib. A typical session to retrieve the NAVPALIB index and the current issue of the Navy News Service might include these lines:

$ ftp   (starts ftp on your system)

ftp> open ftp.ncts.navy.mil   (connects to our system)

login: anonymous   (be sure to spell it right!)

password: (enter your own e/mail address)

ftp> cd pub/navpalib   (moves you to the NAVPALIB area)

ftp> dir   (displays our main directory)

ftp> get Index.txt   (retrieve NAVPALIB index)

ftp> cd news/navnews   (go to NavNews subdirectory)

ftp> get Navnews .txt   (retrieve latest news)

ftp> bye   (close the connection)

 E-mail addresses: The ftpmail service allows you to specify FTP commands within an ordinary e-mail message. The files you request are then returned to you by e-mail, usually within 24 hours. This service enables you to use NAVPALIB even if your only Internet service is e-mail.

You should review the ftpmail help file before using this service. To retrieve it, send this message:

To: ftpmail@decwrl.dec.com   (ftpmail server address)

Subj: Help   (subject is ignored)

help   (the only word in the message text)

To retrieve the current NAVPALIB index, send this message:

To: ftpmail@decwrl.dec.com   (ftpmail server address)

Subj: Latest NavNews   (subject is ignored)

reply yourname@yourhost   (put your e-mail address here)

connect ftp.ncts.navy.mil   (the NAVPALIB host address)

chdir pub/navpalib   (change to main NAVPALIB directory)

get Index.txt   (get the file)

quit   (tell ftpmail we're finished)

🏛 Government agency acronym: DOD

👥 Contact person & title: Henrietta Wright, SYSOP

💻 Contact person's e-mail address: navpalib@opnav-emh.navy.mil

☎ Contact person's voice phone number: 703-695-5471

📠 Contact person's Fax phone number: 703-695-3478

✉ Mailing address: Navy Office of Information, Code OI-3, Washington, DC 20350-1200

DESCRIPTION

"The Navy Public Affairs Library (NAV-

PALIB) is the Internet counterpart of the Navy Leadership Policy Bulletin Board (NLPBB).

NAVPALIB contains a wide variety of general-interest, Navy-related materials, including Navy news, speeches, Congressional testimony, and much more. The "Index.txt" file in the main NAVPALIB directory lists all available files."

NAVPALIB doesn't exhibit fancy graphics or sounds, but it is rich in content. The number of text files available is extensive.

NavyOnLine

⌨N Acronym for online service: NavyOnLine

🌐 Internet address(es): URL:http://www.navy.mil/

💻← E-mail addresses: navyonline@ncts.navy.mil

🏛 Government agency acronym: USN

👥 Contact person & title: The NavyOnLine Management Team

💻← Contact person's e-mail address: navyonline@ncts.navy.mil

Excerpts from the NavyOnLine fact sheet: "—NavyOnLine is the idea that information generated by the Navy ought to be easily accessible online, both within the Navy and to the public, in organized ways. NavyOnLine is an effort both to make Navy information more widely available and to provide tools to help people find what they are looking for.

—The NavyOnLine home page is intended to be a central gateway for beginning an explo-ration of the Navy's online resources. Its goal is to help you get started, to provide a road map for the Navy's portion of the information superhighway. The NavyOnLine home page will lead you to a wide variety of information by and about the Navy.

—The current NavyOnLine fact sheet is available through the World Wide Web:

> http://www.navy.mil/navyonline/ nolintro.txt

or by anonymous FTP

> ftp://ftp.navy.mil/pub/navyonline /nolintro.txt

or by sending an electronic mail message to

> navyonline-request@ncts.navy.mil"

If you feel like you don't get all of the military news you want from television or radio, NavyOnLine's WWW server is the place to visit. You will find enough Navy information here to sustain your interest for hours. Chances are you will come back often.

Next Generation Computer Resources BBS

⌨N Acronym for online service: NGCR BBS

💻) Online service number(s): 703-902-3169, FedWorld 703-321-8020

Log on: Standard BBS for BBS and anonymous for ftp.

🌐 Internet address(es): ftp, Gopher, WWW ngcrbbs.jmb.bah.com, telnet fedworld.gov then gateway to NGCR BBS

🏛 Government agency acronym: SPAWAR

👥 Contact person & title: Jeannine Reilly

💻 Contact person's e-mail address: reilly_jeanine@bah.com

☎ Contact person's voice phone number: 703-902-5317

🖨 Contact person's Fax phone number: 703-902-3388

✉ Mailing address: Booz, Allen & Hamilton, 8283 Greensboro Drive, McLean, VA 22102

DESCRIPTION

"Next Generation Computer Resources (NGCR) Standards are open system computer resource hardware and software standards capable of meeting the Navy's Mission Critical Computer Resources (MCCR) requirements in the mid-1990s and beyond. By standardizing interfaces, protocols and services, NGCR standards will permit program managers and system developers to design and build MCCR systems with enhanced levels of product commonality and interoperability."

ANNOTATION

The NGCR BBS has working groups dealing with the following areas:

- Database Management Systems Interface Standard Working Group, DISWG
- High-Performance Network, HPNWG, and Standards Work Group
- Survivable Adaptable Fiber-Optic Embedded Network, SAFENET
- Backplane
- Operating Systems Standards Working Group, OSSWG

- Graphics Interface Standards Working Group, GISWG
- Project Support Environment Standards Working Group, PSESWG
- High-Speed Data Transfer Network Standard Working Group (HSDTN)

Research, Development, & Acquisition Management Information System RBBS

🖥 Acronym for online service: PPCUG/RDAMIS BBS

🖥 Online service number(s): 703-614-4114, FedWorld BBS 703-321-8020

🌐 Internet address(es): telnet fedworld.gov then gateway to PPCUG/RDAMIS BBS

🏛 Government agency acronym: USN

👥 Contact person & title: John Forbes/SYSOP, Ron Honey/Co-SYSOP, Fred Kolbrenner/Co-SYSOP, Donna Sellinger/Co-SYSOP

☎ Contact person's voice phone number: Ron Honey 703-695-0611

✉ Mailing address: Research, Development & Acquisition Management Information System, Pentagon, SC730, 1000 Navy Pentagon, Washington, DC 20350-1000

DESCRIPTION

"The PCCUG/RDAMIS BBS is operated by the director, Resources and Evaluation, Washington, D.C., to provide marketing information and a forum for its staff and members of the Pentagon PC Users Group. The board is organized as a public bulletin board."

The PPCUG/RDAMIS BBS has lots of files, is well organized, and a little scary to log onto. The introductory messages are intimidating. It's clear that the SYSOPS don't want crank calls from people wanting to get into the Pentagon. Those interested in starting a war by tapping into a Pentagon BBS will be sorely disappointed. There is no sensitive information here. Once past this barrier the BBS has much to offer a wide audience. Most of the files have little or nothing to do with the DoD, USN, or any other government agency. The BBS is popular and logging on may be a task since it only has one phone line.

DEPARTMENT OF EDUCATION

ABLEDATA Database of Assistive Technology & National Rehabilitation Information Center

☎ Parent organization: National Institute on Disability and Rehabilitation Research

💻ᴺ Acronym for online service: NARIC & ABLEDATA

💻) Online service number(s): 301-588-9284, 301-427-0280, FedWorld BBS 703-321-8020.

🌐 Internet address(es): telnet fedworld.gov (then dd115)

💻← E-mail addresses: naric.@cap.gwu.edu

🏛 Government agency acronym: DOE

👥 Contact person & title: Dan Mendling

☎ Contact person's voice phone number: 800-227-0216; 301-588-9284 (both numbers are TT compatible)

🖨 Contact person's Fax phone number: 301-587-1967

✉ Mailing address: NARIC & ABLEDATA, 8455 Colesville Rd., Suite 935, Silver Spring, MD 20910

DESCRIPTION

"ABLE INFORM is a computer bulletin board system produced and maintained by NARIC and ABLEDATA. NARIC and ABLEDATA are funded by the National Institute on Disability and Rehabilitation Research, U.S. Department of Education, and operated by Macro International Inc. Our mission: to provide an "Electronic Information Center" to accompany our work as an information and referral resource in all areas of assistive technology, rehabilitation, and disability.

This BBS provides free access to:

• Databases

• Resource guides and fact sheets

• Various rehabilitation/disability related files and programs

• Electronic mail conferences

• Advertisements for preowned assistive technology"

ANNOTATION

For the disabled, or those involved with the disabled, this is a gold mine of data, networking opportunities, and files. If you know of anyone with a disability, or somebody who works with the disabled, tell them about ABLEDATA and encourage them to use this valuable resource.

Education Board

🖳N   Acronym for online service: ED Board

🖳)   Online service number(s): 202-260-9950, FedWorld BBS 703-321-8020

🌐   Internet address(es): telnet fedworld.gov then telnet to ED Board.

🏛   Government agency acronym: DOED

👥   Contact person & title: George Wagner, SYSOP

☎   Contact person's voice phone number: 202-708-7811

✉   Mailing address: Department of Education, 7th & D Streets, SW, Building ROB3, Washington, DC 20202-4726

DESCRIPTION

"Information available on ED Board.

Grant Combined Application Notice—Notice published in the Sept. 21, 1992, Federal Register inviting applications for many fiscal year 1993 grant programs. Notice includes information on application availability dates and deadline dates for many programs (text document).

Guide to Grant Programs—Electronic version of ED publication with general information about the Department's grant programs, including program eligibility requirements and program office phone numbers (text document).

Database of grant program announcements—Database on announced grant programs which is searchable by program office, Federal Register announcement publishing date, or current availability.

Application for the Education Solicitation Mailing List—Application form and instructions to be added to the contract bidders list at ED (text document).

Guide to Doing Business with the Department of Education—general information about contracting with the Department of Education (text document).

List of contract requests for proposals (RFPs) as published in the Commerce Business Daily (text document).

FY 1993 Forecast of Contract Opportunities—Descriptions of possible upcoming contracting opportunities at the Department (text document)."

ANNOTATION

I was able to obtain most of the information about ED Board, and several of the documents describing the BBS, by searching for the words "Department of Education" on a Gopher server. The FedWorld connection was unreliable.

EDWeb, US Department of Education Gopher, and INet

🖳N   Acronym for online service: Institutional Communications Network (INet)

   Log on: (No telnet services available to public)

🌐   Internet address(es): ftp.ed.gov

🖳←   E-mail addresses: wwwmaster@inet.ed.gov gopher-adm@inet.ed.gov inetmgr@inet.ed.gov

🏛   Government agency acronym: ED

👥   Contact person & title: Keith Stubbs, Director, Education Information Resources Division, OERI

🖳←   Contact person's e-mail address: inetmgr@inet.ed.gov

☎ Contact person's voice phone number: 202-219-1547

✉ Mailing address: INet Project Manager, U.S. Department of Education, Office of Educational Research and Improvement/EIRD, 555 New Jersey Ave. N.W., Room 214b, Washington, DC 20208-5725

DESCRIPTION

"Individuals with access to the Internet can tap a rich collection of education related information at the U.S. Department of Education (ED), including:

- General Information about the Department's Mission, Organization, Key Staff, and Programs
- Information about Key Departmental Initiatives, such as GOALS 2000, Technology, Family issues, School-to-Work Programs, and Elementary and Secondary Schoolwide Projects.
- Full-text Publications for Teachers, Parents, and Researchers
- Statistical Tables, Charts, and Data Sets
- Research Findings and Syntheses
- Directories of Effective Programs
- Directory of Education-related Information Centers
- Announcements of New Publications and Data Sets
- Press Releases
- Funding Opportunities
- Event Calendars
- Searchable ED Staff Directory
- Pointers to Public Internet Resources at R&D Centers, Regional Laboratories, ERIC Clearinghouses, and other ED-Funded Institutions

- Pointers to other Education Related Internet Resources

The Department's Internet site is maintained by the Office of Educational Research and Improvement (OERI) on its Institutional Communications Network (INet). While still focusing primarily on research, improvement, and statistical information, INet also contains substantial information about other ED programs and initiatives sponsored by ED offices outside of OERI."

ANNOTATION

This is a nicely constructed server with lots of content. If your interests run to education you will find depth and quality in the information available here.

Office of Educational Research and Improvement Electronic Bulletin Board

👥 Parent organization: Office of Educational Research and Improvement

🖥N Acronym for online service: OERI BBS

🖥) Online service number(s): 800-222-4922

👥 Contact person & title: Sharon Robinson, Assistant Secretary for Educational Research & Improvement

☎ Contact person's voice phone number: 800-424-1616, 202-219-1513 in Washington, DC.

✉ Mailing address: Office of Educational Research and Improvement, Educational Information Branch, 555 New Jersey Avenue, NW, Washington, DC 20208-5641

"The Office of Educational Research and Improvement (OERI) is a part of the U.S. Department of Education. Its mission is to improve the quality of American education—to help the nation reach its goal of excellence in all areas of instruction for all students at all school levels. The agency collects and interprets data, assesses student achievement, supports basic and applied research, links research to effective practice, promotes the use of educational technology, advances innovative school improvement projects, strengthens library services, and disseminates information.

In many ways, OERI is responsible for most education research and development at the Federal level. OERI looks for answers to questions about every aspect of teaching and learning and sponsors programs, all of which have a single objective: improve American education.

OERI produces many types of research-based information and materials that can enhance learning in the home, in the classroom, and in the community. They are designed to satisfy the requirements of students, parents, teachers, administrators, librarians, and policy makers at every level of education. Individuals, schools, localities, and states are encouraged to use these education resources.

The more than 150 printed products from OERI every year range from low-priced publications for parents in the "Helping Your Child Learn" series to comprehensive statistical reports such as the annual Condition of Education. The free OERI Bulletin reports quarterly on OERI activities, new publications, and upcoming grant competitions. Cooperative publishing with private organizations has put some 2.75 million copies of OERI materials into print at no cost to the Federal Government."

OERI is a wonderful BBS, but you may never reach it unless OERI gets its Internet Gopher set up. It took me more than an hour of dialing to get connected. Once connected I was impressed with the amount of quality educational information and software available. The complete file listing is about 30 pages long. Amiga, Apple, Atari, Commodore, MS-DOS, and Tandy files are nicely divided into directories.

Rehabilitation Services Administration BBS

Acronym for online service: RSA BBS

Online service number(s): 14,400 bps 202-205-5574, 2,400 bps 202-401-6147, FedWorld BBS 703-321-8020

Internet address(es): telnet fedworld.gov then gateway to RSA BBS

Contact person & title: Teri Darter, SYSOP

Contact person's voice phone number: 202-205-8444

Mailing address: Department of Education, Rehabilitation Services Administration, 330 C Street, SW, Washington, DC 20202

"This BBS is for the use of all persons and organizations having an interest in programs funded under the Rehabilitation Act and the Randolph Sheppard Act; i.e. interest in 1) the Vocational Rehabilitation, Independent Living, Supported Employment, Randolph/Sheppard, and/or Client Assistance programs; 2) other discretionary grant programs administered by RSA; and/or 3) related areas."

The RSA BBS is awkward to negotiate, partly as a result of the software it uses, but by reading the new user's manual carefully and following instructions you will be rewarded with access to a large storehouse of rehabilitation information.

DEPARTMENT OF ENERGY

Center for Computational Sciences WEB Server

💻 Acronym for online service: CCS

🏠 Parent organization: Oak Ridge National Laboratory Environmental Sciences Division

🌐 Internet address(es): http://www.esd.ornl.gov/

💻 E-mail addresses: webmaster@www.esd.ornl.gov

👥 Contact person & title: Forrest Hoffman

💻 Contact person's e-mail address: webmaster@www.esd.ornl.gov

☎ Contact person's voice phone number: 615-576-7680

🖨 Contact person's Fax phone number: 615-576-8543

✉ Mailing address: Oak Ridge National Laboratory Environmental Sciences Division, P.O. Box 2008, Oak Ridge, TN 37831-6036

DESCRIPTION

None was provided.

ANNOTATION

I could not connect with this server, but I had better luck connecting with http://www.ccs.ornl.gov/ which is the ORNL Computer Sciences WWW server. A message on that home page said that the server was under construction. By the time you read this both systems should be more operational.

Stanford Linear Accelerator Center WEB Server

💻 Acronym for online service: Stanford Linear Accelerator Center WWW

🌐 Internet address(es): WWW www.slac.stanford.edu, ftp ftp.slac.stanford.edu

💻 E-mail addresses: user@slac.stanford.edu (Generic E-mail address for SLAC)

🏛 Government agency acronym: SLAC

👥 Contact person & title: H. V. White, SLAC Webmaster

💻 Contact person's e-mail address: bebo@slac.stanford.edu

☎ Contact person's voice phone number: 415-926-2907

🖨 Contact person's Fax phone number: 415-926-3329

✉ Mailing address: Stanford Linear Accelerator Center, 2575 Sand Hill Road, Mail Stop 97, SLAC, Menlo Park, California 94025

"The Stanford Linear Accelerator Center (SLAC) is a national laboratory operated by Stanford University for the US Department of Energy. SLAC has been in continuous use for over 25 years in a national research program that has made major contributions to our understanding of nature. Of particular note, two Nobel prizes have been awarded for High Energy Physics discoveries made at SLAC. The Center is one of a handful of laboratories worldwide that stands at the forefront of research into the basic constituents of matter and the forces that act between them.

SLAC does experimental and theoretical research in elementary particle physics using electron beams, plus a broad program of research in atomic and solid-state physics, chemistry, biology, and medicine using synchrotron radiation. Scientists from all parts of the United States and throughout the world participate in this work. There are active programs in the development of accelerators and detectors for high energy physics research and of new sources and instrumentation for synchrotron radiation research.

SLAC was founded in 1962, and the Stanford Synchrotron Radiation Laboratory (SSRL) came into being in 1979 as a national users' facility. SSRL became part of the SLAC facility in 1992. Their combined staff is currently about 1400, of whom 150 are Ph.D. physicists. At any given time, there are typically 300–400 physicists from other institutions participating in the high energy physics program and 600 scientists in the synchrotron radiation program.

SLAC has the following major facilities:

- The Linac, a three-kilometer (or two-mile) long linear accelerator, capable of producing electron and positron beams with energies up to 50 GeV
- SPEAR, a storage ring 80 meters in diame-
ter now used as a synchrotron radiation source
- PEP, a 30 GeV colliding-beam storage ring, 800 meters in diameter, now being upgraded to serve as a B meson factory
- SLC, a 100 GeV electron-positron linear collider
- Major particle detection facilities, such as ESA and SLD"

If your interests run toward high-powered physics, splitting atoms, and such, this is a great destination. If you explore the WWW pages carefully you will find considerable information here. SLAC is a National Lab run by Stanford University under a contract from the DOE.

Commission Issuance Posting System

👀 Parent organization: Federal Regulatory Commission

🖥 Acronym for online service: CIPS

🖥 Online service number(s): 2,400 bps 202-208-1397, 9,600 bps 202-208-1781

🏛 Government agency acronym: DOE

👥 Contact person & title: Vicky A. Bailey, Commissioner

☎ Contact person's voice phone number: 202-208-2304

✉ Mailing address: Federal Regulatory Commission, Commission Issuance Posting System, 1000 Independence Avenue, SW, Washington, DC 20585

"CIPS is a bulletin board service that provides timely access to Commission information and daily issuances. CIPS is not the official version of a Commission issuance. There may be instances where the CIPS version differs from the official issuance. The official Commission issuance is the paper copy issued by the Office of the Secretary available through the Public Reference Room.

Access to CIPS is free of charge to the user and you are permitted up to 60 minutes of connect time for each call. CIPS is available for 23 hours every day. It is not available between 8:00 A.M. and 9:00 A.M. Monday through Friday."

ANNOTATION

FERC-CIPS provides texts of the Department of Energy's regulatory proceedings. It also lists items like the status of court litigation being handled by the Solicitor's Office, the fee schedule for use of Federal lands, filing fee rates, and 1,200 plus lines of descriptions of downloadable files of regulatory proceedings.

If you are using Datastorm's Procomm telecommunications software you may not be able to connect to the FERC-CIPS BBS. There is a known incompatibility problem between the BBS and Procomm software. The only way I was able to work around this problem was to use another telecommunication software product.

EIA Electronic Publishing System

⌨ Acronym for online service: EPUB

💻) Online service number(s): 202-586-2557

🏛 Government agency acronym: DOE

👥 Contact person & title: Bill Foster

☎ Contact person's voice phone number: 202-586-6310

✉ Mailing address: Department of Energy, Electronic Publishing System, EPUB, 1000 Independence Avenue, SW, Washington, DC 20585

DESCRIPTION

EPUB is divided into the following sections:

- Coal
- Nuclear and Electric Reports
- Oil & Gas Reports
- Energy Forecast Reports
- Monthly Energy Review Tables
- EIA Publications Directory
- Press Releases
- Monthly Petroleum Import Data
- Energy Information Contacts
- Upcoming Analyses and Publications
- Performance Profiles of Maj. Energy Producers
- Monthly Energy Review Features
- End-Use Consumption Surveys
- Petroleum Supply Monthly
- Help Files

ANNOTATION

EPUB's information is probably most useful to professionals in the energy field or journalists looking for current energy-related data. There is no messaging system on EPUB.

Energy Efficiency and Renewable Energy Network WWW Server

- Parent organization: Office of Energy Efficiency and Renewable Energy

- Acronym for online service: EREN

- Internet address(es): http://www.eren.doe.gov

- E-mail addresses: webmaster@beijing.dis.anl.gov

- Contact person's e-mail address: ENERGYINFO@delphi.com

- Mailing address: Office of Energy Efficiency and Renewable Energy, P.O. Box 3048, Merrifield, VA 22116

DESCRIPTION

"The Energy Efficiency and Renewable Energy Network (EREN) is a multimedia, Internet-based information system. EREN is a gateway to worldwide information sources that contain maps, images, video, sound, text, and information on energy efficiency and renewable energy. EREN is a World Wide Web (WWW) site developed for the Department of Energy's (DOE) Office of Energy Efficiency and Renewable Energy by Argonne National Laboratory, the National Renewable Energy Laboratory, and Oak Ridge National Laboratory."

ANNOTATION

Watch EREN as it evolves. Their goals, as described under Goals and Future Development, sound ambitious. They are planning an electronic interactive multimedia encyclopedia on energy efficiency and renewable energy.

Energy Information Administration BBS

- Acronym for online service: EIA BBS

- Online service number(s): 202-586-8658

- Government agency acronym: DOE

- Contact person & title: Sandra Wilkins

- Contact person's voice phone number: 202-586-8800

- Contact person's Fax phone number: 202-586-0727

- Mailing address: Department of Energy, Electronic Publishing System, EPUB, 1000 Independence Avenue, SW, Washington, DC 20585

DESCRIPTION

This BBS is slow. I had almost forgotten how slow file transfers seemed with 2,400 bps transfer rates. However, the energy-related files available here are worth the wait if you are interested in feature articles such as "Quarterly Coal Report," "Monthly Energy Review," "Natural Gas Monthly," or "Petroleum Supply Annual."

ANNOTATION

This BBS did not answer the last time I called. You may want to check with the SYSOP for additional information if you can't get online.

Federal Information Exchange

- Acronym for online service: FIE

- Online service number(s): 800-783-3349, in the Washington, DC, area 301-258-0953

🌐 Internet address(es): telnet fedix.fie.com or 192.111.228.33

💻 E-mail addresses: fedix@fedix.fie.com

🏛 Government agency acronym: DOE

👥 Contact person & title: Neal A. Castles, Communications Coordinator

💻 Contact person's e-mail address: ncastles@fedix.fie.com

☎ Contact person's voice phone number: 301-975-0103

🖨 Contact person's Fax phone number: 301-975-0109

✉ Mailing address: Federal Information Exchange, Inc., 555 Quince Orchard Road, suite 200, Gaithersburg, MD 20878

DESCRIPTION

"FEDIX and MOLIS, Online services developed by Federal Information Exchange, Inc., are the information links between the Federal government and academia.

FEDIX databases provide Online information on Federal research and educational opportunities, program contracts, scholarships, research equipment, and minority opportunities.

MOLIS databases provide capability information on 104 Historically Black Colleges and Universities (HBCUs) and 32 Hispanic-serving institutions (HSIs) in the following categories: research centers and equipment, pre-college and education programs, scholarships, and fellowships, revenues and expenditures, degrees and enrollment, faculty profiles and administrative personnel.

Science and engineering student profiles and grant/contract activity will soon be available online. An electronic mail system is available for messaging between the user and the system operators."

ANNOTATION

FEDIX and MOLIS are not operated by Federal agencies. They are operated by Federal Information Exchange, Inc. The reason they are listed here and not in another section is that these services are supported by Federal money through the Department of Energy.

FEDIX is huge. Casually looking through FEDIX's offerings quickly created 130 pages of screen capture. In their brochure, Federal Information Exchange, Inc., says that FEDIX should be used by: Federal agencies, colleges and universities, pre-college institutions, medical schools, industry, associations, hospitals, media, and libraries. They go on to say that the following types of individuals should also use their system: Faculty, researchers, administrators, students, educators, counselors, librarians, and writers. I agree with them completely. If you belong to one of these categories they probably have information that you would find beneficial. When you log on, be prepared to explore for a while to find what you are looking for.

Fossil Energy Telenews Service

💻 Online service number(s): 202-586-6496

🏛 Government agency acronym: DOE

👥 Contact person & title: Bob Porter, Director

☎ Contact person's voice phone number: 202-586-6503

🖨 Contact person's Fax phone number: 202-586-5146

✉ Mailing address: Office of Communications, Room 4G085, 1000 Independence Avenue, SW, Washington, DC 20515

DESCRIPTION

"FE TELENEWS is designed to provide rapid, up-to-date information about or related to the Office of Fossil Energy... including news releases, speeches, Congressional testimony, and other information from the Federal FOSSIL ENERGY program."

"BULLETINS
- Describes most recent Fossil Energy news releases.
- Gives schedules for upcoming speeches, testimony, special events, etc.
- Provides status of Fossil Energy budget. FILES
- Scan headlines and retrieve Fossil Energy News Releases issued since 01/01/85.
- Receive texts of Fossil Energy speeches, testimony, etc. COMMUNICATIONS
- Leave Comments to Fossil Energy staff— readable only by "system operator" (Bob Porter, Public Information Officer)
- Leave Messages for any TELENEWS user."

ANNOTATION

The Fossil Energy Telenews Service is another specialized information distributor of the Department of Commerce. Its focus is coal, oil, and gas data. It also has sections devoted to the Strategic Petroleum Reserve, Naval Petroleum/Oil Shale Reserves, speeches, testimony, background, 1989

Budget Descriptions, Commerce Business Daily Notices, and Assistance Programs.

Megawatts

💻 Acronym for online service: Megawatts

💻 Online service number(s): 202-586-0739

🏛 Government agency acronym: DOE

👥 Contact person & title: Bruce Birnbaum, Division Director

☎ Contact person's voice phone number: 202-586-2216

📠 Contact person's Fax phone number: 202-586-1217

✉ Mailing address: Department of Energy, 1000 Independence Avenue, Washington, DC 20585

DESCRIPTION

"Public Domain/Shareware files. No conferences."

ANNOTATION

The title and source of Megawatts would lead one to expect to find lots of information about the Department of Energy here. Unfortunately, that is not the case. Aside from a couple of bulletins there was almost no Department of Energy information available. The files were several years out of date when I last logged on.

DEPARTMENT OF HEALTH AND HUMAN SERVICES

Administration for Children and Families BBS

💻 Acronym for online service: ACF BBS

💻) Online service number(s): 800-627-8886, 202-401-5800, FedWorld 703-321-8020

🌐 Internet address(es): telnet fedworld.gov then gateway to ACF BBS

🏛 Government agency acronym: HHS

👥 Contact person & title: Kevin R. Fine, Computer Specialist

💻 Contact person's e-mail address: Kevin R Fine@OISM.DASN.A@ACF.WDC

☎ Contact person's voice phone number: 202-401-5682

✉ Mailing address: The Administration for Children & Families, 370 L'Enfant Promenade, SW, Washington, DC 20477

DESCRIPTION

"There isn't much on this system except bits and pieces of information about the Administration for Children and Families. Including:

- Fact-Sheets about each ACF program offices
- ACF Press Releases
- Some information about the new Child Support Enforcement Network (CSENET)
- Information about the Low Income Heating Energy Assistance Program (LIHEAP) ...and the list keeps growing!

If you'd like to see more ACF information available through the ACF BBS, please contact our program offices and tell them so!"

ANNOTATION

I disagree with the statement that "There isn't much on this system..." The ACF BBS has many valuable files on topics like:

- Child Abuse
- Child Care
- Child Support Collection
- Emergency Assistance
- Runaway and Homeless Youth
- Tribal Job Opportunities

If you are a professional dealing with, or a client of, family services you may find the resources here worth exploring. Journalists will appreciate the active press release document area.

FDA Electronic Bulletin Board

🔝 Parent organization: Food and Drug Administration

💻 Acronym for online service: FDA BBS

💻) Online service number(s): 301-594-6849, 301-594-6857

Log on: Standard BBS on dial-up numbers. Use "bbs" as response to "login" request on telnet.

🌐 Internet address(es): telnet fdabbs.fda.gov

🏛 Government agency acronym: FDA

👥 Contact person & title: Bill Haag

☎ Contact person's voice phone number: 301-443-7318

✉ Mailing address: Parklawn Computer Center (PCC), Food and Drug Administration, 5600 Fisher Lane, Room 2B59, Rockville, MD 20857

DESCRIPTION

Topics covered by the FDA BBS include:

- News releases
- Enforcement Reports
- Drug and Device Product Approvals Lists
- Centers for Devices and Radiological Health Bulletins
- Text from Drug Bulletins
- Current Information on AIDS
- FDA Consumer Magazine Index and Selected Articles
- FDA Federal Register Summaries by Subject
- Summaries of FDA Information
- Index of News Releases and Answers
- FDA Federal Register Summaries by Publication Date
- Text of Testimony at FDA Congressional Hearings
- Speeches Given by FDA Commissioner and Deputy
- Veterinary Medicine News
- Upcoming FDA Meetings
- Import Alerts
- Online User's Manual

ANNOTATION

The FDA BBS is of concern only to those of us who eat, drink, and take medication. Whether you are interested in the "FDA Review of Penile Implants," "Canned Tuna," or "Hearing Aids," there is a file on this BBS that is relevant to you or someone in your family.

FDA Guidance BBS

🖥N Acronym for online service: FDA/DMMS

🖥) Online service number(s): 800-222-0185, 301-594-6850, FedWorld 703-321-8020

🌐 Internet address(es): telnet fdabbs.fda.gov or fedworld.gov then gateway to FDA/DMMS BBS

🏛 Government agency acronym: FDA

👥 Contact person & title: Edward Mueller, Deputy Director, Division of Mechanics and Materials.

💻← Contact person's e-mail address: epm@fdadr.cdrh.fda.gov

☎ Contact person's voice phone number: 301-443-7003

📠 Contact person's Fax phone number: 301-443-5259

✉ Mailing address: Food and Drug Administration, Center for Devices and Radiological Health, 12200 Wilkins Avenue, Rockville, MD 20852

DESCRIPTION

"The Center for Devices and Radiological Health is making informal guidance documents available to the public on this experimental PC-based Bulletin Board System. This system gives users ready access to documents and provides a direct method for communicating comments to the appropriate FDA staff.

The Center has been developing the guidance documents to enable medical device developers and evaluators to identify the types of data and analysis that the FDA needs to adequately assess the safety and effectiveness of a product before it is marketed. Guidance documents have been developed for products in the Premarket Approval (PMA), Premarket Notification (510 (k)), and Investigational Device Exemption (IDE) categories, many of these through interactive comment by experts in the medical, scientific, and industrial communities. To encourage this, the FDA is making these documents available for use and for comment through the PC-based BBS.

The BBS is presently located in the Center's Division of Mechanics and Materials Science in Rockville, MD. Those who are familiar with PC-based bulletin boards may wish to note that the FDA is using the Remote Bulletin Board System (RBBS) PC software Version 17.3.

The BBS operates using Remote Bulletin Board System (RBBS) software, but can be accessed by any telecommunications program. Its files are stored as WordPerfect 5.1 documents compressed in ZIP format. These files can be uncompressed using the PKUNZIP program which is also available on the BBS. Pictorial or graphics information is in WordPerfect's WPG format or PCX file format. If you use WordPerfect 5.1 to print or view these documents they will be properly interpreted and printed. Other wordprocessing programs will require conversion."

ANNOTATION

The following are random file descriptions from the FDA Guidance BBS: "Draft of Suggested Information for Reporting Extracorporeal Shock Wave Lithotripsy Device Shock Wave Measurements. Guidance to Manufacturers on the Development of Required Postmarket Surveillance Study Protocols Under Sections 522 (a) (1) of the Federal Food and Drug, and Cosmetic Act."

A typical FDA Guidance BBS user might be a manufacturer of medical devices looking for FDA guidelines that deal with their product.

Indian Health Services Bulletin Board System

🖵N   Acronym for online service: IHS BBS

🖵)   Online service number(s): FedWorld 703-321-8020

🌐   Internet address(es): telnet fedworld.gov then gateway to IHS BBS

🏛   Government agency acronym: HHS

👥   Contact person & title: Sid Sand, SYSOP

☎   Contact person's voice phone number: 301-443-2554

✉   Mailing address: Indian Health Service, 6500 Fishers Lane, Room 4B08, Parklawn Bldg., Rockville, MD 20857

DESCRIPTION

None available.

ANNOTATION

This system was not yet online when the book went to press.

National Head Start BBS

🖵N   Acronym for online service: NHS BBS

🖵)   Online service number(s): 800-477-8278, 301-985-7902, FedWorld 703-321-8020

Log on: Standard BBS. "This BBS is not open to individuals who are not associated with the Head Start community. The 800# is for the convenience of Head Start."

🌐 Internet address(es): telnet fedworld.gov then gateway to NHS BBS

🏛 Government agency acronym: HHS

👥 Contact person & title: Tillie Bayless, SYSOP

☎ Contact person's voice phone number: 800-688-1675, 301-985-7990

✉ Mailing address: Head Start, University of Maryland, University College, University Blvd. at Adelphi Rd., College Park, MD 20742-1630

DESCRIPTION

Not enough information available to form a description.

ANNOTATION

When I logged on HHS BBS I was only given access to a couple of minimal services, so I can't report what the Head Start BBS has to offer or to whom. The SYSOP said that because of nuisance calls by children to their 800 number, the BBS only allows access to a specific clientele with direct interest in Head Start programs. Even though you will see this BBS listed in the FedWorld directory, don't log on to it. You won't have access to much. If you are professionally involved with Head Start, contact the SYSOP by phone or letter for instructions on how to gain full access.

National Institute of Dental Research BBS

🖥 Acronym for online service: NIDR BBS

🖥 Online service number(s): 800-358-2221, FedWorld 703-321-8020

Log on: Immediately after requesting the gateway to the NIDR BBS switch your telecommunications software to E-7-1 Half Duplex. After that you will be asked for your name and organization.

🌐 Internet address(es): telnet wylbur.cu.nih.gov or telnet fedworld.gov then gateway to NIDR BBS

🏛 Government agency acronym: HHS

👥 Contact person & title: Carla G. Flora, Chief, Management Information Systems and Analysis Section, National Institute of Dental Research

💻 Contact person's e-mail address: florac@wwpo.nidr.nih.gov

☎ Contact person's voice phone number: 301-594-7645

📠 Contact person's Fax phone number: 301-594-7655

✉ Mailing address: National Institutes of Health, National Institute of Dental Research, Bethesda, MD 20892

DESCRIPTION

"NIDR ONLINE—a National Institute of Dental Research computer program—is now available to the dental research community. The program provides access to the latest news about NIDR research and development activities, conference schedules, a variety of directories, requests for grants and contracts (RFPs and RFAs), Physician Scientist and Dentist Scientist Awardees, and much more. The system also stores lists of NIDR publications and provides a means of ordering them directly through the computer's message system.

NIDR developed ONLINE to help dental libraries speed up their access to Institute information. The service is available on TYMNET and is free to users through a public database."

ANNOTATION

The NIDR is one of the most difficult-to-use BBSs described in this book. When you connect with this BBS through FedWorld you are told to change your system to Half Duplex. If you don't, anything you type will not show up on your computer monitor. Once you get into the BBS one of the options presented is the NIH Education Bulletin Board. If you select that option and try to leave a message, you will find that a simple ASCII upload will not work. Additionally, the way to exit the Education BBS is said to be a BREAK. Control C doesn't work nor does any other key on my keyboard. I had to break the connection to get out. If you try to call the NIH Education BBS using the 800 direct dial up number you won't be able to log on. I tried typing every log-on message I knew, and all I got were error messages and no connection. Using this BBS may be more difficult than going to a dentist.

National Institute on Alcohol Abuse and Alcoholism BBS

👀 Parent organization: Health and Human Services

🖥 Acronym for online service: NIAAA BBS

🖥 Online service number(s): FedWorld

703-321-8020

🌐 Internet address(es): telnet fedworld.gov then gateway to Quick Facts or NIAAA BBS

🏛 Government agency acronym: HHS

👥 Contact person & title: Gerry Williams

💻 Contact person's e-mail address: $get.pccjes2.bitnet

☎ Contact person's voice phone number: 202-842-7600

📠 Contact person's Fax phone number: 202-842-0418

✉ Mailing address: Cygnus Corporation, Suite 200, 1400 Eye Street, NW, Washington, DC 20005

DESCRIPTION

"The purpose of the BBS is to disseminate alcohol-related statistical data from the NIAAA and AEDS and facilitate communication between users of the data"

ANNOTATION

The NIAAA BBS is not large, it does not have many public messages or any message threads. Its menu structure is not standard. Use it and you will hate having to type a question mark every time you want to see a menu. You may also find the request for a password to enter a library a little disconcerting. Even with these limitations, this is a useful BBS. Chances are that someone you know is an alcoholic, abuses alcohol, or is the child of an alcoholic. You may be able to help or understand them better with the information you find here.

The following is a listing of the file libraries of the NIAAA BBS.

LIBRARY	Files	Description
MAIN	04	The Main LIB
ABUS_DEP	06	Alcohol Abuse and Dependency
ALERTS	26	Text of NIAAA's "Alcohol Alert" Issues
CONSUME	18	Alcohol Consumption
ECONOMIC	12	Economic Costs of Alcohol
MORBID	08	Morbidity: Hospital Discharges
MORTALTY	22	Mortality—Cirrhosis & Traffic Crashes
NDATUS	17	Nat'l Drug & Alc. Treatment Unit Survey
OTHER	04	Miscellaneous files
PATTERNS	33	Patterns of Drinking
PRIVATE	05	Private Library

There are 155 files distributed among 11 Libraries.

National Institutes of Health Grant Line Bulletin Board

🖥️N Acronym for online service: NIHGL (DRGLINE)

🖥️) Online service number(s): 301-402-2221, FedWorld 703-321-8020

Log on: Standard BBS, but set your terminal at even parity, 7 data bits, 1 stop bit, and Half Duplex. When you get a response indicating that you have been connected, then type ',GEN1' (the comma is mandatory) and press ENTER; you will be prompted by the NIH system for INITIALS?. Type 'BB5' and press ENTER. You will then be prompted for ACCOUNT?. Type 'CCS2' and press ENTER.

When connecting to NIHGL through FedWorld, use your normal set up until you connect with NIHGL then set your terminal or software to even parity, 7 data bits, 1 stop bit, and Half Duplex. When you log off of NIHGL you must reset your terminal or software to your default.

To access the NIH Grant Line in an interactive Internet session, the user should telnet to WYLBUR.CU.NIH.GOV and when a message has been received that the connection is open, type ',GEN1' (the comma is mandatory). At the INITIALS? prompt, type 'BB5' and at the ACCOUNT? prompt, type 'CCS2'. This should put the user into the DRGLINE Bulletin Board (also known as NIH Grant Line at NIH).

🌐 Internet address(es): telnet fedworld.gov, telnet wylbur.cu.hih.gov,

🏛️ Government agency acronym: NIH

👥 Contact person & title: Dr. John C. James, Assistant Director for Special Projects and moderator of NIHGL.

☎️ Contact person's voice phone number: 301-594-7270

✉️ Mailing address: National Institutes of Health Grant Line, WW, 109, Bethesda, MD 20892

DESCRIPTION

"The purpose of NIH Grant Line is to make program and policy information of the Public Health Service (PHS) agencies rapidly available to the biomedical research community.

Most of the research opportunity information available on this bulletin board is derived from the weekly publication, "NIH Guide for Grants and Contracts," consisting of Notices, RFAs, RFPs (announcements of availability), Numbered Program Announcements, and statements of PHS policy. The electronic version known as E-Guide is available for electronic transmission each week, sometimes a day or two in advance of the nominal Friday publication dates. The material consists predominantly of statements about the research interests of the PHS Agencies, Institutes, and National Centers that have funds to support research in the extramural community.

A relatively new feature that has been added is a monthly listing of new NIH Awards, and a cumulative FY 93 New Awards to date. Under development is an order form to obtain NIH publications from DRG's Grants Information Office.

The information found on the NIH Grant Line is grouped into three main sections: (1) short News Flashes that appear without any prompting shortly after you have logged on; (2) Bulletins that are for reading; and (3) Files that are intended mainly for downloading."

ANNOTATION

The switching back and forth between Half and Full Duplex and changing communications protocols makes it a nuisance to connect to NIHGR. Having to follow special log-on instructions is a pain. However, once connected there is valuable information available to those interested in National Institutes of Health grant information. Researchers and journalists will find the information useful. Browsers will probably find titles like "Microstimulators and Macrotransducers for Functional Neuromuscular Stimulation" less than entertaining.

National Institutes of Health Information Center

🖥ℕ Acronym for online service: NIH Info Center

💻⟩ Online service number(s): 800-644-2271, 301-480-5144, FedWorld 703-321-8020

🌐 Internet address(es): telnet fedworld.gov then gateway to NIH Info Center

🏛 Government agency acronym: NIH

👥 Contact person & title: Dennis Rodrigues, SYSOP

💻 Contact person's e-mail address: dennis_rodrigues%nihod31.bitnet.@cu.nih.gov

☎ Contact person's voice phone number: 301-496-6610

📠 Contact person's Fax phone number: 301-402-1434

✉ Mailing address: National Institutes of Health Information Center, Building 31, Room 2B09, Bethesda, MD 20892

DESCRIPTION

"Welcome to the NIH INFORMATION CENTER! This Bulletin Board System (BBS) has been established to serve students, medical professionals, reporters, science writers and members of the public with information about the National Institutes of Health (NIH) and the medical research it supports. It is brought to you by the Office of Communications, a staff office to the Director of NIH."

This BBS is everything a well-run government online resource should be. It has a wide range of files that deal with the NIH. You can download a history of the NIH, a map of its buildings and grounds, a map of the surrounding streets, and even a Metro map of the area. There are telephone number lists for NIH institutes, centers, and divisions available.

Read through the list of files. Chances are you will find one or many files you will want to download and read. When I browsed the file area I found several files to download. For example, I downloaded:

HIST_MED.INT "Surfing the Internet for information on medicine." I forwarded this to a friend who is a curator at the Smithsonian Institution.

MELATON.TXT "Tiny oral doses of melatonin can put people to sleep." Perhaps this information will help me sleep better.

EXERART.TXT "Exercise keeps aging arteries young and flexible."

METRO.GIF "Metrorail system map in GIF format." I will use this map to find my way around Washington, DC, when I visit my sister and brother-in-law.

WOMEN.TXT "Fact sheet on women and HIV infection." I downloaded this for my wife who teaches a women's studies class.

Office of the Assistant Secretary for Health BBS

Acronym for online service: OASH BBS

Online service number(s): FedWorld 703-321-8020

Internet address(es): telnet fedworld.gov then gateway to OASH BBS

Government agency acronym: HHS

Contact person & title: Ted Foor, SYSOP

Contact person's voice phone number: 202-690-6248

Mailing address: Office of the Assistant Secretary for Health, 200 Independence Avenue, SW Room 738G, Washington, DC 20201

DESCRIPTION

"This is a public service electronic bulletin board for the exchange of information and non-commercial software. This board specializes in the following:

• Distribution of governmental information about Health

  Secondarily, the BBS offers—

• Private conferences for PHS Agencies"

ANNOTATION

The OASH BBS has file sections on the following health-related topics:

HIV/AIDS Files Areas

• Weekly MMWR's from CDC
• AIDS DAILY provided by NAC
• AIDS INFORMATION Category
• National Library of Medicine's AIDS Bibliogrp
• Federal Register Notices on HIV/AIDS
• Public Health Service Press Releases on AIDS
• National Commission on AIDS, Reports
• CDC National AIDS Clearinghouse

- Surgeon General's Speeches/Editorials (HIV/AIDS)
- Health Related Files Areas (Non-AIDS)

DEPARTMENT OF HOUSING AND URBAN DEVELOPMENT

Housing and Urban Development News and Events Bulletin Board

🖥️ Acronym for online service: HUD-N&E BB

💻 Online service number(s): FedWorld 703-321-8020

🌐 Internet address(es): telnet fedworld.gov then gateway to HUD-N&E BB

🏛️ Government agency acronym: HUD

👥 Contact person & title: Jack Flynn

☎️ Contact person's voice phone number: 202-708-0685 ext. 113

✉️ Mailing address: Housing and Urban Development News and Events Bulletin Board, 451 7th Street, NW, Washington, DC 20410

DESCRIPTION

"Maintained for the nation's news media and HUD's regional and field offices—24 hours a day, seven days a week."

ANNOTATION

The day that I logged onto this BBS the following message was displayed:

"This software package is about to be replaced. All users will be required to re-register under the new software package. However, until it is actually is replaced you'll find new materials such as the HUD reorganization plan now available to download or read on screen. Go to Field News or FYI Conferences in MAIL."

When I used the commands described I couldn't find anything to look at or download. The sections of the BBS that were operational were interesting. For example, you can read biographies of the top HUD personnel and find out facts like where the director received his degrees and the names of his children.

DEPARTMENT OF THE INTERIOR

Automated Vacancy Announcement Distribution System BBS

🖥️ Acronym for online service: AVADS BBS

💻 Online service number(s): FedWorld 703-321-8020

🌐 Internet address(es): telnet fedworld.gov then gateway to AVADS BBS

🏛️ Government agency acronym: DOI

✉️ Mailing address: Department of the Interior, 1849 C Street, NW, Washington, DC 20240

DESCRIPTION

The AVADS BBS provides information on job vacancies for bureaus within the Department of the Interior. There are no messaging services provided. Full listings can be downloaded as files.

Are you looking for a job at the Department of the Interior? If you are, this is the place to look.

Bureau of Mines Electronic Bulletin Board Network

💻 Acronym for online service: BOM-BBN

💻) Online service number(s): 202-501-0406, FedWorld BBS 703-321-8020.

🌐 Internet address(es): telnet fedworld.gov

🏛 Government agency acronym: USGS

☎ Contact person's voice phone number: 202-502-9448, Answering machine 202-501-0406

✉ Mailing address: United States Bureau of Mines, Department of the Interior, 810 Seventh St., NW, Washington, DC 20241

DESCRIPTION

"The U.S. Bureau of Mines Bulletin Board is a joint effort from within the U.S. Bureau of Mines to provide timely and accurate data to its users. The Bureau covers the research & development and information analysis of the mineral industry both domestic and abroad. The USBM Bulletin Board is one of the many automated information systems produced by the U.S. Bureau of Mines.

Current information on minerals and mineral-related publications from the U.S. Bureau of Mines (USBM) is now available through an easy-to-use automated Fax response system. The MINES FaxBack service allows callers to retrieve information and order publications for delivery to their Fax machines in minutes, 24 hours a day, 7 days a week. MINES FaxBack allows the USBM to make some of its monthly and quarterly Mineral Industry Survey publications on mineral commodities available to the public as soon as they are released and sent to the printer, two to three weeks earlier than the date of their being mailed out.

From the touch-tone handset of any Fax machine, dial (412) 892-4088."

ANNOTATION

Searching through the Bureau of Mines BOM-BBN may not immediately grab your attention unless you are a miner or someone associated with the mining industry. However, there are text files with descriptions like " Fires in Abandoned Mines" and "Spontaneous Coal Mine Combustion" that sound interesting enough to download and read for general knowledge. BOM-BBN is an excellent resource for journalists and researchers working on mining or mineral-related subjects.

Earthquake & Geomagnetic Online Information System

💻 Acronym for online service: OLIS-QED

💻) Online service number(s): OLIS 1,200 bps 303-273-8673 and 303-273-8678. 2,400 bps 303-273-8672. 300-1,200 bps 800-358-2663. FedWorld 703-321-8020.

Log on: For telnet connections use "QED" as your username.

🌐 Internet address(es): telnet neis.cr.usgs.gov or telnet Fedworld.gov then gateway to QED.

🏛 Government agency acronym: USGS/
NEIC

👥 Contact person & title: Stuart
Koyanagi or Pamela Tatalaski, NEIC
Operations

💻 Contact person's e-mail address:
sedas@neis.cr.usgs.gov

☎ Contact person's voice phone number:
303-273-8500

🖨 Contact person's Fax phone number:
303-273-8450

✉ Mailing address: U.S. Geological
Survey, MS-967, Federal Center, Box
25046, Denver, CO 80225-0046

DESCRIPTION

The Earthquake and Geomagnetic Online
Information System provides quick determinations of earthquake epicenters, lists of
recent earthquakes, and values of geomagnetic field elements, such as magnetic decli-
nation. If the prompt "GLDSV1>" appears,
type "C NEIS"; if "Username:" appears, type
"QED."

ANNOTATION

The opening menu for OLIS/QED provides
four options:

Q   for Quick Epicenter Determinations
     (QED)
L   for Earthquake Lists (EQLIST)
M   for Geomagnetic Field Values (GEO-
     MAG)
X   to log out

Option M requires that you provide lati-
tude and longitude values to display data. If
you select M and see the message that suggests that you contact Norman Peddie
regarding problems or suggestions, ignore

it. Mr. Peddie retired in May 1994. The message was still being displayed in July 1994.

Some of the information found on
QED/OLIS is very technical. The geomagnetic field values were typical of the highly
technical information. However, the earthquake lists were interesting and easy to
understand.

If you are interested in additional information related to this online service look
at the entry for National Earthquake
Information Center BBS.

Minerals Management Service Online Information Service

🖳 Acronym for online service: MMS BBS

💻 Online service number(s): 703-787-
1225, FedWorld BBS 703-321-8020

🌐 Internet address(es): telnet
fedworld.gov

🏛 Government agency acronym: DOI

👥 Contact person & title: Marcia Oliver,
SYSOP

☎ Contact person's voice phone number:
703-787-1032

✉ Mailing address: OCS Information
Program, Office of Offshore Statistics
and Information, Mineral
Management Service, 381 Elden Street,
MS 4610, Herndon, VA 22070-4817

DESCRIPTION

"The Outer Continental Shelf Information
Program (OCSIP) was mandated by the 1978
amendments to the OCS Lands Act (43 U.S.C.
1352). Recently re-named to the Office of
Statistics and Information (OSI), the program

is charged with providing to the public information that describes oil and gas related activities in each of the four OCS regions of the Minerals Management Service (MMS), an agency of the U.S. Department of the Interior.

The OSI has historically made this information available, free of charge, in two types of documents (summary reports and indices). The format of this publication series was recently modified in recognition of the many changes that have occurred in the offshore program of the MMS in the ten years since inception of the OSI. As an adjunct to this modification the OSI will now make available many of its files containing statistical and tabular data, in a downloadable format, through this electronic bulletin board service (BBS).

The purpose of this BBS is to provide interested parties with a relatively current electronic source of information related to the exploration and development of the oil and gas resources of the OCS.

In addition to this BBS, the OSI will continue to make its information available to the public in a redesigned series of reports. The OSI now produces an annual OCS LEASING AND OPERATIONS PROCEDURES report (formerly the Index); a streamlined, annual UPDATE report covering activities in each of the four MMS OCS Regions (formerly the Summary Report); a biennial NATIONAL OCS COMPENDIUM that presents historical information on all of the OCS Regions; an OCS DIRECTORY OF FEDERAL AND STATE AGENCIES AND THEIR OCS RESPONSIBILITIES; a quarterly statistical newsletter, and, a MAP SERIES for each of the four OCS Regions."

ANNOTATION

Don't pass up the news tips files on this BBS if you are researching information on oil and gas resources. It would be nice if there were a better means of finding out contents of files. Seeing pages of files with descriptions like "News Clips, April 22, 1994," isn't really helpful to new users.

National Earthquake Information Center BBS

🖥N Acronym for online service: NEIC BBS

🖥) Online service number(s): 300–9,600 bps 303-273-8508

Log on: Log in as "GUEST" without a password or become a registered member by entering "NEW".

🏛 Government agency acronym: USGS

👥 Contact person & title: Pamela Tatalaski, SYSOP

💻← Contact person's e-mail address: Leave mail via BBS

☎ Contact person's voice phone number: 303-273-8500

🖨 Contact person's Fax phone number: 303-273-8450

✉ Mailing address: U.S. Geological Survey, MS-967, Federal Center, Box 25046, Denver, CO 80225-0046

DESCRIPTION

"The electronic bulletin board system provides both the scientific community and the general public with information on seismology and geomagnetism. Users may leave or read messages and upload or download files.

Users may customize their own searches and obtain daily earthquake information."

ANNOTATION

The NEIC BBS is divided into the following subboards:

AMSEIS	Amateur Seismology
EPIC	Earthquake Data Base CD-ROM files
GEOM	Geomagnetic files
IMP	Interactive Mapping Program
MAIN	Main BBS files
PDE	Preliminary Determination of Epicenters
SEIS	General Seismology Files
WCH	Weather Channel

The following message was captured from the BBS. It sounds ominous, so if you are interested in this area you should log on and express your opinion soon.

Attention all users:

"As you may know, government projects are subject to periodic review. This BBS is being examined to see if it is serving any purpose or if it should be terminated. If you have any opinion (either way), please post a message to me expressing your views.

We solicit your input at all times anyway and are particularly interested in your additional needs or desires. Our intent is to provide timely and accurate information to anyone who needs it."

If you are interested in additional information related to this online service, look at the entry for Earthquake & Geomagnetic Online Information Service.

Office of Environmental Policy and Compliance BBS

🖳ᴺ Acronym for online service: OEPC BBS

🖳⟩ Online service number(s): 202-208-7119, FedWorld 703-321-8020

🌐 Internet address(es): telnet fedworld.gov then gateway to OEPC BBS

🖳← E-mail addresses: sspecht@ios.doi.gov

🏛 Government agency acronym: DOI

👥 Contact person & title: Steve Specht, SYSOP

☎ Contact person's voice phone number: 202-208-3811

📠 Contact person's Fax phone number: 202-208-6970

✉ Mailing address: Office of Environmental Policy and Compliance, MS 2340, Department of the Interior, 1849 C Street, NW, Washington, DC 20240

DESCRIPTION

"The purpose of this bulletin board system is to facilitate communications between the Office of Environmental Policy and Compliance (OEPC), other Bureaus and offices within the Department of the Interior, other Federal, state, and local agencies, and the general public.

We welcome inquiries of all kinds related to the missions of OEPC, and we will try to be responsive to all questions. Please be as specific as you can, and address inquiries to appropriate OEPC staff or division, if known.

Other Federal agencies that have official business with OEPC are encouraged to use the OEPC BBS to make inquiries about the status of review comments, and other matters of mutual concern.

Above all, please let us know what you would like to see on this board, and how we may better serve your interests."

On my first visit to the OEPC BBS I found files that were immediately useful and interesting. I downloaded CRYSTAL.ASC, an ASCII file containing a press release about the Crystal City Trail Connector linking bicycle trails in Arlington, VA. I also downloaded BLOSSOMS.ASC, a file about the Washington, DC–area cherry blossoms. Both of these files were in the file area "Area National Parks." There are numerous file areas of interest and a good messaging area available on the OEPC BBS. While pondering what I thought about OEPC, I couldn't find any criticism except that I wished there were more files available and more messages to read. For example, I would like to have been able to download more files describing the DC-area National Parks (in depth), walking tour maps, lists of events, and more. Perhaps the success of this BBS will encourage its managers to dedicate more resources to it.

United States Geological Survey Bulletin Board System

🖥️N   Acronym for online service: USGS BBS

💻)   Online service number(s) 703-648-4168

🏛️   Government agency acronym: USGS

👥   Contact person & title: Joe Kempter and Jerry McFaul, SYSOPs

☎️   Contact person's voice phone number: 703-648-7194

✉️   Mailing address: United States Geological Survey, Department of the Interior, 119 National Center, Reston, VA 22092

The USGS BBS offers three conferences:

- SYSOPS: For Registered SYSOPS of other PC Boards
- CD-ROM: For those interested in CD-ROM technology
- Geology: For those interested in Geologic Technology

According to the SYSOPs, their CD-ROM and Geologic Conferences are their most popular. This BBS contains a small collection of interesting and unique files related to geological surveys. The conferences could be a good source for expertise about geology. Journalists may find the USGS press releases posted here a valuable resource.

Americans with Disabilities Electronic BBS

🖥️N   Acronym for online service: CRS-BBS

💻)   Online service number(s): 202-514-6193, FedWorld 703-321-8020

🌐   Internet address(es): telnet FedWorld

🏛️   Government agency acronym: DOJ

👥   Contact person & title: Robin Deykes, SYSOP

☎️   Contact person's voice phone number: 202-307-0663 V/TDD, 800-877-8339 Federal Relay

✉ Mailing address: Department of Justice, Public Access Section, P.O. Box 66738, Washington, DC 20035

DESCRIPTION

"The ADA authorizes the Department of Justice to provide technical assistance to individuals and entities that have rights or responsibilities under the Act. This BBS has been established to assist the general public in obtaining access to information for understanding and complying with the ADA.

The information on this system is informal guidance about the provisions of the ADA."

ANNOTATION

The CRS-BBS is organized around the following topics in the main menu:

- Regulatory
- ADA Overview
- Enforcement
- Employment
- Government
- Business
- Telecommunications
- Transportation
- Standards
- Grants
- New Technologies

There are not many files in each of the sections, but those listed could be very useful to someone with a disability and to researchers looking for information about the Americans with Disabilities Act (ADA). The file "Q&A.ASK" is particularly useful if you have questions about the ADA.

Executive Office for U.S. Attorneys BBS

🏛 Government agency acronym: DOJ

👥 Contact person & title: Carol Sloan, Acting Assistant Director of Office Automation

☎ Contact person's voice phone number: 202-501-8220

✉ Mailing address: Department of Justice, Office of Office Automation, 601 D Street NW, Room 6320 , Washington, DC 20530

DESCRIPTION

This BBS is an internal government agency BBS and not available for public access.

ANNOTATION

You may find this BBS listed in other sources, but don't bother calling the numbers you find, because you won't be allowed to log on.

National Criminal Justice Reference Service Electronic Bulletin Board

🖥 Acronym for online service: NCRJS BBS

💻 Online service number(s): FedWorld 703-321-8020

🌐 Internet address(es): telnet fedworld.gov

🏛 Government agency acronym: DOJ

👥 Contact person & title: Vivian Workman, SYSOP

☎ Contact person's voice phone number: 301-251-5115

✉ Mailing address: National Criminal Justice Reference Service BBS, Department of Justice, P.O. Box 6000, Rockville, MD 20850

DESCRIPTION

"The National Criminal Justice Reference Service (NCJRS) Electronic Bulletin Board is a public service established by the National Institute of Justice to share current information from the following participating Office of Justice Programs agencies: National Institute of Justice, Office of Juvenile Justice and Delinquency Prevention, Bureau of Justice Statistics, Office for Victims of Crime, and Bureau of Justice Assistance.

It is part of the NCJRS information network effort to help individuals and organizations involved in criminal justice policy and research obtain and share information, experiences, and views.

The bulletin board provides users with—
• Continuing conferences with other users about key policy and research issues.

• News and reviews of criminal justice developments, activities, and new publications.

• Opportunities to participate online in surveys on emerging issues and practices.

• An indexed library of information about criminal justice policy.

• Electronic mail and document transfer.

Some information will come from NCJRS, which collects reports and studies from many sources. Some will come from users who wish to share information they have produced or found and have entered it into the network. And some of the most valuable information will be created online, as users comment on materials, exchange ideas, ask and answer questions, or participate in surveys. The more users contribute, the more valuable the network will be.

ANNOTATION

The NCJRS BBS is one of the most difficult-to-use bulletin boards I have logged onto. The means by which you navigate through the BBS are not made clear until you are well into it. A couple of commands you may find useful are Ctrl N which enables you to page through a section and Ctrl P which enables you to page backward.

DEPARTMENT OF LABOR

Labor News BBS

💻N Acronym for online service: Labor News

💻) Online service number (s): 202-219-4784

🏛 Government agency acronym: DOL

👥 Contact person & title: Don Berry, SYSOP

☎ Contact person's voice phone number: 202-219-8831, TDD 800-326-2577

📠 Contact person's Fax phone number: 202-219-8699

✉ Mailing address: U.S. Department of Labor, Office of Public Affairs, Room S-1004, 200 Constitution Avenue, NW, Washington, DC 20210

DESCRIPTION

"U.S. Department of Labor's electronic bulletin board service, LABOR NEWS, is provided by the Secretary of Labor's Office of Affairs.

LABOR NEWS was established in 1991 in response to the sharp increase in the number of organizations and individuals able to receive and transfer information via remote computers. At minimal cost to the Department, the service has substantially enhanced and expanded immediate public access to a wide variety of important Labor Department information. The service is available to anyone having a computer and phone modem and is free to users except for any telephone toll charges they may incur.

The service's original focus was on the news media which can use it to see and, if they desire, print out any Department release including such widely watched ones as the monthly unemployment figures and the consumer price index. Responding to user interest, the service has expanded to offer a broad range of information including publications, regulations, reports, nationwide Federal job listings, public forums on labor-related subjects, and similar material from all of the Department's agencies.

LABOR NEWS began with a single phone line and a surplus personal computer. Today, sixteen phone lines serve thousands of registered users and interest in the service continues to grow."

ANNOTATION

Do you need a "Brief History of the U.S. Department of Labor," accounts of fatal accidents in the workplace, reports on the labor trends in Thailand, lists of publications dealing with women in the workplace, "20 Facts About Women Workers," or a description of the Native American Indian Program? If you do, Labor News is the place to look. Labor News has a rich assortment of useful and interesting files for researchers, employers, and workers.

Wage and Service Contract Appeals BBS

Acronym for online service: WSCA BBS

Online service number(s): 800-735-7396, FedWorld 703-321-8020

Internet address(es): telnet fedworld.gov then gateway to WSCA BBS

Government agency acronym: DOL

Contact person & title: Gerald Krizan, SYSOP

Contact person's voice phone number: 202-219-9039

Mailing address: Department of Labor, Wage and Service Contract Appeals BBS, 200 Constitution Avenue NW, Washington, DC 20210

DESCRIPTION

"...the Electronic Reference Library offered as a service of the U.S. Department of Labor, Wage Appeals Board and Board of Service Contract Appeals. This Federal BBS provides legal reference materials for our Boards' statutory program areas."

ANNOTATION

The resources available on the WSCA BBS may be especially valuable to legal researchers and scholars looking for Service Contract Appeals and Wage Appeals decisions in downloadable full-text form.

DEPARTMENT OF STATE

Consular Affairs Bulletin Board

🖥 Acronym for online service: CABB

💻) Online service number(s): 202-647-9225, FedWorld 703-321-8020

Log on: Standard BBS without password.

🌐 Internet address(es): telnet Fedworld.gov then gateway to CABB

👥 Contact person & title: Wallis Doerge, Public Affairs Specialist

☎ Contact person's voice phone number: 202-647-1488

✉ Mailing address: U.S. Department of State, Consular Affairs , 2201 C Street, NW, Room 5807, Washington, DC 20520

DESCRIPTION

"The Consular Affairs Bulletin Board provides information on international travel for U.S. citizens. It includes information on travel advisories, U.S. passports, the types of assistance provided by Citizens Consular Services and the Citizens Emergency Center, and visa information for aliens wishing to come to the United States. It also permits access to the information contained on the Overseas Security Advisory Council (OSAC) Electronic Bulletin Board.

The following is from the opening menu of CABB:

- About the Consular Affairs Bulletin Board
- Passport Information for U.S. Citizens

- Emergency Services Available to U.S. Citizens Abroad
- Non-emergency Information for U.S. Citizens
- Consular Information Sheets & Public Announcements
- Travel Information on Specific Subjects or Regions
- Visa Information
- OSAC Bulletin Board (Incident Reports)
- User Instructions
- Search All Bulletins (Full Text)
- Download Summary Files

If you have a personal computer and a modem, you can also access Consular Information Sheets and Travel Warnings through the Official Airlines Guide (OAG). The OAG provides the full text of Consular Information Sheets and Travel Warnings on many online computer services. To obtain information on accessing Consular Information Sheets and Travel Warnings through OAG on any of the following computer services, call the OAG Electronic Edition at 1-800-323-4000.

CompuServe, Dialcom, Dialog, Dow Jones News/Retrieval, General Videotex-Delphi, NewsNet, GEnie, IP, Sharp, iNet-America, iNet-Bell of Canada, Telenet, Western Union-Easylink.

CompuServe subscribers may type GO STATE at any "!" prompt.

Infosys America Inc. also provides the full text of Consular Information Sheets and Travel Warnings through Travel Online BBS on the SmartNet International Computer Network in the U.S., Canada, and overseas. The (modem) telephone number for Infosys America is (314) 625-4054.

Interactive Office Services, Inc. offers online travel information in Travel+Plus through the networks listed below. For information on access, call Travel+Plus at (617) 876-5551 or 1-800-544-4005.

Delphi, MCI (RCA Hotline) Unison Bell South TUG FTCC Answer Bank

The Overseas Security Electronic Bulletin Board provides State Department Consular Information Sheets and Travel Warnings as a free service (purchase of necessary software required) for American firms doing business overseas. Apply to the Executive Director, Overseas Security Advisory Council (DS/OSAC), Department of State, Washington, DC 20522-1003.

By Computer Reservation System (CRS)

The following computer reservation systems (CRS) maintain State Department Consular Information Sheets and Travel Warnings. This information can be accessed by entering the CRS codes listed below.

APOLLO—For the index, enter: S*BRF/TVLADV For the full text of Consular Information Sheets and Travel Warnings, enter: TD*DS/ADV

DATAS II—For full text of Consular Information Sheets and Travel Warnings, enter: G* _ (country)_

PARS—For the index, enter: G/AAI/TVL

Travel Document Systems, Inc. provides the full text of Consular Information Sheets and Travel Warnings to the following reservation systems:

SABRE—Enter: N*/ADVISORY INDEX

SYSTEM ONE—Enter: GG SUP TD ADV

In Western Europe, SYSTEM ONE is accessed through the AMADEUS system and APOLLO through the GALILEO system."

ANNOTATION

I will never leave the U.S. again without consulting CABB, and you shouldn't either. There is just too much valuable free information on CABB to pass up. What you learn from CABB could save your life, or at least

make your life a little safer, once you venture out into the foreign world.

The Department of State's Bureau of Consular Affairs also offers an automated Fax system providing similar information. To receive an index for the Fax system call 202-647-3000 using your Fax machine. Follow the instructions to receive the index. Additional prompts will be given for ordering documents.

PerMfanNet BBS

⌨N   Acronym for online service: PerManNet BBS

⌨)   Online service number(s): 703-715-9832, FedWorld BBS 703-321-8020

🌐   Internet address(es): telnet fedworld.gov then gateway to PerManNet BBS

💻   E-mail addresses: info@permanet.org, support@permanet.org

👥   Contact person & title: Mark Prado, Systems Operator

☎   Contact person's voice phone number: 703-715-8473

🖨   Contact person's Fax phone number: 703-715-7982

✉   Mailing address: PerManNet, Inc., 11425 South Lakes Drive, Reston, VA 22091

DESCRIPTION

"PerManNet serves a variety of interest groups including:

- associates of the U.S. Agency for International Development (division of the U.S. Department of State), incl. non-Govt. orgns.

- scientific researchers (space development, longevity & health, other)
- writers and global networkers
- those needing access to the Internet, or certain message conferences
- those looking for state-of-the-art PC communications software
- those looking for reliable personal computers for turnkey networks and certain other areas of more esoteric interest.
- Coming soon: ARPA conversion of defense industries to commercial ones!"

ANNOTATION

PerManNet is a large BBS with many valuable resources. It also offers limited access to the Internet. Government employees equipped with computers and modems will find PerManNet an easy on ramp to the Internet. The message area of PerManNet is lively and interesting to read. The Frequently Asked Questions (FAQ) section contains a wealth of information about a wide variety of subjects. The files area is extensive.

Connecting to PerManNet through Fed-World and a telnet connection can be frustrating. The only successful means of downloading a file through telnet, according to Bob Bunge of FedWorld, is through Kermit or ASCII. Unfortunately, PerManNet does not support the Kermit protocol. That means that if you want to download files you will have to call PerManNet directly rather than going through the Internet, telnet, or FedWorld's Internet connection. This problem is not unique to PerManNet and it is likely that the problem will be resolved when the BBS SYSOPS incorporate Kermit into their bulletin board software or establish their own Internet connections. Even with these limitations PerManNet is worthy of your exploration.

St. Olaf College Internet and BITNET Distribution Point for the US State Department Travel Warnings and Consular Information Sheets

Internet address(es): mailing list: travel-advisories@stolaf.edu

(to subscribe:) travel-advisories-request@stolaf.edu

ftp: ftp.stolaf.edu:/pub/travel-advisories

URL: http://www.stolaf.edu/network/travel-advisories.html

Contact person & title: Craig Rice

Contact person's e-mail address: cdr@stolaf.edu

Contact person's voice phone number: 507-646-3631

Contact person's Fax phone number: 507-646-3096

Mailing address: Academic Computing Center, St. Olaf College, 1510 St. Olaf Avenue, Northfield, MN 55057-1097

DESCRIPTION

"St. Olaf College is the Internet and BITNET distribution point for the U.S. State Department Travel Warnings and Consular Information Sheets. We administer a mailing list for timely distribution of the warnings and information sheets, as well as make them available via Gopher, FTP and WWW."

This WWW server provides information similar to the Consular Affairs BBS, but in a more graphical format.

DEPARTMENT OF TRANSPORTATION

Air Transportation Division (AFS-200) BBS

□N Acronym for online service: ATD BBS

💻) Online service number(s): 202-267-5231, FedWorld BBS 703-321-8020

Log on: Abbreviated standard BBS

🌐 Internet address(es): telnet fedworld.gov then gateway to ATD BBS

🏛 Government agency acronym: DOT

👥 Contact person & title: Tom Penland

☎ Contact person's voice phone number: 202-267-3460

✉ Mailing address: The Federal Aviation Administration, Air Transportation Division (AFS-200), 800 Independence Avenue, SW, Room 306A, Washington, DC 30591

DESCRIPTION

The Air Transport BBS provides information about transport category, small aircraft, rotorcraft helicopters, and Flight Standardization Board documents.

ANNOTATION

I downloaded a couple files from the ATD BBS, at random, to see what they contained. The filenames didn't provide much of a clue about their contents. The content of the files was technical and of little interest to anyone not involved in Air Transportation Division topics. However, those interested in ATD topics will be impressed with the number of files available and the quality of information provided.

Airport BBS

□N Acronym for online service: Airport BBS

💻) Online service number(s): 202-267-5205, FedWorld 703-321-8020

🌐 Internet address(es): telnet fedworld.gov then gateway to Airport BBS

🏛 Government agency acronym: DOT/FAA

👥 Contact person & title: Rick Marinelli, SYSOP

💻← Contact person's e-mail address: rmarinelli@hq.faa.gov

☎ Contact person's voice phone number: 202-267-7669

📠 Contact person's Fax phone number: 202-267-5383

✉ Mailing address: The Federal Aviation Administration, AAS-100, 800 Independence Avenue, SW, Washington, DC 20591

DESCRIPTION

"PURPOSE

The FAA AIRPORTS Bulletin Board's purpose is to provide a method to distribute information of interest to airport operators and designers. This will include various computer programs and updated versions of Advisory Circulars originated by the Office of Airport Standards. These are generally Advisory Circulars in the 150 series.

FEATURES

As most other Boards that are open to the public, it also has other options that can be used:

- Electronic messaging.
- Bulletins.
- Conferences for the free exchange of information among users.
- A database for downloading files (to guard against the spread of computer viruses, uploading will be possible only through special arrangements with the SYSOP).
- An on-line version of AC 00-2.X, Advisory Circular Checklist. Our version is always more current than the hard copy.
- A database of information found on FAA form 5010, Airport Master Record. To save space, we have selected a limited number of fields to display. Leave a comment to the sysop to request additional fields, and we'll see if we can accommodate your request.
- An on-line version of the Signs and Marking Supplement (SAMS).
- An on-line version of the Certified Airport Lighting Equipment List.
- On-line Certalerts.
- Downloadable enplanement and cargo data.
- A list of draft Advisory Circulars currently out for public comment.
- Airports Calendar of Events."

ANNOTATION

Airport BBS's files, messages, bulletins, and announcements are specifically directed toward airport operators and designers.

However, even those with just a casual interest in airport workings may find this BBS worth the visit. It is well run and organized.

Read the FAQ file to find answers to frequently asked questions. It will save you time and effort if you have a question about the FAA.

Department of Transportation WWW Server

💻) Online service number(s): 1 (800) 665-6087 (starting Jan 95) will provide modem access up to 14.4 to Gopher, web server and bbs systems.

Log on: Follow screen instructions

🌐 Internet address(es): http://www.dot.gov, gopher.dot.gov, ftp.dot.gov

💻← E-mail addresses: Webmaster@dot.gov

🏛 Government agency acronym: DOT

👥 Contact person & title: Gus Coronel, Internet Administrator

💻← Contact person's e-mail address: gus@mailstorm.dot.gov

☎ Contact person's voice phone number: 202 366-4715

🖨 Contact person's Fax phone number: 202 366-4776

✉ Mailing address: US Dept. of Transportation, 400 7th St. SW, Room PL-206, Washington, DC 20590

DESCRIPTION

"The main point of entry for all Department of Transportation on-line services. Provides gateways to all Federal Transportation related bulletin boards and on-line servers, including:

- The Federal Aviation Administration
- The Federal Highways Administration
- The Federal Transit Administration
- The Federal Railroads Administration
- The Maritime Administration
- The National Highway Safety Administration
- The Office for Commercial Space
- The Transportation Inspector General
- The Saint Lawrence Seaway Development Corporation
- The Bureau of Transportation Statistics
- The Transportation Research and Special Projects Administration
- The US Coast Guard
- and others"

Like other new U.S. Government WWW servers, the graphics found here are great and the organization of information is logical and easy to use. If your computer can handle it, look at the video.

FAA Office of Environment & Energy BBS

⌨N   Acronym for online service: AEE BBS

🖥)   Online service number(s): 202-267-9647, FedWorld 703-321-8020

     Log on: Before you can gain access to public areas you need approval from the SYSOP.

🌐   Internet address(es): telnet fedworld.gov then gateway to AEE BBS

🏛   Government agency acronym: FAA

👥   Contact person & title: Steve Vahovich

💻←   Contact person's e-mail address: svahovich@mail.hq.faa.gov

☎   Contact person's voice phone number: 202-267-3559

🖨   Contact person's Fax phone number: 202-267-5594

✉   Mailing address: Federal Aviation Administration, Office of Environment & Energy , 800 Independence Avenue, SW, AEE-120, Washington, DC 20591

"The Office of Environment & Energy (AEE) Federal Aviation Administration has placed on-line a bulletin board to support public and private conferences and file exchange areas dealing with noise, pollution and controls."

If you are not a client of the FAA and AEE, and are not interested in the FAA's noise-modeling files, there is no reason to contact this BBS.

Federal Highway Electronic Bulletin Board System

⌨N   Acronym for online service: FEBBS

🖥)   Online service number(s): 9,600 bps 202-366-3175, 2,400 bps 202-366-3764, Voice help is available at 202-366-1120

Government agency acronym: FHWA

👥 Contact person & title: Carl Shea and Donna Avallone, SYSOPs

☎ Contact person's voice phone number: Shea 202-366-9022, Avallone 202-366-9037

✉ Mailing address: Federal Highway Administration, Information Systems Division, 400 7th St., SW, Washington, DC 20590

DESCRIPTION

"FEBBS is intended for informal communications among Federal Highway Administration staff and interested members of the public about the Federal Highway and Motor Carrier programs and the information technology that supports those programs."

ANNOTATION

If you are interested in detailed information about Federal Highway Administration, this is the BBS. FEBBS is small and not as information rich as other Federal BBSs, but it is well organized and easy to use.

Headquarters Bulletin Board

💻 Acronym for online service: FAAHQ BBS

💻 Online service number(s): 202-267-5697, FedWorld 703-321-8020

🌐 Internet address(es): telnet fedworld.gov then gateway to FAAHQ BBS

🏛 Government agency acronym: DOT

👥 Contact person & title: Michael L. Lee, Program Analyst

💻 Contact person's e-mail address: mlee@hq.faa.gov, lee3961@delphi.com, michael.lee@wdn.com

☎ Contact person's voice phone number: 202-267-3332

📠 Contact person's Fax phone number: 202-267-3324

✉ Mailing address: Federal Aviation Administration, APO-120, Room 934A, 800 Independence Avenue, SW, Washington, DC 20591

DESCRIPTION

"This bulletin board is jointly supported by the Federal Aviation Administration's (FAA) Office of Aviation Policy, Plans, and Management Analysis, the Office of Public Affairs, and the Executive Director for Acquisition and Safety Oversight. The purpose of the board is to provide an alternative outlet for the exchange of information and data between the FAA and its user community, other Federal government departments and agencies, and the general public.

This computer bulletin board also provides an alternative means of intra-agency communications between the FAA's headquarters, the regions, the Aeronautical Center and the Technical Center. The bulletin board provides a means of sharing information through various bulletins, message conferences, and various informational text files, public domain software, and shareware programs.

This bulletin board is open to anyone, including members of the general public, who are actively engaged in or interested in aviation and/or the activities for which the FAA is responsible. The Offices that support the operation of this electronic bulletin board system believe this rather unique means of communication will prove beneficial to the FAA community and the public at large."

Michael Lee, the SYSOP of the FAAHQ BBS, deserves recognition for being one of the most helpful SYSOPS I encountered during the compilation of this book. While I was online to the FAAHQ BBS, Lee introduced himself using the chat mode of his telecommunications software. We exchanged a dozen or so lines of information about ourselves, then Lee took me on a tour of his BBS. Lee's attitude of openness and pride in his BBS makes him refreshingly unique.

The FAAHQ BBS has an excellent message system. The messages are interesting and so are the threads of the messages. The bulletin and file areas are worthy of exploration if you are an airplane pilot or frequent airline passenger.

Maritime Administration, Information Resources Management, MARlinspike BBS

▯N   Acronym for online service: MARlinspike BBS

▯)   Online service number(s): 202-366-8505, FedWorld 703-321-8020

🌐   Internet address(es): telnet fedworld.gov then gateway to MARlinspike BBS.

🏛   Government agency acronym: MARAD

👥   Contact person & title: Terry Jones, SYSOP

☎   Contact person's voice phone number: 202-366-4181

✉   Mailing address: Maritime Administration, Information Resources Management, 400 Seventh Street, SW, Room 8311, Washington, DC 20590

DESCRIPTION

MARlinspike is divided into the following sections:

- Public Affairs
- International Trade
- Domestic Trade
- National Cargo
- Port and Intermodal
- Technology Assessment Legislation.

ANNOTATION

If you are curious about what the Maritime Administration does, you may want to download INTROMAR.TXT from the MARlinspike BBS. It will, in about 10 pages, provide you with a clear overview of the Maritime Administration. Other files found on MARlinspike include news announcements, bulletins, and more.

MARlinspike is narrowly focused, so you won't see files or discussion on anything other than Maritime Administration–oriented topics.

For more information about MARlinspike contact Deborah Johnson at 800-9US-FLAG.

NAVSTAR GPS Information Center Bulletin Board

🏠   Parent organization: U.S. Coast Guard

🖳 Acronym for online service: GPSIC BBS

🖳 Online service number(s): 703-313-5910, FedWorld 703-321-8020

🌐 Internet address(es): telnet fedworld.gov then gateway to USCG.

🏛 Government agency acronym: USCG

👥 Contact person & title: Michael Reese, SYSOP

☎ Contact person's voice phone number: 703-313-5900

✉ Mailing address: United State Coast Guard, 7323 Telegraph Avenue, Alexandria, VA 22310

DESCRIPTION

"This bulletin board's purpose is to provide civil GPS users access to system information on a continuous basis. The information is updated 24 hours a day, as messages are received; however

Information is not 'real time'. There are delays involved in generating, transmitting, and processing messages.

This BBS is currently in a test and evaluation stage.

Technical data on GPS status is available in three reports from GPS Operational Control:

Notice Advisory to Navstar Users (NANU), which provide notification of changes, outages, periods of unusability, etc.

Almanacs, which contain numerical parameters describing each satellite, and can be used to predict coverage and visibility.

Status reports, which contain info on satellite planes, clocks, current advisories, etc.

These reports are available in the Satellite Information Group (FORUMS) section of the BBS. Some background information and a status summary are also available.

Help on using the BBS is available at the '?' prompt. ('?' is context sensitive.) In general, 'X' usually returns you to the previous menu, while 'Exit' returns you to the main menu. When menu selections are listed in short form (just a series of letters), the long form can be obtained by pressing [cr]. Further notes on BBS shortcuts are contained in the 'Shortcuts' section.

This bulletin board service is FREE, except for whatever you pay your phone company. However, the BBS software is capable of assessing charges for service, in the form of 'credits' used. We are using the credits only as a means of limiting access time for individual users, and do not anticipate that anyone will run out, with normal use of the BBS."

ANNOTATION

Although this BBS is accessible through the Internet by using FedWorld, I found the FedWorld connection extremely slow. The response time for typing a command was often several minutes. File download attempts were unsuccessful through Fed-World.

Safety Data Exchange Bulletin Board

🖳 Acronym for online service: FAA SAFETY BBS

🖳 Online service number(s): 800-426-3814, FedWorld 703-321-8020

Log on: Follow instructions carefully. The password is "SAFETY."

🌐 Internet address(es): telnet fedworld.gov then gateway to FAA Safety Exchange.

🏛 Government agency acronym: FAA

👥 Contact person & title: Ben Morrow, SDR Coordinator

☎ Contact person's voice phone number: 816-426-3580

🖨 Contact person's Fax phone number: 816-426-2169

✉ Mailing address: Federal Aviation Administration, ACE-103, 601 E. 12th Street, Kansas City, MO 64106

DESCRIPTION

"The SAFETY DATA EXCHANGE BULLETIN BOARD is operated by the FAA's Small Airplane Directorate in Kansas City, MO, solely for the exchange of safety related information on AMATEUR-BUILT AND ULTRALIGHT aircraft."

ANNOTATION

If you are thinking of building an ultralight aircraft you may want to look through the list of approved kits found here. Look for changes in the BBS after August 1994.

One of the nongovernment aviation oriented BBSs listed on this BBS may also be worth exploring: Sport Aircraft Builders BBS 8 P.M.–8 A.M. 908-755-5371.

DEPARTMENT OF THE TREASURY

Customs Electronic Bulletin Board

🏠 Parent organization: United States Customs Service

🖥 Acronym for online service: CEBB

🖥 Online service number(s): 703-440-6155, FedWorld 703-321-8020

🌐 Internet address(es): telnet to fedworld.gov then gateway to CEBB.

🏛 Government agency acronym: USCS

👥 Contact person & title: Sue Coppola

☎ Contact person's voice phone number: 703-440-6236

🖨 Contact person's Fax phone number: 703-440-6293

✉ Mailing address: United States Custom Service, 7681 Boston Blvd., Springfield, VA 22153

DESCRIPTION

"CEBB makes available to the public the following Customs information: quota status, currency conversion rates, directives pertaining to trade and importation; NAFTA and MOD Act requirements; a listing of Intellectual Property Rights registered with Customs; news releases; Federal register notices; operating instructions for the trade community; administrative messages on antidumping and countervailing duty; and information from Canadian Customs."

ANNOTATION

"Dramatic Late Evening Air Chase Nets Millions in Smuggled Marijuana" was the first file title I read on the CEBB. The next was "U.S. Customs Returns 14th Century Art to Italy." The content of these stories was just as exciting as their titles. CEBB also maintains a huge file collection dealing with nearly every aspect of customs.

Journalists with writer's block should log on to the CEBB and scan the file titles for article ideas. Chances are they will discover fresh new stories. Some additional file titles that caught my attention were: "Organized

Crime Rings," "Liquidation Instructions for Whiskbrooms," and "Will the Real California Pistachio Nut Please Stand Up?" My tastes in file titles may not paint an accurate picture of CEBB. There are many more titles dealing with more mundane subjects such as global trade, tariffs, countervailing duties, NAFTA, and trademark counterfeiting. CEBB is easy to use and it is interesting to explore.

CEBB is closed on Mondays from 6:00 A.M. to 9:00 A.M. EST for maintenance.

Electronic Filing Service Bulletin Board

☗ Parent organization: Internal Revenue Service

🖳ᴺ Acronym for online service: 1040 BBS

🖳⟩ Online service number(s): 202-799-0221, FedWorld 703-321-8020

🌐 Internet address(es): telnet fedworld.gov gateway to

🏛 Government agency acronym: IRS

👥 Contact person & title: Susanne Thomas

☎ Contact person's voice phone number: 202-283-0459

✉ Mailing address: Internal Revenue Service Headquarters, Department of the Treasury, 1111 Constitution Avenue, NW, Washington, DC 20224

DESCRIPTION

The 1040 BBS is specifically oriented toward IRS electronic filing issues.

ANNOTATION

When I logged on to the 1040 BBS I was only

able to read bulletins. The messaging, files, doors, and other sections were not accessible.

Financial Management Service

🖳ᴺ Acronym for online service: FMS BBS

🖳⟩ Online service number(s): 202-874-6817, 202-874-6953, 202-874-7034, 202-874-6872, 202-874-8608, FedWorld 703-321-8020

🌐 Internet address(es): telnet fedworld.gov then gateway to FMS-BBS

👥 Contact person & title: Stephen Vajs, SYSOP

☎ Contact person's voice phone number: 202-874-6943, Voice mail 202-874-6995

🖨 Contact person's Fax phone number: 202-874-7321

✉ Mailing address: Financial Management Service, Room 312A, Liberty Center Building, 401 14th Street, SW, Washington, DC 20227

DESCRIPTION

"The FMS Inside Line was established to provide an easy method of access to the Inventory Management Standards project team, its products and guidelines, and related financial management guidelines, tools, and texts."

FMS also provides update information on:

• Current interest rate, both Prompt Payment and Current Value of Funds Rates Inventory Management

• Collection Practices

• Disbursement Practices

- Cash Management Certification
- Collection Specification Worksheet
- Accounts for Funds Held Outside of the Treasury
- FMS conferences

The Inside Line provides access to documents and software including:

- Cash Management Tools
- Inventory Management Assistance
- Policy Texts
- Historical Interest Rate Data
- Forms and Applications

ANNOTATION

The FMS BBS also maintains a Fax-on-Call system (202-874-8616) that works very nicely. Call the number and listen to the instructions. Image number 1 is an index to documents available. Get the index first, then call back to request other documents.

Statistics of Income Division BBS

Parent organization: Internal Revenue Service

Acronym for online service: SOI BBS

Online service number(s): 202-874-9574, FedWorld 703-321-8020

Internet address(es): telnet fedworld.gov then gateway to SOI BBS #104

Government agency acronym: IRS

Contact person & title: Jim Willis and Kristine Zahm, SYSOPs

Contact person's voice phone number: 202-874-0277, 202-874-0273

Contact person's Fax phone number: 202-874-0922

Mailing address: Internal Revenue Service, Statistics of Income Division, Foreign Operations Section, CP:S:R, P.O. Box 2608, Washington, DC 20013-2608

DESCRIPTION

"The sole purpose of this BBS is to disseminate statistical information to the public. This BBS cannot accept any uploaded files except comments."

ANNOTATION

The IRS SOI BBS has statistical files on the following topics which are also the file area names:

- Individual Public Use Files
- Corporate Public Use Files
- Sole Proprietorship Public Files
- Partnership Public Use Files
- U.S. Corporation Foreign Files
- Non-SOI Public Use Files
- Tax Exempt Organization Files
- Private Foundation Public Files
- County Income Data by State Files
- Published Papers by SOI
- U.S. Possession Public Files
- International Boycott Files
- Taxpayer Usage Study Files
- State to State Migration Files
- Documentation of Various Reports
- Personal Wealth Public Files
- Estate Public Use Files

- Census, County Business Pattern
- Excerpts from the SOI Newsletter
- Individual Foreign Earned Income
- Excise Tax Public Files
- Projections (from Research Div.)
- SOI 1990 Individual by State Files
- SOI 1991 Individual by State Files
- SOI 1992 Individual by State Files

Surety Bond Branch BBS

⌂ Parent organization: Financial Management Service

🖥N Acronym for online service: SBB-BBS

🖥) Online service number(s): 202-874-7214, FedWorld 703-321-8020

🌐 Internet address(es): telnet fedworld.gov

🏛 Government agency acronym: Dept. of Treasury-FMS

👥 Contact person & title: Dorothy E. Martin, Manager, Surety Bond Branch

☎ Contact person's voice phone number: 202-874-6850

📠 Contact person's Fax phone number: 202-874-6533

✉ Mailing address: Surety Bond Branch, Financial Management Service, U.S. Department of the Treasury, 401-14th Street, SW, Room 262C, Washington, DC 20227

DESCRIPTION

"This Bulletin Board enables you to VIEW the companies that are recognized by the Treasury Department, for Federal bonding and to DOWNLOAD the entire document to your computer, for hard copy production, or to PRINTSCREEN.

Copies of Circular 570 continue to be available by contacting this office, however, we anticipate this computerized listing will replace the hard copies normally requested from our office."

ANNOTATION

If Surety Bonds are part of your business vocabulary, you may find the content of the SBB-BBS interesting and valuable. Otherwise, you may find little of interest here.

DEPARTMENT OF VETERANS AFFAIRS

VA Vendor Bulletin Board System

🖥N Acronym for online service: VA Vendor BBS

🖥) Online service number(s): "(202) 233-6971 for D.C. and local calling area, (800) SELL-2-VA toll-free long distance ONLY, (800) 735-5282 (numerical representation)"

Log on:
"Note! Open to businesses only.
As a new user you will be automatically logged off the systems until you have registered by sending a request asking for access. To do this simply send a request on your company's letterhead or Fax to:
Department of Veterans Affairs (711)
Attn.: Jeremy Cohen
810 Vermont Avenue, NW

Washington, DC 20420 or FAX: (202) 233-4726"

🌐 Internet address(es): telnet Fedworld.gov then use gateway to VA Vendor BBS. Connect to SBA Online then use gateway to VA Vendor BBS

💻 E-mail addresses: N/A

🏛 Government agency acronym: VA

👥 Contact person & title: Jeremy Cohen, SYSOP

☎ Contact person's voice phone number: 202-233-6219

🖨 Contact person's Fax phone number: 202-233-4726

✉ Mailing address: Department of Veterans Affairs, 810 Vermont Avenue, NW, Washington, DC 20420

DESCRIPTION

"The BBS is intended to be used for businesses who believe they have products or services that may benefit VA and wish to know about potential contracts. Users are able to download all types of acquisition documentation such as RFPs, RFQs, APRs and DPAs. Also special announcements, CBD ads, telephone directories of VA acquisitions personnel, organizational charts of VA acquisitions and other types of information that may be deemed conducive to good business."

ANNOTATION

If you are like me and you don't know an RFP from an RFQ, you probably don't have any reason to request an account on the VA Vendor BBS. If you do have business here, you will want to know that this BBS is closed on weekends and only open from 8:00 A.M. to 8:00 P.M. EST.

Chapter 11

INDEPENDENT ESTABLISHMENTS AND GOVERNMENT CORPORATIONS

CONSUMER PRODUCT SAFETY COMMISSION

Consumer Product Safety Commission (CPSC) Internet Gopher

- Internet address(es): Gopher cpsc.gov

- E-mail address(es): info@cpsc.gov

- Government agency acronym: CPSC

- Contact person & title: Ken Giles

- Contact person's voice phone number: 301-504-0580 ext. 1184

- Contact person's Fax phone number: 301-504-0862

- Mailing address: U.S. Consumer Product Safety Commission, Office of Public Affairs, Washington, DC 20707

DESCRIPTION

"The U.S. Consumer Product Safety Commission (CPSC) is now on the INTERNET, joining other Federal Government agencies on the "information superhighway." Consumers can electronically access the commission's recent news releases about recalls and product hazards along with the agency's current calendar of meetings.

CPSC's INTERNET address, cpsc.gov, is available on the agency's Gopher server. INTERNET users can search news releases to download the recall information onto their computers. A brief menu item lists the commission's responsibilities and describes how consumers can report hazardous products to the agency. Questions or comments about CPSC's information on the INTERNET may be sent to: info@cpsc.gov.

The U.S. Consumer Product Safety Commission's mission is to protect the public from unreasonable risks of injury and death associated with consumer products. CPSC believes that by making safety information quickly and easily available, more injuries and deaths can be prevented.

NOTE: To report an unsafe consumer product or a product-related injury, consumers should call the Commission's toll-free hot line at (800) 638-2772. A teletypewriter for the speech or hearing impaired is available at (800) 638-8270. Product hazards also may be reported to info@cpsc.gov."

I was curious if I would find anything useful to me personally on the CPSC Gopher. Exploring the press release section of the Gopher, I found several files that were of immediate interest to me. For example, I discovered that a smoker-cooker I had used for years had a design flaw that could have caused a fire had I used it on a wooden deck. The press release provided an 800 telephone number for the manufacturer and described what the manufacturer offered as a solution to the problem. Parents may be interested in scanning the press releases for toy and children's furniture recalls.

CORPORATION FOR NATIONAL SERVICE

Corporation for National Service

(See description)

🏛 Government agency acronym: CFNC

👥 Contact person & title: Jim Delloso

💻 Contact person's E-mail address: pliaison@aol.com

☎ Contact person's voice phone number: 202-606-5108

✉ Mailing address: Corporation for National Service, 1100 Vermont Avenue, NW, Washington, DC 20525

DESCRIPTION

The Corporation for National Service (CFNC) does not have direct online access through an electronic bulletin board or through the Internet. Instead, CFNC distributes documents electronically through other government agency and commercial online services. Not all CFNC documents are electronically distributed to all online services.

CFNC documents are available from:

- U.S. Dept. of Agriculture Gopher server at ace.esuda.gov
- HandsNet (voice) 408-257-4500. A fee-based commercial service that provides Corporation for National Service documents.
- Peace Corps BBS

Although CFNC does not have direct access, they do have indirect access and that was enough to justify their being listed.

DEFENSE NUCLEAR FACILITIES SAFETY BOARD

Defense Nuclear Facilities Safety Board Gopher

🖥 Acronym for online service: DNFSB Gopher

🌐 Internet address(es): Gopher gopher.dnfsb.gov.

Log on: After connecting to the Gopher select the option "Databases and Network Information/." Next select the option "Defense Nuclear Facilities Safety Board Gopher/."

 E-mail address(es): mailbox@dnfsb.gov

🏛 Government agency acronym: DNFSB

👥 Contact person & title: Carole Morgan

💻 Contact person's E-mail address: mailbox@dnfsb.gov

☎ Contact person's voice phone number: 202-208-6400

🖷 Contact person's Fax phone number: 202-208-6518

✉ Mailing address: Defense Nuclear Facilities Safety Board, 625 Indiana Avenue, NW, Suite 700, Washington, DC 20004

DESCRIPTION

The Defense Nuclear Facilities Safety Board provides:

- The Board's Most Recent Annual Report to Congress
- The Board's Enabling Legislation
- Recommendations Issued to the Secretary of Energy
- Board Member's Biographies
- Federal Register Notices
- Notice of Public Hearings
- Vacancy Announcements
- Trip Reports Transmitted to the Department of Energy
- Correspondence Log of Technical Documents

ANNOTATION

Researchers, journalists, and individuals seeking information about the defense nuclear complex will find the information available on the DNFSB Gopher useful.

If you need more information than is provided here, send your requests to the contact person listed above.

ENVIRONMENTAL PROTECTION AGENCY

Aerometric Information Retrieval System

🖥 Acronym for online service: AIRS

💻 Online service number(s): EPA TTN BBS 919-541-5742

🌐 Internet address(es): telnet ttnbbs.rtpnc.epa.gov then use gateway to AIRS.

🏛 Government agency acronym: EPA

👥 Contact person & title: Angie Shatas, SYSOP

✉ Mailing address: U.S. EPA National Air Data Branch, MD-14, Research Triangle Park, NC 27711

DESCRIPTION

"The focus of the AIRS BBS is to encourage the exchange of information among State and local agencies that utilize AIRS documents and information. AIRS BBS is operated by the National Air Data Branch (NADB) of the Office of Air Quality Planning and Standards.

The AIRS BBS maintains the current AIRS-LETTER; relevant brochures, pamphlets, and bulletins; and information on meetings, conferences, training seminars, and permits. User-supplied AIRS-related demonstration software is circulated, as well as EPA PC-based AIRS related software. All AIRS User's Manuals and Guides are available for download. The AIRS bulletin board also contains a current listing of AIRS Contact Personnel. Answers to frequently asked question are available, as well as public and private electronic mail for use in obtaining information from the AIRS user community"

ANNOTATION

The AIRS BBS is reached through the EPA TTN BBS.

Air Pollution Training Institute

⌨ Acronym for online service: APTI

💻) Online service number(s): EPA TTN BBS 919-541-5742

🌐 Internet address(es): telnet ttnbbs.rtpnc.epa.gov.

🏛 Government agency acronym: EPA

👥 Contact person & title: Betty Abramson, SYSOP

✉ Mailing address: U.S. Environmental Protection Agency, OAQPS, Annex MD-17, Research Triangle Park, NC 27711

DESCRIPTION

"The Air Pollution Training Institute (APTI) offers the widest scope of air pollution training in the United States. Funded by the U.S. Environmental Protection Agency, APTI develops instructional material for and provides technical assistance to training activities conducted in support of the nation's regulatory programs of air pollution abatement.

EPA-sponsored lecture and laboratory courses, using APTI materials, are scheduled at several locations across the country. Self-instructional courses, providing opportunities for individual training at home or in place of employment, are obtainable from APTI. Training material is continually updated, and individual courses undergo periodic major revision. APTI publishes a 'Chronological Schedule of Air Pollution Training Courses'; generally once a year. This publication describes the training being offered with a description of the APTI courses and how to obtain the training.

If you would like a copy of 'Chronological Schedule of Air Pollution Training Courses,' contact the Registrar at (919) 541-2497."

ANNOTATION

The APTI BBS is reached through the EPA TTN BBS.

Alternative Treatment Technology Information Center

⌨ Acronym for online service: ATTIC

💻) Online service number(s): 703-908-2138, FedWorld 703-321-8020

🌐 Internet address(es): telnet fedworld.gov then gateway to ATTIC

🏛 Government agency acronym: EPA

👥 Contact person & title: Dan Sullivan, Project Manager, Mike Entner and Robert McCurdy SYSOPS

☎ Contact person's voice phone number: Hot line 703-908-2137, Dan Sullivan 908-321-6677

☎ Contact person's Fax phone number: 908-906-6990

✉ Mailing address: Office of Research & Development, U.S. Environmental Protection Agency, 2890 Woodbridge Avenue, MS-106, Edison, New Jersey 08837-3679

DESCRIPTION

"The Alternative Treatment Technology Information Center (ATTIC) is a comprehensive computer database system providing up-to-date information on innovative treatment technologies. ATTIC provides access to several independent databases as well as a mechanism for retrieving full-text documents of key literature. The system provides information you need to make effective decisions on hazardous waste clean-up alternatives. It can be accessed with a personal computer (PC) and modem 24 hours a day, and there are no user fees.

The Treatment Technology Database contains information on:

- Biological Treatment
- Chemical Treatment
- Physical Treatment
- Solidification/Stabilization
- Thermal Treatment

Approximately 150 publications from EPA's Off of Research and Development have been abstracted and included in this database to provide information on the treatment and disposal of spilled oil and chemicals. This small database is being expanded to include key literature produced by organizations other than EPA."

ANNOTATION

ATTIC is another sharply focused BBS. Its content is nearly all related to alternative treatment technology. A sample bulletin title is a good example of ATTIC's content: "Wastes Generated during the Manufacture of Chlorinated Toluenes Listed as Hazardous."

Ambient Monitoring Technology Information Center BBS

🖵 Acronym for online service: AMTIC

🖵 Online service number(s): EPA TTN BBS 919-541-5742

🌐 Internet address(es): telnet ttnbbs.rtpnc.epa.gov then use gateway to AMTIC BBS.

🏛 Government agency acronym: EPA

👥 Contact person & title: Ed Hanks, SYSOP

✉ Mailing address: Ambient Monitoring Technology Information Center (AMTIC), U.S. Environmental Protection Agency (EPA), Office of Air Quality Planning and Standards (OAQPS), TSD/MRB (MD-14), Research Triangle Park, NC 27711

DESCRIPTION

"The AMTIC BBS is centered around the exchange of ambient monitoring related information. At the present time the AMTIC electronic bulletin board system contains information on all the Reference and Equivalent methods for the criteria pollutants. As the system evolves, it will also contain all the TO Methods and other noncriteria pollutant methodologies. The AMTIC BBS already contains all federal Regulations pertaining to ambient monitoring. It also contains ambient monitoring QA/QC related information and some information on ambient monitoring related publications. There is also available information on ambientmonitoring news, field and laboratory studies of interest, and available related training. A bulletin board is a dynamic system, and this one is expected to grow quickly."

ANNOTATION

The AMTIC BBS is reached through the EPA TTN BBS.

BLIS BBS

⌨N   Acronym for online service: BLIS BBS

🖥)   Online service number(s): EPA TTN BBS 919-541-5742

🌐   Internet address(es): telnet ttnbbs.rtpnc.epa.gov then use gateway to BLIS.

🏛   Government agency acronym: EPA

👥   Contact person & title: Joe Steigerwald, SYSOP

☎   Contact person's voice phone number: 919-541-2736

🖷   Contact person's Fax phone number: 919-541-0072

✉   Mailing address: U.S. Environmental Protection Agency, MD-13, Research Triangle, NC 27711

DESCRIPTION

"The BLIS BBS contains information from the Reasonably Available Control Technology (RACT)/Best Available Control Technology (BACT)/Lowest Achievable Emission Rate (LAER) Clearinghouse. This information is distilled from air permits submitted by most

of the State and local air pollution control programs in the United States. The data is meant to assist State/local agency personnel and private companies in determining what types of controls other air pollution agencies have applied to various sources. The BLIS database option allows the user to do interactive searches of the database."

ANNOTATION

The BLIS BBS is reached through the EPA TTN BBS.

Clean Air Act Amendments Bulletin Board

⌨N   Acronym for online service: CAAA BBS

🖥)   Online service number(s): EPA TTN BBS 919-541-5742

🌐   Internet address(es): telnet ttnbbs.rtpnc.epa.gov then use gateway to CAAA BBS.

🏛   Government agency acronym: EPA

DESCRIPTION

"The Clean Air Act Amendments Bulletin Board System (CAAA BBS) is designed to provide access to information on the Clean Air Act amendments of 1990. Through this electronic information dissemination vehicle, the CAAA BBS allows regulators, the regulated community and members of the general public to easily obtain access to that information that is relevant to the Clean Air Act (CAA) amendments of 1990. In this manner, the task of understanding, implementing and complying with the requirements of the new law will be made easier."

The CAAA BBS is reached through the EPA TTN BBS. For contact information contact the EPA TTN BBS SYSOP.

Cleanup Information Bulletin Board System

📺N   Acronym for online service: CLU-IN

💻)   Online service number(s): 301-589-8366, Help line 301-589-8368, FedWorld 703-321-8020

🌐   Internet address(es): telnet fedworld.gov then gateway to CLU-IN BBS

🏛   Government agency acronym: EPA

👥   Contact person & title: Gary Turner, EPA Project Manager

☎   Contact person's voice phone number: 703-308-8827

🖨   Contact person's Fax phone number: 703-308-8528

✉   Mailing address: U.S. Environmental Protection Agency, Office of Solid Waste and Emergency Response, Technology Innovation Office (5102W), 401 M. St., SW, Washington, DC 20460

DESCRIPTION

"The Cleanup Information Bulletin Board System (CLU-IN) is designed for hazardous waste cleanup professionals who need current information on innovative technologies and remediation and would like to consult with other professionals online. CLU-IN is used by those involved in the cleanup of Superfund, Resource Conservation and Recovery Act corrective action, and underground storage tank sites. Users include EPA and other Federal and State personnel, consulting engineers, technology vendors, remediation contractors, researchers, community groups, and individual citizens.

CLU-IN offers many different types of information from many sources. Some items are intended to be read online; others may be copied to your computer for use at your convenience. In addition to the examples below, the message exchange on CLU-IN is an excellent source of up-to-date information.

Text of Articles from EPA Newsletters:

Tech Trends. Provides descriptions and performance data for innovative technologies that actually have been applied in the field. Five issues per year.

Ground Water Currents. Provides information on the development and demonstration of innovative groundwater remediation techniques. Reports on technologies, new regulations that impact groundwater remediation, discussions on issues such as DNAPLs, and information on conferences and publications.

Bioremediation in the Field. An information update on applying bioremediation to site cleanup. Offers articles describing treatability studies underway, a table detailing CERCLA, RCRA, UST, and TSCA sites planning, operating, or having completed bioremediation projects, and technical support and publications offered by EPA.

EPA HQ Library's OERR Infoline. A current awareness tool from the EPA library including references to upcoming meetings and conferences, new journal articles, EPA reports, reference works, and other documents.

More EPA Publications:

Compendium of Superfund Program Publications. Lists of Superfund Directives by title, subject, and EPA directive and report numbers, as well as directions on how to order the documents.

Innovative Treatment Technologies: Semi-Annual Status Report. Offers information on applications of innovative treatment technologies for remedial and removal actions, organized in extensive tables providing detailed site-specific information.

TIO's Innovative Technology Bibliography. Provides descriptions and order numbers for publications related to all aspects of the choice and application of innovative technologies.

Other Regularly Updated Information:

Training Calendars. Quarterly updates provide titles, dates, and locations of courses, organized by EPA Region, and provide a contact and phone number to register.

RCRA/CERCLA/OUST/EPCRA Hot line Monthly Report. Commonly asked questions and answers about regulations. Also details new publications.

Federal Register. Summaries of recent notices related to Hazardous Waste and Ground Water. Citations for all EPA regulations.

Commerce Business Daily. Weekly update containing the text of Commerce Business Daily announcements for hazardous waste remediation.

National Priorities List:

Upcoming Conferences, Workshops, and Demonstrations of Innovative Technologies.

Databases:

UST Case Study Data System. Contains over 200 case studies that were developed to support RCRA rule and guidance development activities affecting facility location, RCRA corrective action, and closure.

Risk Reduction Engineering Laboratory (RREL) Treatability Database. Provides a thorough review of the effectiveness of proven, commercially available treatment technologies for the removal or destruction of chemicals from media such as municipal and industrial wastewater, drinking water, groundwater, soil, debris, sludge, and sediment.

Air Methods Database. A database of methods for measuring the levels of toxic pollutants in ambient and indoor air."

ANNOTATION

The description provided by CLU-IN provides a good indication of the content of this BBS. What it doesn't tell you is how well run and organized CLU-IN is. The structure of the BBS and its commands are nicely designed and consistent. Researchers will find the search features useful and easy to use.

Cleanup Standards Outreach Bulletin Board System

🖳N Acronym for online service: CSO BBS

🖳) Online service number(s): Washington DC Metro area local number 703-790-0825, 800-700-7837, FedWorld 703-321-8020

🌐 Internet address(es): telnet fedworld.gov then gateway to CSO BBS

🏛 Government agency acronym: EPA

👥 Contact person & title: Barbara Hostage

✉ Mailing address: U. S. Environmental Protection Agency, Mail Stop 6603J, 401 M. Street, SW, Washington, DC 20460

DESCRIPTION

"In recent years, the public, industry and federal facility managers have become increasingly aware of the problems associated with contamination of the environment by releases of radioactive materials. The Office of Radiation and Indoor Air (ORIA) has been approached by the Department of Energy and other organizations, who have requested that ORIA assist them in developing and implementing programs to control and abate contamination of the environment caused by radionuclides.

It is the goal of this BBS to be of assistance to those members of the public, industry, and federal entities who are attempting to understand and comply with environmental regulations which apply to radionuclides."

ANNOTATION

Unless you have an immediate relationship with radioactive materials, you may not find it worth your time to explore this BBS. The efforts of this BBS are directed specifically at disseminating information about radioactive clean-up efforts.

Clearinghouse for Inventories and Emission Factors

🖥N Acronym for online service: CHIEF BBS

🖥) Online service number(s): EPA TTN BBS 919-541-5742

🌐 Internet address(es): telnet ttnbbs.rtpnc.epa.gov then use gateway to CHIEF BBS.

🏛 Government agency acronym: EPA

👥 Contact person & title: Michael Hamlin, Chief SYSOP

☎ Contact person's voice phone number: 919-541-5232

✉ Mailing address: Clearinghouse for Inventories and Emission Factors (CHIEF), U.S. Environmental

Protection Agency, MD-14, Research Triangle Park, NC 27711

DESCRIPTION

"The CHIEF BBS provides access to tools for estimating emissions of air pollutants and performing air emission inventories. CHIEF will serve as EPA's central clearinghouse for the latest information on air emission inventories and emission factors. Emission estimation data bases, newsletters, announcements, and guidance on performing inventories will be included in CHIEF."

ANNOTATION

The CHIEF BBS is reached through the EPA TTN BBS.

Compliance Information BBS

🖥N Acronym for online service: COMPLI BBS

🖥) Online service number(s): EPA TTN BBS 919-541-5742

🌐 Internet address(es): telnet ttnbbs.rtpnc.epa.gov then use gateway to COMPLI BBS.

🏛 Government agency acronym: EPA

👥 Contact person & title: Walter White, SYSOP

☎ Contact person's voice phone number: 703-308-8704

✉ Mailing address: U.S. Environmental Protection Agency Headquarters, 401 M. Street, SW, Washington, DC 20460

"The COMPLI BBS contains three databases. They are:

- NARS National Asbestos Registry System. A listing of all asbestos contractors, their inspections and the results of them. This database is used to target contractors for inspection.
- Determinations Index. This is a compilation of clarifications and determination issued by the EPA concerning selected subparts of the Federal Register. It consists of two major parts: NSPS determinations and NESHAP determinations.
- Woodstoves. A database of EPA Certified Woodstoves and Woodstove manufacturers.

This COMPLI BBS is maintained by EPA—Stationary Source Compliance Division (SSCD)."

ANNOTATION

The COMPLI BBS is reached through the EPA TTN BBS

Control Technology Center BBS

🖥 Acronym for online service: CTC BBS

🖥 Online service number(s): EPA TTN BBS 919-541-5742

🌐 Internet address(es): telnet ttnbbs.rtpnc.epa.gov then use gateway to CTC BBS.

🏛 Government agency acronym: EPA

👥 Contact person & title: Joe Steigerwald, SYSOP

☎ Contact person's voice phone number: 919-541-2736

📠 Contact person's Fax phone number: 919-541-0072

✉ Mailing address: U.S. Environmental Protection Agency, MD-13, Research Triangle, NC 27711

DESCRIPTION

"The CTC is a cooperative effort for engineering assistance to State and local air pollution control agencies (and private companies to an extent) by the Air and Engineering Research Laboratory and the Office of Air Quality Planning and Standards. It is a cooperative effort with the State and Territorial Air Pollution Program Administration (STAPPA) and the Association of Local Air Pollution Control Officials (ALAPCO)."

The CTC provides three levels of assistance:

- HOTLINE—(919) 541-0800
- Engineering Assistance
- Technical Guidance

The CTC's goal is to provide technical support to State and local agencies and the EPA's Regional Offices in implementing air pollution control programs. The CTC assists regulatory and permitting agencies, but does not provide policy guidance and compliance advice which is the responsibility of the EPA Regional Office. CTC services are available at no cost to State and local air pollution control agencies and EPA Regional Offices. Other government agencies may use the HOTLINE for technical assistance or to order CTC documents."

ANNOTATION

The CTC BBS is reached through the EPA TTN BBS.

Drinking Water Information Exchange

🖳 Acronym for online service: DWIE BBS

💻) Online service number(s): 800-932-7459, FedWorld BBS 703-321-8020

🌐 Internet address(es): telnet fedworld.gov then gateway to DWIE BBS

💻← E-mail address(es): FidoNet 1:277/260

🏛 Government agency acronym: EPA

👥 Contact person & title: Brad Maust, System Operator

💻← Contact person's E-mail address: jbm@wvnvaxa.wvnet.edu

☎ Contact person's voice phone number: 800-624-8301, 304-293-4191

🖨 Contact person's Fax phone number: 304-293-3161

✉ Mailing address: Drinking Water Information Exchange, West Virginia University, NRCCE, NDWC, P.O. Box 6064, Morgantown, WV 26506-6064

DESCRIPTION

"The National Drinking Water Clearinghouse (NDWC) provides small systems with basic advice. Technical Services Coordinator David Pask, P. Eng., said 'If our resources don't allow for immediate assistance, we will investigate the matter, then get back in touch with callers.'"

ANNOTATION

Drinking water is a concern to all of us, so the DWIE BBS should be carefully moni-tored, especially by researchers, journalists, and concerned citizens. It has a large file section and active message areas. The DWIE BBS's hardware is underpowered. It only has a 2,400 bps modem and only 80 megabytes of space on its hard disk, but it makes up for these deficiencies by providing high-quality information.

Drinking Water Information Processing Support BBS

🖳 Acronym for online service: DRIPSS BBS

💻) Online service number(s): 800-229-3737, 703-339-0420 FedWorld BBS 703-321-8020

🌐 Internet address(es): telnet fedworld.gov then gateway to DRIPPS BBS

🏛 Government agency acronym: EPA

👥 Contact person & title: Arnetta Davis, SYSOP

☎ Contact person's voice phone number: 202-260-2803

✉ Mailing address: Environmental Protection Agency, 401 M Street, SW, Washington, DC 20460

DESCRIPTION

"This electronic bulletin board system (BBS) is provided by the U.S. Environmental Protection Agency (EPA) to facilitate the exchange of information between various environmental professionals supporting EPA's missions. This BBS should be considered a government information source.

This BBS provides a wealth of information pertaining to water rules, regulations, systems operations, and other related health issues. You are encouraged to use the E-mail system to post questions to other users concerning regulatory issues, plant operations, etc. You are also encouraged to respond to other users requests for information and to upload any computer programs, worksheets, databases, forms, etc. that they have found to be useful in their work so that others may share in their success."

DRIPSS is available from 4:00 A.M. to 2:00 A.M. 7 days a week. From the content of the messages it seems that DRIPSS may be facing funding difficulties. That might explain why most of the files I found on DRIPSS were nearly a year old.

Emission Measurement Technical Information Center

⌨N   Acronym for online service: EMTIC BBS

💻)   Online service number(s): EPA TTN BBS 919-541-5742

🌐   Internet address(es): telnet ttnbbs.rtpnc.epa.gov then use gateway to EMTIC BBS.

🏛   Government agency acronym: EPA

👥   Contact person & title: Michael Ciolek, SYSOP

☎   Contact person's voice phone number: 919-541-4921

✉   Mailing address: U.S. EPA OAQPS/TSD/EMB, Mail Drop 19, Research Triangle Park, NC 27711

"The EMTIC BBS provides technical guidance on stationary source emission testing issues, particularly to people who conduct and/or oversee emissions tests in support of the development and implementation of emission standards, emission factors, and State implementation plans."

The EMTIC BBS is reached through the EPA TTN BBS.

Environmental Protection Agency's Online Library System (OLS)

⌨N   Acronym for online service: OAQPS

💻)   Online service number(s): 919-549-0720. Use Half Duplex, Even Parity, 7 data bits per character, and one stop bit.

Log on: At the first system prompt select "OLS."

🌐   Internet address(es): telnet epaibm.rtpnc.epa.gov. At the first menu, select "Public Access." At the second menu select "OLS."

🏛   Government agency acronym: EPA

👥   Contact person & title: R.K. Thorn

☎   Contact person's voice phone number: 919-541-2777

📠   Contact person's Fax phone number: 919-541-1405

✉   Mailing address: U.S. Environmental Protection Agency, Library Services Office, MD-35, 86 Alexander Drive, Research Triangle Park, NC 27711

"The Online Library System (OLS) is a computerized list of bibliographic citations compiled by the EPA Library network. EPA provides this menu-driven, user-friendly system at no cost to support public access to environmental information. The only charges what will be incurred through use of the system are telecommunications charges.

OLS includes several related databases that can be used to locate books, reports, articles, and information on a variety of topics. The material in OLS is updated every two weeks, and can be searched by numerous access points, such as title, author, and keyword."

OLS provides the following resources:
"National Catalog. Citations and summaries on environmentally related topics encompassing biology, chemistry, ecology, and other basic sciences and EPA reports distributed through the National Technical Information Center.

Hazardous Waste. Citations and summaries for key materials on hazardous waste.

ACCESS EPA. Over 300 entries for EPA and other public sector information sources such as hot lines, clearinghouses, etc.

Clean Lakes. Citations and summaries on topics relating to lake management, protection, and restoration.

Regional Files. Selected items owned by the regional libraries."

ANNOTATION

Using the correct telecommunication software setting is essential to logging into OLS. Once you are connected, do not attempt to use any options other than OLS. If you do select another option, you will find yourself being asked for identification numbers that you won't be able to supply. There seems to be no way of getting back to the menu without logging off OLS and reconnecting. Avoid the hassle and follow the instructions.

Environmental Protection Agency's Office of Research and Development BBS

- Acronym for online service: ORD BBS
- Online service number(s): 513-569-7610
- Government agency acronym: EPA
- Contact person & title: Charles W. Guion, System Operator
- Contact person's voice phone number: 513-569-7272
- Contact person's Fax phone number: 513-569-7566
- Mailing address: Center for Environmental Research (CERI), 26 Martin L. King Drive, Mail Stop G75, Cincinnati, OH 45268

DESCRIPTION

"Created to serve as a forum for the exchange of scientific and technical research information both within and external to the U.S. EPA. Includes an online, text-searchable database of every ORD publication produced since 1976."

ANNOTATION

When you connect to the ORD BBS, you will be presented with the options below. Select only the ORD option. All other options will request a user identification and password that you won't be able to provide.

Welcome to the U.S. EPA Cincinnati Network PAD

CINSNA   for 3270 Access Via VAX/SNA Gateway

IBMPSI   for Line Mode Access to IBM Mainframes

OACIN   for Access to the Cincy PRIME

MAIL   for Access to Agency Electronic Mail

          (ALL-IN-ONE)

ORDBBS   Office of Research and Development Bulletin Board

The ORD BBS is a well-run BBS with lots of resources dealing with environmental research. The message system is well used and contains interesting leads to other environmental resources.

Gulfline BBS

⌨N Acronym for online service: GMP BBS

💻) Online service number(s): 800-235-4662, 601-688-2677, 601-688-7018, FedWorld BBS 703-321-8020

🏛 Government agency acronym: EPA

👥 Contact person & title: Kay McGovern, SYSOP

☎ Contact person's voice phone number: 601-688-1065, 601-688-2522

✉ Mailing address: Environmental Protection Agency, Gulf of Mexico Program Office, Building 1103, Stennis Space Center, MS 39529

DESCRIPTION

"The system is being made available in support of the Gulf of Mexico Program.

This system may be used by the public in support of Gulf of Mexico Program objectives. Such use is considered official government business."

ANNOTATION

The first time you log onto the GMP BBS you will not have full access privileges. This BBS only permits verified users full access. However, once you get full access you will probably be able to satisfy your curiosity about the Gulf of Mexico Project.

National Air Toxics Information Clearing House BBS

⌨N Acronym for online service: NATICH BBS

💻) Online service number(s): EPA TTN BBS 919-541-5742

🌐 Internet address(es): telnet ttnbbs.rtpnc.epa.gov then use gateway to NATICH BBS.

🏛 Government agency acronym: EPA

👥 Contact person & title: Vasu Kilaru, SYSOP

✉ Mailing address: U.S. Environmental Protection Agency, OAQPS, Mail Drop 13, Research Triangle Park, NC 27711

DESCRIPTION

"NATICH is an information service cooperatively provided by USEPA, the State and Territorial Air Pollution Program Administrators (STAPPA), and the Association of Local Air Pollution Control Officials (ALAPCO) to support their efforts at controlling toxic (noncriteria) air pollutants. Thus, the clearinghouse is designed to facilitate the exchange of information among

Federal, State, and local agencies concerned with control of toxic air pollutants.

To achieve this goal the clearinghouse annually collects, classifies, and disseminates information submitted by State and Local (S/L) agencies regarding their air toxics programs. In addition, NATICH also provides information on current federal activities in controlling air toxics.

In an effort to keep up-to-date with the information needs of the user community (STAPPA/ALAPCO), the clearinghouse is currently reevaluating its services. After this critical review, some of the contents of NATICH are likely to change; these changes will be incorporated into the bulletin board version of NATICH."

ANNOTATION

The NATICH BBS is reached through the EPA TTN BBS.

New Source Review

🖥 Acronym for online service: NSR BBS

💻 Online service number(s): EPA TTN BBS 919-541-5742

🌐 Internet address(es): telnet ttnbbs.rtpnc.epa.gov then use gateway to NSR BBS.

🏛 Government agency acronym: EPA

👥 Contact person & title: Dennis Crumpler, SYSOP

✉ Mailing address: U.S. Environmental Protection Agency, MD-15, Research Triangle Park, NC 27711

DESCRIPTION

"The NSR BBS provides material and information pertaining to New Source Review (NSR). The user can search the abstracted index of the 'New Source Review Prevention of Significant Deterioration and Nonattainment Area Guidance Notebook' by selected keywords or a customized text word or text string."

ANNOTATION

The NSR BBS is reached through the EPA TTN BBS.

Nonpoint Source Program BBS

🖥 Acronym for online service: NPS BBS

💻 Online service number(s): 301-589-0205, FedWorld 703-321-8020

🌐 Internet address(es): telnet fedworld.gov then gateway to NPS BBS

🏛 Government agency acronym: EPA

👥 Contact person & title: Elaine Bloom, Project Leader

☎ Contact person's voice phone number: 202-260-3665

✉ Mailing address: U.S. Environmental Protection Agency, Office of Water, NPS Information Exchange (4503F), 401 M. Street, SW, Washington, DC 20460

DESCRIPTION

"The Nonpoint Source Bulletin Board System (NPS BBS) is an interactive telecommunications system that provides timely NPS information, a forum for open discussion, and the ability to share computer text and program files. The NPS BBS has a broad watershed focus and is accessible to anyone with a computer and a modem. It is sponsored by the U.S. Environmental Protection Agency and is free. Its users include Federal, State, and local agency personnel, university researchers, businesses, and concerned individuals."

ANNOTATION

The NPS BBS is large, well run, easy to use, and contains lots of information dealing with wetlands in the form of files, bulletins, and messages. If you have an interest in wetlands, you will find something useful on the NPS BBS.

Office of Mobile Sources Bulletin Board System

💻ᴺ Acronym for online service: OMS BBS

💻⁾ Online service number(s): EPA TTN BBS 919-541-5742

🌐 Internet address(es): telnet ttnbbs.rtpnc.epa.gov then use gateway to OMS BBS.

🏛 Government agency acronym: EPA

👥 Contact person & title: Craig Harvey, SYSOP

☎ Contact person's voice phone number: 313-668-4237

🖷 Contact person's Fax phone number: 313-668-4531

✉ Mailing address: U.S. Environmental Protection Agency, EPSD/ECSB, 2565 Plymouth Road, Ann Arbor, MI 48105

DESCRIPTION

"The purpose of the bulletin board is to provide the user with information pertaining to mobile source emissions, including regulations, test results, models, guidance, etc.
What you will find on the OMS BBS:

- Office of Mobile Sources Contact List
- OMS Rule-making Packages and Reports per the Clean Air Act
- Vehicle and Engine Certification Guidance
- Fuel Economy Information
- Vehicle Emissions Models (e.g., MOBILE5)
- Public Awareness Information ("Fact Sheets")
- Other Relevant Mobile Source Emission Documents"

ANNOTATION

The OMS BBS is reached through the EPA TTN BBS.

Office of Radiation and Indoor Air BBS

💻ᴺ Acronym for online service: ORIA BBS

💻⁾ Online service number(s): EPA TTN BBS 919-541-5742

🌐 Internet address(es): telnet ttnbbs.rtpnc.epa.gov then use gateway to ORIA BBS.

🏛 Government agency acronym: EPA

👥 Contact person & title: Dale Hoffmeyer, SYSOP

💻← Contact person's E-mail address: hoffmeyer.dale@epamail.epa.gov

☎ Contact person's voice phone number: 202-233-9228

📠 Contact person's Fax phone number: 202-233-9629

✉ Mailing address: US EPA Office of Radiation & Indoor Air, 401 M St. SW (6602J), Washington, DC 20460

DESCRIPTION

"The goal of the Environmental Protection Agency's (EPA) Office of Radiation and Indoor Air is to protect the public and the environment from exposures to radiation and indoor air pollutants.

The Office develops protection criteria, standards, and policies and works with other programs within the EPA and other agencies to control radiation and indoor air pollution exposures; provides technical assistance to states through the EPA's regional offices and other agencies having radiation and indoor air protection programs; directs an environmental radiation monitoring program; responds to radiological emergencies; and evaluates and assesses the overall risk and impact of radiation and indoor air pollution. The Office is the EPA's lead office for intra- and interagency activities coordinated through the Committee for Indoor Air Quality. It coordinates with and assists the Office of Enforcement in enforcement activities where the EPA has jurisdiction. The Office disseminates information and works with state and local governments, industry and professional groups, and citizens to promote actions to reduce exposures to harmful levels of radiation and indoor air pollutants."

ANNOTATION

The ORIA BBS is reached through the EPA TTN BBS.

The Pesticide Information Network

🖥 Acronym for online service: PIN

💻 Online service number(s): 703-305-1919, FedWorld 703-321-8020

🌐 Internet address(es): telnet fedworld.gov then gateway to PIN BBS

💻 E-mail address(es): davies-hilliard.leslie@epamail.epa.gov

🏛 Government agency acronym: EPA

👥 Contact person & title: Constance A. Haaser and Leslie Davies-Hilliard

☎ Contact person's voice phone number: Haaser 703-305-5455, Davies-Hilliard 703-305-7499.

📠 Contact person's Fax phone number: 703-305-6309

✉ Mailing address: U.S. Environmental Protection Agency, Office of Pesticide Programs, EFED, EFGWB, 7507C, 401 M Street, SW, Washington, DC 20460

DESCRIPTION

"The Pesticide Information Network (PIN) is an interactive database containing current and historic pesticide information. It is a free service offered by the U.S. Environmental Protection Agency, Office of Pesticide Programs (OPP). It was created as an information tool for environmental management designed to promote a Federal, State and local partnership in data gathering and information exchange.

In late 1994 the PIN will expand into a multi-access network capable of supporting four simultaneous online dial-in users. (Internet access is not available at this time.) This enhancement of the PIN will greatly broaden

---

the system's accessibility, information base, and capabilities.

The data sets to be available on the PIN are:

BIOLOGICAL PESTICIDES (BPD): The BPD contains information on the U.S. EPA's OPP biotechnology decisions, rules, documents, and meetings.

ECOLOGICAL INCIDENT INFORMATION SYSTEM (EIIS): The EIIS is a collection of reported incidents where nontarget organisms, such as birds, fish, or plant species, have been adversely affected by pesticides.

ENVIRONMENTAL FATE AND EFFECTS (EFE): The EFE is comprised of data resulting from the pesticide registration data requirements as specified in 40 CFR Part 158. (Soon to be implemented.)

PESTICIDE APPLICATOR TRAINING: The PAT is a bibliographic reference of pesticide-applicator training available in each state.

PESTICIDE MONITORING INVENTORY (PMI): The PMI is a compilation of pesticide monitoring projects performed by Federal, State and local governments and private institutions. Information on each project includes a contact person, the pesticides and environmental media sampled, sampling locations, and an abstract. The Pesticides in Groundwater Database (PGWDB) will be added to the PMI, providing data for groundwater monitoring projects.

REGULATORY INFORMATION (REG): The REG contains the Pesticides in Special Review data set, the Canceled and Suspended Pesticides data set and the Restricted Use Products (RUP) data set. The RUP is a listing of all pesticide products, including canceled products, that have been classified as Restricted Use Pesticides under 40 CFR Part 152, Subpart I.

In addition to the pesticide information, user services provided by the PIN include:

I.   PIN System User Guide
II. PIN Contacts Directory
III. Listing of EPA Product Managers
IV. Restricted Use Products Report
V.   Biological User's Guide
VI. State and County FIPS Codes (Federal Information Processing Standards)
VII. Miscellaneous Pesticide Information
   A. CAS, PC Code (Shaughnessey), Case, & Caswell Numbers
   B. Synonym Names
   C. Chemical Classification
   D. Pesticide Category
   E. MCL (Maximum Contaminant Level)
   F. LHA (Lifetime Health Advisory Levels)"

ANNOTATION

If you want to make use of the files available on the PIN BBS, reading the instructions located in the DOWNLOAD INSTRUCTIONS section is essential. The instructions are extensive, and you will need to capture them as they go by on the screen. By reading the instructions, you will gain insight as to the usefulness of the databases.

Support Center for Regulatory Air Models

⌨ Acronym for online service: SCRAM BBS

📞 Online service number(s): EPA TTN BBS 919-541-5742

🌐 Internet address(es): telnet

ttnbbs.rtpnc.epa.gov then use gateway to SCRAM BBS.

 Government agency acronym: EPA

Contact person & title: Dennis Atkinson, SYSOP

Contact person's voice phone number: 919-541-0518

Contact person's Fax phone number: 919-541-2357

✉ Mailing address: Support Center for Regulatory Air Models, U.S. EPA, OAQPS, TSD, SRAB, MD 14, Research Triangle Park, NC 27711

DESCRIPTION

"The SCRAM BBS is the Agency's primary source for the acquisition of the computer code for the regulatory air models. Changes to the models, including updates, corrections, and new regulatory codes are main features of the SCRAM. In addition, SCRAM contains surface and mixing height meteorological data, which is required for some models.

The new user can obtain a quick review for BBS services by browsing through the main menu options. In addition to code, model-related news and important bulletins concerning model modifications, status, etc. are provided. An especially important feature is the 'Model Change Bulletin' provided for each model/program. MCB#1 lists information on the initial status of that model; new MCB's are posted for each model as required."

ANNOTATION

The SCRAM BBS is reached through the EPA TTN BBS.

Technology Transfer Network

Online service number(s): 919-541-5742

Internet address(es): telnet ttnbbs.rtpnc.epa.gov

Government agency acronym: EPA

Contact person & title: Hersch Rorex, SYSOP

Contact person's E-mail address: rorex.h@epamail.epa.gov

Contact person's voice phone number: 919-541-5637

Contact person's Fax phone number: 919-541-2357

✉ Mailing address: U.S. Environmental Protection Agency, Office of Air Quality Planning and Standards, TSD, SRAB Mail Drop 14, Research Triangle Park, NC 27711

DESCRIPTION

"The Office of Air Quality Planning and Standards (OAQPS) Technology Transfer Network (TTN) is a network of independent Bulletin Board Systems (BBSs) that provides technical information, documents, files, and messages related to the control of air pollution."

ANNOTATION

The Technology Transfer Network (TTN) network includes the following bulletin boards:

- AIRS—Aerometric Information Retrieval Systems
- AMTIC—Ambient Monitoring Technology Information Center

- APTI—Air Pollution Training Institute
- BLIS—RACT/BACT/LAER Information Systems
- CAAA—Clean Air Act Amendments
- CHIEF—Clearinghouse for Inventories/Emission Factors
- COMPLI—COMPLIance Information on Stationary Sources of Air Pollution
- CTC—Control Technology Center
- EMTIC—Emission Measurement Technical Information Center
- NATICH—National Air Toxics Information Clearinghouse
- NSR—New Source Review
- OMS—Office of Mobile Sources
- ORIA—Office of Radiation and Indoor Air
- SCRAM—Support Center for Regulatory Air Models

Wastewater Treatment Information Exchange BBS

🖥ᴺ Acronym for online service: WTIE BBS

🖥) Online service number(s): 800-544-1936, 304-293-5969, Fedworld 703-321-8020

🌐 Internet address(es): telnet fedworld.gov

🏛 Government agency acronym: EPA

👥 Contact person & title: Brad Maust, SYSOP

💻← Contact person's E-mail address: jbm@wvnvaxa.wvnet.edu

☎ Contact person's voice phone number: 800-624-8301, 304-293-4191

📠 Contact person's Fax phone number: 304-293-3161

✉ Mailing address: Small Flows Clearing House, P.O. Box 6064, Morgantown, WV 26506-6064

DESCRIPTION

"The National Small Flows Clearinghouse (NSFC) is an advocate of alternative technologies for wastewater treatment for small communities that cannot afford to implement conventional technologies. In order to provide services to a national audience, the NSFC is constantly seeking information from various sources as well as means for effectively disseminating this information."

ANNOTATION

WTIE BBS's list of available files clearly demonstrates that wastewater treatment is its main concern. There are files of interest to individuals, communities, and cities dealing with the question of wastewater. Although I live in a city and wastewater is not an immediate concern, I still found files worth downloading and reading. For example, the toilets in my 90-year-old house will soon require replacement. The file "TOILET.TXT" "Laboratory tests measures performance of low-flow toilets" provided interesting insights about new water-saving toilets—they don't work as well as the older water guzzlers. Read WTIE BBS's file list carefully and you will probably find something relevant to your situation.

The WTIE BBS message section is well used and provides a forum for informative discussions. If you use an off-line mail reader, use the QWK option from the main menu to download batches of messages.

EQUAL EMPLOYMENT OPPORTUNITY COMMISSION

Equal Employment Opportunity Commission

ANNOTATION

No services available, but Internet services are being discussed.

EXPORT-IMPORT BANK OF THE U.S.

Eximbank Bulletin Board

🖥N Acronym for online service: Eximbank BBS

🖥) Online service number(s): FedWorld BBS 703-321-8020.

🌐 Internet address(es): telnet fedworld.gov and gateway to Eximbank BBS

👥 Contact person & title: Susan Hein, SYSOP

☎ Contact person's voice phone number: 202-566-4490

🖨 Contact person's Fax phone number: 202-566-7542

✉ Mailing address: Export-Import Bank of the U.S., Marketing Division, 811 Vermont Avenue, NW, Washington, DC 20571

DESCRIPTION

"This Bulletin Board is for use by Exporters, Bankers, Researchers, Governmental, and oth-ers interested in the export of U. S. goods and services overseas."

ANNOTATION

"What is the Export-Import Bank?" was the first question that came to mind when I came across the Eximbank BBS. That answer was quickly supplied by reading bulletin number 1 "What is Eximbank?" The following is an excerpt from that bulletin:

"The Export-Import Bank of the United States (Eximbank) is an independent U.S. Government agency that helps finance exports of U.S. goods and services. Over the past 58 years, Eximbank has assisted more than $270 billion in U.S. exports.

WHAT DOES EXIMBANK DO?

Eximbank facilitates export financing of U.S. goods and services by matching the effect of export credit subsidies from other governments and by absorbing reasonable credit risks that are beyond the current reach of the private sector. It helps U.S. exporters obtain preexport financing by guaranteeing their repayment of export-related working capital loans from commercial lenders. It helps exporters extend credit to their foreign customers by covering the political and commercial risks of nonpayment. It encourages commercial financing of U.S. exports by guaranteeing repayment of loans made to foreign buyers of U.S. exports. It encourages foreign buyers to purchase U.S. exports by offering competitive, fixed-rate loans."

If you want to know more about the Export-Import Bank, read the rest of this bulletin online. If you are still hungry for more information, read some of the 40 other bulletins or select one of the many informational files for downloading.

Eximbank does not provide messaging service or non-Export-Import Bank files for download.

FEDERAL COMMUNICATIONS COMMISSION

Public Access Link

🖥 Acronym for online service: PAL

🖥) Online service number(s) 301-725-1072

🏛 Government agency acronym: FCC

☎ Contact person's voice phone number: 202-634-1833

✉ Mailing address: Federal Communications Commission Common Carrier Bureau, Domestic Facilities Division, Room 6101, 2025 M St., NW, Washington, DC 20554

DESCRIPTION

The following is a copy of the opening screen of the PAL BBS. It provides a good description of what is available:
"1—Access Equipment Authorization Database
2—Definitions—Terms/Codes used in Application Records
3—Applying for an Equipment Authorization (1/92)
4—Other Commission Activities and Procedures (8/92)
5—Laboratory Operational Information
6—Public Notices (6/93)
7—Bulletins/Measurement Procedures (3/93)
8—Rule Makings (8/93)
9—Help
a—Information Hotline (2/93)
b—Processing Speed of Service (12/93)
c—Test Sites on File per Sec 2.948 (1/94)
d—Advanced Television Service Schedule Of Meetings"

ANNOTATION

PAL is a simple and small BBS with a single purpose. This is not a BBS where you could invest hours downloading files of interest to the general public. However, it is an effective means of delivering information about specific FCC operations.

FEDERAL DEPOSIT INSURANCE CORPORATION

Federal Deposit Insurance Corporation Gopher

🖥 Acronym for online service: FDIC Gopher

🌐 Internet address(es): Gopher fdic.sura.net, ftp fdic.sura.net

Log on: When using ftp use "anonymous" as your I.D. and "guest" as your password.

💻 E-mail address(es): postmaster@fdic.gov

🏛 Government agency acronym: FDIC

👥 Contact person & title: Robert Molyneux

☎ Contact person's voice phone number: 703-516-5819

✉ Mailing address: Federal Deposit Insurance Corporation, 550 Seventeenth St., NW., Washington, DC 20429

DESCRIPTION

"The Federal Deposit Insurance Corporation promotes and preserves public confidence in banks and protects the money supply by providing insurance coverage for bank deposits and periodic examinations of insured State-chartered banks that are not members of the Federal Reserve System."

ANNOTATION

Most likely, your bank displays the letters FDIC on its advertising literature as a means of convincing you that your money is safe in their hands. Do you know what the FDIC is, what it does, or what it means to you and your money? To find out the answer to these questions, use Gopher to access the FDIC. Once connected, read or download the file "Your Insured Deposit" or "YID.TXT" or one of the "About" files. You can also obtain these and other files by anonymous ftp from the FDIC.

If you explore FDIC's online services through ftp there are a few extra instructions you may need to find the FDIC. First, use the "cd pub" command to move to the publications directory. Next, use the "cd fdic" command to enter the FDIC directory. To see what files are available type "dir" and press "Enter." Gopher is much easier to use and provides access to the same information.

FEDERAL ELECTION COMMISSION

Federal Election Commission's Direct Access Program

💻ᴺ Acronym for online service: DAP

💻) Online service number(s): (Call 800-424-9530 or 202-219-3730 locally for access procedure information)

🏛 Government agency acronym: FEC

👥 Contact person & title: Data Systems Division

☎ Contact person's voice phone number: 800-424-9530

✉ Mailing address: Federal Election Commission, Data Systems Division, 999 E Street, NW, Washington, DC 20463

DESCRIPTION

Information available on DAP includes "Records of:

- Contributions by individuals, PACs, and political party committees
- "Soft Money" or nonfederal contributions to national parties
- Financial status reports on all candidates and committees, including latest total receipts, total disbursements, cash-on-hand, and debt amounts
- Listings including names, addresses, connected organizations, and reports filed by all committees
- Data from FEC press releases, including popular "Top 50" rankings of various financial activities

And...

- Individual contributor searches that DAP users the ability to perform global searches by an individual's name, place of business, or occupation, city, state, zip code, and date of contribution.

Plus...

- Listings of FEC Advisory Opinions and court case abstracts."

The FEC's DAP costs $20 per hour. There are no sign-up fees. However, you have to pay in advance in one-hour increments. Reporters are urged by the FEC to contact the Press Office at 202-219-4155 for additional press-related information.

FEDERAL EMERGENCY MANAGEMENT AGENCY

Federal Emergency Management Agency WWW Server

💻 Acronym for online service: FEMA WWW Server

🌐 Internet address(es): URL http://www.fema.gov/

🏛 Government agency acronym: FEMA

👥 Contact person & title: Bill Zellers, Public Affairs

☎ Contact person's voice phone number: 202-646-4600

✉ Mailing address: Federal Emergency Management Agency, 500 C Street, SW, Washington, DC 20472

DESCRIPTION

"The Federal Emergency Management Agency is the focal point within the Federal Government for emergency planning, preparedness, mitigation, response, and recovery. The Agency works closely with State and local governments by funding emergency programs and providing technical guidance and training. The coordinated activities at the Federal, State, and local lev-

els ensure a broad-based emergency program to protect public safety and property."

ANNOTATION

The FEMA WWW server looks great. However, its graphics take forever to load even at 28,800 bps. The design and content are excellent. The home page has buttons titled, Who We Are, What We Do, Preparing For A Disaster, Help After A Disaster, I Want To Know, Library, News Desk, and Master Index. This design makes it easy to find the information you are looking for quickly and easily.

State and Local Emergency Management Data Users Group BBS

💻 Acronym for online service: SALEM-DUG BBS

💻 Online service number(s): 202-646-2887

🏛 Government agency acronym: FEMA

👥 Contact person & title: Bill Lent, President of SALEMDUG

☎ Contact person's voice phone number: 301-499-8050

✉ Mailing address: Prince George's County, Office of Emergency Preparedness, 7911 Anchor Street, Landover, MD 20785

DESCRIPTION

"The State and Local Emergency Management Data Users Group (SALEMDUG) is an association of State, local, and FEMA emergency management personnel who share an interest in fostering the use of computers to support emergency management programs and activities. The purpose of the organization is to promote the exchange of information, to encourage standardization throughout the emergency management community, and to work together to facilitate the application of computer technology to emergency management problems and the transfer of automated data processing information among all levels of government.

The membership of SALEMDUG includes 31 states, several local civil defense organizations, FEMA Headquarters and all FEMA regions. Six standing committees have been established and an annual meeting is conducted to inform members of new technology, provide a forum for discussion, and provide the opportunity for sharing ideas and software applications.

FEMA has fostered and supported SALEMDUG. This bulletin board has been established by FEMA to support the group. The SALEMDUG BBS provides a means of communication between its geographically dispersed members, shares information through bulletins and messages, and offers a means of exchanging public domain software and shareware programs.

The SALEMDUG BBS is open to anyone, including members of the general public, who are affiliated with or have an expressed interest in the area of Emergency Management. FEMA hopes that this rather unique means of communication will prove beneficial to you in this important arena.

The System Operators of this board (SYSOP) is Diana Wade (202-646-2571). Suggestions are welcomed and may be left by leaving a message to the SYSOP.

If you are interested in establishing a conference (a separate place on the bulletin board for people to discuss a particular special interest), please let the SYSOP know."

ANNOTATION

If you have a professional or morbid interest in disasters, you will enjoy reading the files and messages posted on SALEMDUG. A sampling of file topics include "Early Morning Heart Attacks—Causes and Information" (AM-ATTK.ZIP), "Disaster Research News," "FEMA Situation Reports," and so on. However, the files didn't seem as up-to-date as I expected.

Journalists, researchers, and the curious will find the resources described on SALEMDUG valuable.

FEDERAL MINE SAFETY AND HEALTH REVIEW COMMISSION

Federal Mine Safety and Health Review Commission

ANNOTATION

No online services available. Federal Mine Safety and Health Review Commission decisions are available from WESTLAW (See Commercial Online Information Providers.)

FEDERAL RESERVE SYSTEM

Federal Reserve Bank of Dallas Info Board

▭ⁿ Acronym for online service: FED FLASH

▭⟩ Online service number(s): 800-333-1953, 214-922-5199

👥 Contact person & title: Karen Gee, SYSOP

☎ Contact person's voice phone number: 214-922-5178

✉ Mailing address: Public Affairs Department, Federal Reserve Bank of Dallas, 2200 N. Pearl Street, Dallas, TX 75201

DESCRIPTION

"We currently have available a wide array of southwest and national economic and banking data."

The following is a listing of directories from Fed Flash:

- Background of Federal Reserve System
- Calendar of Events and Economic Education Programs
- Releases, Speeches and T-bill Rates
- Dallas FED Publications
- Dallas FED's Ag Survey
- Dallas FED's Southwest Economy
- Dallas FED's Economic Review
- Table of Recent Regional Economic Data
- Leading, Coincident, and Lagging Indicators
- TX and LA Retail Sales
- TX, LA, and NM Construction
- District Agricultural Land Values
- TX, LA, and U.S. Energy
- Household Survey Unemployment
- Household Survey Civilian Labor Force
- Household Survey Employment
- TX, LA, and NM Personal Income
- Prices and Wages
- TX Non-Ag Employment by Major SIC Code
- LA Non-Ag Employment by Major SIC Code
- NM Non-Ag Employment by Major SIC Code
- 11th District Banks' Financial Data
- U.S. Non-Ag Employment by Major SIC Code
- Monetary Data
- Miscellaneous U.S. Macro Data
- Dallas FRB Economic Research Notes
- Industrial Production and Capacity Utilization
- Dallas FED Trade-Weighted Value of the Dollar

ANNOTATION

Although Fed Flash has a messaging system, there were only three messages listed when I logged on. It is clear that the usefulness of this BBS lies in its data.

Federal Reserve Economic Data

☎ Parent organization: Federal Reserve Bank of St. Louis.

🖳 Acronym for online service: FRED

🖳 Online service number(s): 314-621-1824

👥 Contact person & title: Tom Pollmann, Senior Research Associate

🖳 Contact person's E-mail address: pareto!pollmann@wupost.wustl.edu

☎ Contact person's voice phone number: 314-444-8562

🖨 Contact person's Fax phone number: 314-444-8731

✉ Mailing address: Research and Public Information Department, Federal

Reserve Bank of St. Louis, P. O. Box 442, St. Louis, MO 63166

DESCRIPTION

"FRED provides:

- Current economic and financial data
- Historical data on monetary and business variables
- Regional economic data for Missouri, Arkansas, Kentucky, Tennessee, Illinois, Indiana, and Mississippi
- And more"

ANNOTATION

FRED was useful on the first call. I downloaded a file (H10) which contained the Federal Exchange Rates for the previous week. The data was in text format and separated into columns by tabs. This formatting permitted me to import the file into my wordprocessing program and later make a table from it. I could then import the table into spreadsheet software. Having the data open as a spreadsheet enabled me to visualize it in graphical form and perform interesting comparisons.

All of the files on FRED are listed in downloadable files named "FILES.ZIP" or "FILES.EXE."

KIMBERELY

☖ Parent organization: Federal Reserve Bank of Minneapolis.

💻) Online service number(s): 612-340-2489

👥 Contact person & title: Carol Dvoracek

☎ Contact person's voice phone number: 612-340-2443

☎ Contact person's Fax phone number: 612-335-2855

✉ Mailing address: Public Affairs, Federal Reserve Bank of Minneapolis, 250 Marquette Avenue, Minneapolis, MN 55401-2171

DESCRIPTION

"KIMBERELY is a public service electronic database offered by the Federal Reserve Bank of Minneapolis, Public Affairs Department. Economic and financial data, and information about the economy and the Federal Reserve are available electronically free of charge except for any long-distance telephone costs incurred.

KIMBERELY was designed for easy access and use by teachers and students, business people, and the general public. Help screens can assist in locating and downloading files. About 500 downloadable files are available, offering:

- Daily financial data
- National economic data, monthly and quarterly
- Economic data for Ninth District states
- Federal Reserve Statistical Releases
- Federal Open Market Committee meeting minutes
- Treasury Securities Auction Results
- Speeches by Board of Governors members and other Fed officials
- Economic condition reports
- Text of Ninth District Fed publications
- Information about educational programs
- Information about U.S. coin and currency
- And more"

Do you know what coin the motto "In God We Trust" first appeared on? How about the first bank note it appeared on? Do you know what "legal tender" means and when it was first used in the United States? Do you know whose face is on the $100,000, $10,000, or $5,000 Federal Reserve notes? How many new dollar notes make a pound of money? Has the United States paper currency ever carried a woman's face? If so, when and whose? Do you want to know where you can find the answers to these questions? The answer is at the KIMBERELY BBS of the Federal Reserve Bank of Minneapolis. The file name you can download for the answers is "INFO.MON" in directory 29, "Money: Facts About U.S. Coin and Currency."

KIMBERELY has more information than just facts about money. There are 30 directories of files covering topics related to the Federal Reserve System. There are two directories dedicated to "Student Programs/Activities" and "Educator Programs/Activities." Don't you wish you had known more about money before you graduated from school?

KIMBERELY does not have messaging services.

Liberty Link

- Online service number(s): 212-720-2652

- Government agency acronym: NY FED

- Contact person & title: Barton R. Sotnick, SYSOP and Staff Director of Press and Community Relations

- Contact person's voice phone number: 212-720-6143

- Contact person's Fax phone number: 212-720-6628

- Mailing address: The Federal Reserve Bank of New York, 33 Liberty Street, New York, NY 10045

"The New York Fed created the bulletin board to broaden the dissemination of information and to make data available in an electronic format.

Among the data available from the bulletin board are computer-usable versions of the New York Fed's daily listing of Treasury securities bid and asked prices and yields, two series of daily foreign exchange rates, weekly Federal Reserve statistics on the nation's money supply, and several other statistical releases. The texts of speeches by New York Federal Reserve Bank senior officers and news releases issued by the New York Fed also are placed on the bulletin board system. All data are in ASCII form and thus are usable by any computer."

The following information was retrieved from the Liberty Link BBS:
"The NEW YORK FED is one of the 12 regional Reserve Banks, which, together with the Board of Governors in Washington, D.C., comprise the Federal Reserve System.

The 'Fed,' as the system is commonly called, is an independent governmental entity created by Congress in 1913 to serve as the central bank of the United States. It is responsible for conducting monetary policy; maintaining the liquidity, safety and soundness of the nation's banking system; and assisting the Federal government's financing operations. The Fed also serves as the banker for the U.S. government and the distributor of its coin and currency. In addition, it has important roles in operating the nation's payments systems, protecting consumers' rights in their dealings with banks and promoting community development and reinvestment.

The 12 Reserve Banks are the operating units of the System, and each serves a specific geographic area of the United States.

The NEW YORK FED serves the Second Federal Reserve District, which consists of all of New York State; the 12 northern counties of New Jersey; Fairfield County, Conn.; Puerto Rico; and the Virgin Islands.

In addition to the responsibilities it shares in common with the other Reserve Banks, the NEW YORK FED has several unique responsibilities; foremost is the implementation of monetary policy. Open market operations are conducted for the System by the NEW YORK FED under the direction of the 12-member Federal Open Market Committee (FOMC).

The NEW YORK FED, representing the Federal Reserve System and the U.S. Treasury, also is responsible for intervening in foreign exchange markets to counter disorderly conditions. Further, the NEW YORK FED serves as fiscal agent in the United States for foreign central banks and official international financial organizations."

Like the other Federal Reserve Bank BBSs listed, the Liberty BBS provides information about the Federal Reserve and regional information. Which Federal BBS you should call depends on what information you are looking for. If you are looking general Federal Reserve information, call the closest area code. If you are looking for regional information, call the BBS that oversees that region.

GENERAL SERVICES ADMINISTRATION

Cooperative Administrative Support Program BBS

⌨N Acronym for online service: CASU-COM BBS

🖥) Online service number(s): 202-501-7707, FedWorld 703-321-8020

🌐 Internet address(es): telnet fedworld.gov then gateway to CASU-COM BBS (#73)

🏛 Government agency acronym: GSA

👥 Contact person & title: Phil LaBonte, Assistant Director

💻← Contact person's E-mail address: phil.labonte@gsa.gov, CompuServe 72204,2470, Prodigy KFGX01A

☎ Contact person's voice phone number: 202-273-4665

🖨 Contact person's Fax phone number: 202-273-4670

✉ Mailing address: Cooperative Administrative Support Program, Office of Workplace Initiatives (CW), 18th & F Streets, NW, Room 7007, Washington, DC 20405

DESCRIPTION

"CASUCOM is the electronic mail and information system for the Federal Cooperative Administration Support Program and is a network of almost 50 sites around the United States. Includes files, public discussion, forums, policy statements, newsletters, public relations, etc. that pertain to the task of improving and lowering the cost of administrative services."

Telecommuters will find the information provided by CASUCOM's "Tcommute" library of files interesting and relevant to their situation.

Be cautious when using the bulletin section of the BBS. If you select the nonstop option for reading the bulletins, you will find that large numbers of bulletins going back several years will pass by before you regain control of your system.

Consumer Information Center BBS

⌨ᴺ   Acronym for online service: CIC-BBS

🖥)   Online service number(s): 202-208-7679, FedWorld 703-321-8020

🌐   Internet address(es): telnet fedworld.gov then gateway to CIC-BBS.

🏛   Government agency acronym: GSA

👥   Contact person & title: Joshua Shleien, SYSOP

☎   Contact person's voice phone number: 202-501-1794

✉   Mailing address: Consumer Information Center, 18th & F Streets, NW, Room 20405, Washington, DC 20405

DESCRIPTION

"The Consumer Information Center's bulletin board system was established in January 1991. Its original purpose was to provide the media with immediate access to new press releases highlighting important consumer information.

Since that time, the system has broadened its scope to appeal to the general public. The 'Consumer Information Catalog,' which lists the more than 200 free and low-cost federal publications distributed from Pueblo, Colorado, can now be accessed electronically. See bulletins 10–24 for publication descriptions and ordering information.

Beginning in July 1993, electronic versions of publications from the 'Catalog' have been added to the system. These are available for download or online viewing. More publications will continue coming online over the next few months.

In sum, this BBS is intended to disseminate consumer information from the Federal Government, through electronic means, to the media and general public.

An extensive library of 'New for Consumers' press releases is also available. These provide useful tips and information on a wide range of subjects including money management, education, buying a house, and protecting yourself from fraud, to name just a few."

ANNOTATION

There are other government BBSs with more files. There are other government BBSs providing more technical data, and there are other government BBSs with more exotic content. However, the CIC-BBS probably has more files of value to more people than any other government BBS. It would be hard to imagine anyone logging into the CIC-BBS and not finding a file they want to read or share with someone else. The reason for this is that we are all consumers, and this BBS has a consumer information file on just about every aspect of consuming. Additionally, it offers lists of publications you can order from the Consumer Information Center.

How useful is the information found here? Downloading "How to protect yourself from HIV and AIDS," NFCAID2.TXT, could save your life.

Federal Information Resources Management Electronic Bulletin Board

🖳 Acronym for online service: GSA/IRM BBS

🖳) Online service number(s): FedWorld BBS 703-321-8020.

🌐 Internet address(es): telnet fedworld.gov gateway to GSA/IRM BBS

🏛 Government agency acronym: GSA

👥 Contact person & title: Gonza Kirksey, SYSOP

☎ Contact person's voice phone number: 202-501-4409

✉ Mailing address: General Services Administration, Federal Information Resources Management, 18th and F Streets, NW, Washington, DC 20405

DESCRIPTION

The following headings were captured from the opening menu and provide an overview of the information on the BBS:

- The Delegations of Procurement Authority
- Regulatory Information
- Subject Matter Area Experts
- The Governmentwide Acquisition Contracts (GWACS)
- List the GWACS Contracts
- GWACS Contracts Listing

- FIRMR Bulletin C-24
- The Reference Center (RC)

ANNOTATION

The GSA/IRM BBS deals mostly with the business of government. If you are involved in doing business with or within the U.S. Government, you will find the information provided interesting.

Federal Real Estate Sales Bulletin Board

🖳 Acronym for online service: FRES BBS

🖳) Online service number(s): Fedworld 703-321-8020

🌐 Internet address(es): telnet fedworld.gov

🏛 Government agency acronym: GSA

👥 Contact person & title: Christy McFarren, SYSOP

☎ Contact person's voice phone number: 202-501-3273

✉ Mailing address: General Services Administration, 18th & F Streets, NW, Room 4242, Washington, DC 20405

DESCRIPTION

"This bulletin board contains the following:

- A general description of the Federal Agencies selling real estate and the types of property they sell and instructions on where to call or write for additional information.
- A list of specific properties available for sale from GSA, the U.S. Postal Service, and the Tennessee Valley Authority.

- A list of GSA regional, field, and central offices.
- A summary of military base closures and realignment activities undertaken by the Secretary of Defense pursuant to recent legislation.
- Instructions on how to capture information in this bulletin board.

GSA provides this bulletin board as a service to both the agencies selling property and the public. Each agency selling real estate will widely advertise the availability of its properties, using such means as local and national newspapers, and mailing lists. The information in this bulletin board is intended to supplement existing advertising.

GSA, working with the other Federal agencies, makes every effort to ensure the accuracy of the information contained in this bulletin board. If you are interested in a specific property, please be sure to contact the person/organization listed as point-of-contact for the latest information on the particular property.

Federal, State, and local governmental agencies, as well as eligible nonprofit organizations, may utilize this bulletin board to obtain information on properties available for Federal transfer or Public Benefit disposal under the terms of the Federal Property and Administrative Services Act of 1949. Write on agency- or organization-letterhead to General Services Administration (DK), Washington, DC 20405 to obtain access instructions.

ANNOTATION

You have probably seen advertisements urging you to purchase information about how to buy Federal land and property cheap. The FRES BB will supply you with some of the same information for free. It will also instruct you where to write for precise, free information from specific government agencies.

Online Schedules System

⌨ Acronym for online service: OSS

💻 Online service number(s): FedWorld BBS 703-321-8020.

🌐 Internet address(es): telnet fedworld.gov then gateway to OSS-BBS.

🏛 Government agency acronym: GSA

👥 Contact person & title: Kathy Granger, Mel Hill, and Mark Graham, SYSOPS

☎ Contact person's voice phone number: 202-501-0002

✉ Mailing address: IRM Reference Center (KML) General Services Administration, 18th & F Streets, NW, Washington, DC 20405

DESCRIPTION

"This system is for general use by both the Federal Government and private individuals to review information provided by vendors authorized to participate in the GSA Multiple Award Schedule (MAS) Program. Information on the system and the systems functions are provided to all users exclusively through a series of specific menu selections."

ANNOTATION

OSS is not a fun BBS. The purpose of this BBS is strictly business. The following are the choices you will have if you log on:

- Contracts and Schedules
- Federal Acquisition Regulation Changes (FAC's)
- Potential Government Sources of ADP Sharing and Computer Support

- Debarred Bidders List
- Financial Management System Software FSC Group 70
- OSS User Instruction Manual
- Vendor Transaction Area
- Utilities Area
- Review System Bulletins
- Send message to SYSOP

If you have an interest in the Online Schedules System, be sure to download the Desk Guide file (DESKGIDE.DOC). It is about 100 pages long, depending on the font size and margins used.

MERIT SYSTEMS PROTECTION BOARD

The Federal Bulletin Board

🖥N   Acronym for online service: FBB

🖥)   Online service number(s): 202-512-1387

🏛   Government agency acronym: The bulletin board is operated by the Government Printing Office.

👥   Contact person & title: Michele Westbrook, Communications Officer

☎   Contact person's voice phone number: 202-653-7200

🖨   Contact person's Fax phone number: 202-653-6203

✉   Mailing address: Merit Systems Protection Board, 1120 Vermont Avenue, NW, Washington, DC 20419

DESCRIPTION

"The Merit Systems Protection Board decisions, studies, and publications are available through the Government Printing Office's Federal Bulletin Board."

ANNOTATION

The Federal Bulletin Board provides some free information, but most of the information they provide is fee-based and requires opening an account with them to obtain files.

NATIONAL AERONAUTICS AND SPACE ADMINISTRATION

Johnson Space Center BBS

🖥N   Acronym for online service: JSC

🖥)   Online service number(s) 713-483-5817

🏛   Government agency acronym: NASA

✉   Mailing address: Media Service Branch, Office of Public Affairs, Lyndon B. Johnson Space Center, Houston, TX 77058

DESCRIPTION

Johnson Space Center's Mission Television Schedule is posted here, but not much else.

ANNOTATION

There are no files to download.

JPL Info BBS

⌨) Online service number(s): 818-354-1333

Log on: Standard BBS 92 procedure is used for the BBS. Use anonymous as your ID and your Internet address as your password when using the ftp site.

🌐 Internet address(es): ftp jplinfo.jpl.nasa.gov

💻 E-mail address(es): newsdesk@jplpost.jpl.nasa.gov

🏛 Government agency acronym: NASA

👥 Contact person & title: Franklin O'Donnell, Deputy Manager

☎ Contact person's voice phone number: 818-354-5011

✉ Mailing address: Public Information Office, Jet Propulsion Laboratory, 4800 Oak Grove Drive, Pasadena, CA 91109-8099

DESCRIPTION

"The purpose of this site is to disseminate information on JPL's activities, including the robotic exploration of the solar system for the American space agency, NASA."

ANNOTATION

The JPL Info BBS is of particular value to science educators and space buffs. Educators will find guides to everything from comets to sunspots. Space buffs will enjoy the numerous graphic images available for downloading. More advanced space buffs will enjoy the status reports from numerous NASA missions. Don't forget to peruse the software library for a variety of software for many computer platforms.

On my first cyber voyage to the JPL Info BBS I downloaded a Windows program that showed me the constellations overhead at any time of the year at any time of the day. I'll be going back for graphics files next time.

NASA Small Business Innovation Research BBS

🖥 Acronym for online service: NASA SBIR BBS

⌨) Online service number(s): 800-547-1811, 202-488-2939

🌐 Internet address(es): FTP coney.gsfc.nasa.gov. Login as "anonymous" and use "guest" as the password.

🏛 Government agency acronym: NASA

👥 Contact person & title: Michael Shillinger, SYSOP

✉ Mailing address: NASA SBIR Headquarters, Code CR, Washington, DC 20546-0001

DESCRIPTION

"This bulletin board was developed to provide the business community with an additional access method for retrieving information about NASA's Small Business Innovation Research (SBIR) and Small Business Technology Transfer (STTR) programs. Using this technology, NASA has responded to the request of many businesses that are seeking to obtain information electronically. On this board you will find the annual solicitation for both the SBIR and STTR programs, Award Lists, procurement information, contact information, and for SBIR, abstracts of past awards, as well as late-breaking information about both programs. This service is being offered as a pilot program and its existence is dependent upon the availability of funding and the support of the bulletin board users.

Since this BBS is primarily serving the small business community, we have provided toll-free telephone access so that use of this service will not create a financial obstacle to full participation in these programs.

This BBS is not:

- Your personal E-mail system
- A general NASA BBS—we do not have space gif's, launch schedules or information on Space Camp.
- A recommended forum for asking SBIR/STTR policy questions."

ANNOTATION

The NASA SBIR BBS is a special purpose BBS as the SYSOP clearly states. Small businesses interested in working with NASA may find SBIR worth exploring.

NASA Spacelink

🖳) Online service number(s): 205 895 0028

🌐 Internet address(es): ftp 192.149.89.61, Domain Name spacelink.msfc.nasa.gov or xsl.msfc.nasa.gov

🏛 Government agency acronym: NASA

👥 Contact person & title: Bill Anderson, Spacelink Administrator

☎ Contact person's voice phone number: 205-544-6360

✉ Mailing address: NASA Spacelink, NASA Marshall Space Flight Center, CA21, Building 4200, Huntsville, AL 35812

DESCRIPTION

"While NASA understands that people from a wide variety of backgrounds will use NASA Spacelink, the system is specifically designed for teachers. The data base is arranged to provide easy access to current and historical information on NASA aeronautics and space research. Also included are suggested classroom activities that incorporate information on NASA projects to teach a number of scientific principles. Unlike bulletin board systems, NASA Spacelink does not provide for interaction between callers. However it does allow teachers and other callers to leave questions and comments for NASA."

ANNOTATION

NASA's Spacelink BBS may be the ultimate resource of NASA and space-related information for educators and space buffs. Printing out a list of all of the files found on Spacelink requires about 100 pages of paper. These files include photos of the Earth from space, photos of other planets, educational software, information about Space Shuttle missions, and much more. There is so much interesting information worthy of downloading on Spacelink that you may have to buy a larger hard disk drive just to make room for it. Spacelink is not a standard system, so paying attention to instructions is very important. If you try to use intuitive keystrokes, you may find yourself immediately logged out. There is no messaging or E-mail system on this BBS except for sending messages to the SYSOP. Spacelink is also slow and hard to reach during Space Shuttle flights, but they say they are planning on making improvements to resolve these problems. Spacelink is easily reached through the Internet by using

NASA and Spacelink as keywords during a Gopher search.

National Space Science Data Center, Online Data and Information Service

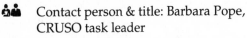 Acronym for online service: NSSDC NODIS

Online service number(s): 301-286-9000, FedWorld BBS 703-321-8020.

Log on: To use the dial-in BBS follow these instructions:

Internet address(es): telnet fedworld.gov and gateway to NSSDC\NASA\Goddard. telnet or ftp nssdca.gsfc.nasa.gov then log in as anonymous and use your E-mail address or "guest" as your password.

Dial 301-286-9000

[CONNECT 1200 (or 2400 or 300)]

Enter several carriage returns

[ENTER NUMBER]

MD

[CALLING 55201 (or 55202)]

[CALL COMPLETE]

Enter several carriage returns

[username:] NODIS or NSSDC

The square brackets [ ] indicate the response of the computer.

Government agency acronym: NASA

Contact person & title: Barbara Pope, CRUSO task leader

Contact person's voice phone number: 301-286-6695

Contact person's Fax phone number: 301-286-1771

Mailing address: National Space Science Data Center, Online Data and Information Service, Goddard Space Flight Center, Greenbelt, MD 20770"

DESCRIPTION

"NODIS provides menu-based access to data and information services provided by NSSDC and by the Space Physics Data Facility. Primarily through the multi-disciplinary Master Directory, NODIS also describes, and enables electronic access (E-links) to data/information/systems remote to NSSDC."

The following are descriptions of some of the subdivisions of NSSDC:
"The Astronomical Data Center (ADC).

This is a system for obtaining information about, and interactively requesting, any of the ADC's more than 700 astronomical catalogs. Catalogs are available on: the NASA Science Internet and NSI/DECnet computer networks; 9-track magnetic tape; microfiche and/or microfilm; hard copy and CD-ROM. Not all catalogs are available in all forms. The Online System will tell you what is available and how it can be sent to you."

"The Space Physics Data System.
The Space Physics Data System (SPDS) serves the four science disciplines encompassed within the programs of the NASA Space Physics Division, namely:

- Cosmic and Heliospheric Physics;
- Ionospheric, Thermospheric, and Mesospheric Physics;
- Magnetospheric Physics; and
- Solar Physics.

Goals of SPDS are to meet the urgent data requirements presented by upcoming new missions while helping to better preserve and improve access to critically important data from both past and present space physics missions. SPDS will initially operate primarily as a demonstration "confederation" of systems now existing and serving a broad constituency of space physics science users. A project coordinator and four discipline coordinators are now being recruited who will act as a science focus in addressing data-related issues."

The Coordinated Heliospheric Observations (COHO) Database
"Space Science Data Center for solar wind magnetic field, plasma, and energetic particle experiments on spacecraft operating partly or wholly in the interplanetary heliospheric environment. In most cases the data parameters have been extracted from the original formats of the archival datasets and loaded into the COHO data base as ASCII data fields. In a few cases COHO holds prearchival versions of datasets being prepared for formal submission to the NSSDC archive at a later date. The data files are organized in experiment-specific directories and accompanied by document files briefly describing the data parameters and formats. Additional COHO subdirectories provide supplementary information about archival data formats, geomagnetic activity indexes, ephemeris datasets for special events, spacecraft launch schedules, and general NASA activities of interest to the heliospheric science community.

In the event that the user actually needs the original datasets, including all data parameters, similar data at higher time resolution, or other related heliospheric datasets, references to such data may be found by accessing data catalogs (NSSDC Master Catalog, NASA Master Directory) on NSSDC's Online Data and Information Service (NODIS). Limited information on such datasets are provided in dataset document files within the COHO data base. Interplanetary data from the IMP-series

satellites in earth orbit are provided through the OMNI data service on NODIS."

Satellite Situation Center.
"This public-access Internet/DECnet directory has been established to facilitate user access to selected parameters of heliospheric interest from datasets archived at the National Satellite Situation Center (SSC) and the SSC Software System are services designed to assist the space physics community in planning and analyzing studies of the Earth's magnetosphere. These services are jointly developed and operated by the Space Physics Data Facility (SPDF) and the National Space Science Data Center (NSSDC) at NASA Goddard Space Flight Center."

The Solar-Terrestrial Energy Program (STEP)
"STEP (Solar-Terrestrial Energy Program) is a SCOSTEP-sponsored international program whose main scientific goal is to advance the quantitative understanding of the coupling mechanisms that are responsible for the transfer of energy and mass from one region of the solar-terrestrial system to another.

This STEP Bulletin Board is intended to facilitate communication among STEP participants, and to inform those participants of the goals and activities of STEP of the overall and individual STEP Working Groups and Research Projects."

ANNOTATION

I have harbored a question about space research since childhood: Where does all the data from space flights go? I found the answer in the Space Physics section of NSSDC.
"NASA has conducted many rocket and spacecraft missions over the years and has also collaborated in ground-based experiments. From these endeavors many valuable (and some not-

so-valuable) scientific and technical data have been gathered.

After a third of a century of space physics data acquisition, what do we now do with all these perishable data?

Many of the NASA data sets have been archived in the National Space Science Data Center (NSSDC) at Goddard Space Flight Center in Maryland. Most of the data sets from spacecraft operated by the National Oceanic and Atmospheric Administration are archived in the National Geophysical Data Center (NGDC) located in Boulder, Colorado, and other data sets are archived at various regional data centers. Yet there are undoubtedly a great many data sets that reside with the instrument's principal investigators or associate researchers at various universities, colleges, and aerospace laboratories—data that are not now included in the national archiving effort.

Some of these data may be in danger of becoming unreadable due to deterioration of the data medium (magnetic tape print-through, iron oxide shedding, etc.), due to loss of knowledge of what the data bits mean (incomplete documentation or lack of documentation), and perhaps due to loss of insightful knowledge of the instrument operation as principal and associate investigators retire or leave the space physics field."

There is even more space data to explore through ftp sites on the Internet, and many of those are listed in various parts of NSSDC.

When you log on to NSSDC, you are given the option of using a text oriented interface or a windowed interface. If you want to capture to a file what goes by on the monitor, select the text interface. If you want to see what an advanced windowed user interface looks like, select the other option.

Space Telescope Electronic Information Service

📡 Parent organization: NASA Space Telescope Science Institute.

🖥 Acronym for online service: STEIS

🌐 Internet address(es): ftp ftp.stsci.edu, Gopher stsci.edu 70, URL http://stsci.edu/top.html

💻 E-mail address(es): odea@stsci.edu

👥 Contact person & title: Dr. Chris O'Dea

💻 Contact person's E-mail address: odea@stsci.edu

☎ Contact person's voice phone number: 410-338-2590

🖨 Contact person's Fax phone number: 410-338-5085

✉ Mailing address: STScI, 3700 San Martin Dr., Baltimore, MD 21218

DESCRIPTION

The Space Telescope Electronic Information Service (STEIS) is an ftp, Gopher, WAIS, and WWW server, which provides information about the Hubble Space Telescope to the astronomical community and to the public. STEIS contains information about the telescope, its instruments, data-reduction software, and telescope schedule. A large collection of publicly available images of interesting objects is also available in several formats (GIF, TIFF, JPEG).

ANNOTATION

If you are looking for an outer space experience, this is the WWW server to visit. The graphics are fantastic and plentiful. The information available is extensive. This is a great server to visit for anyone with an interest in space.

NATIONAL ARCHIVES AND RECORDS ADMINISTRATION

Federal Register Electronic News Delivery

🖳ᴺ Acronym for online service: FREND

🖳⟩ Online service number(s): 202-275-0860, 202-275-0898, 202-275-1538, FedWorld 703-321-8020

Log on: Abbreviated standard BBS

🌐 Internet address(es): telnet fedworld.gov then gateway to FREND 1 or 2

🏛 Government agency acronym: NARA

👥 Contact person & title: Ernie Sowada, SYSOP

☎ Contact person's voice phone number: 202-523-3447

✉ Mailing address: Office of the Federal Register (NF-A), National Archives and Records Administration, Washington, DC 20408

DESCRIPTION

"FREND is operated by the Office of the Federal Register, which is part of the National Archives, in Washington DC.
Its purpose is to provide fast access to:

• Public Law Numbers, as we assign these to bills signed by the President.

• Listings of Federal Register documents on public inspection.
• Tables of Contents of recent Federal Registers. FREND is designed as an electronic finding aid. This means that you can use it to get information about Public Laws or Federal Register documents, but NOT the text of those laws or documents."

ANNOTATION

FREND has two addresses on FedWorld, FREND1 and FREND2.

NATIONAL CREDIT UNION ADMINISTRATION

National Credit Union Bulletin Board System

🖳ᴺ Acronym for online service: NCUA BBS

🖳⟩ Online service number(s): FedWorld 703-321-8020

🌐 Internet address(es): telnet fedworld.gov then gateway to NCUA BBS

🏛 Government agency acronym: NCUA

👥 Contact person & title: Carey Savage, SYSOP

☎ Contact person's voice phone number: 703-518-6335

✉ Mailing address: National Credit Union Administration, 1776 G Street, NW, Washington, DC 20456

DESCRIPTION

"The National Credit Union Administration Board is responsible for chartering, insuring, supervising, and examining Federal credit unions and administrating the National Credit Union Share Insurance Fund. The Board also manages the Central Liquidity Facility, a mixed-ownership government corporation whose purpose is to supply emergency loans to member credit unions."

National Endowment for the Humanities BBS

🏠 Parent organization: National Endowment for the Humanities

💻 Online service number(s): 202-606-8688

🏛 Government agency acronym: NEH

👥 Contact person & title: Amy Lifson

☎ Contact person's voice phone number: 202-606-8435

🖨 Contact person's Fax phone number: 202-606-8420

✉ Mailing address: National Endowment for the Humanities, 1100 Pennsylvania Avenue, NW, Washington, DC 20506

ANNOTATION

On the NCUA BBS you will find files and messages related to topics described in the description. This is not a general purpose BBS.

The file topics found on the NCUA BBS include:

- Rules and Regulations
- FPR Guide
- Supervisory Committee Manual
- Press Releases
- Financial Trends Report
- Newsletter
- User Assistance
- Final Regulations
- NCUA New Phone Numbers
- Board Calendar
- Bylaws
- Federal Credit Union Act
- FFIEC EDP Handbook
- Proposed Regulations
- Opinion Letters
- Letters to Credit Union
- Proposed Chartering Policy
- Legislation
- Vacancy Announcements–All Sources
- 5300 Information

DESCRIPTION

The Bulletin Board can give you information on grants, deadlines, and humanities events.

ANNOTATION

History academicians will find the National Endowment for the Humanities BBS of interest because of the information provided on obtaining grants. Others will find it interesting to read about the goings on at the NEH.

NATIONAL SCIENCE FOUNDATION

FinanceNet

🏠 Parent organization: Joint Financial Management Improvement Program

🖥 Acronym for online service: FNet

🌐 Internet address(es): gopher.financenet.gov, WWW http://www.financenet.gov/, ftp.financenet.gov, telnet.financenet.gov, Usenet: news.financenet.gov

💻 E-mail address(es): info@financenet.gov; e-mail-info@financenet.gov

🏛 Government agency acronym: NSF

👥 Contact person & title: Preston Rich, Co-Chair FinanceNet Core Team

💻 Contact person's E-mail address: Preston.Rich@nsf.gov

☎ Contact person's voice phone number: 703-306-1282

📠 Contact person's Fax phone number: 703-306-0287

✉ Mailing address: Joint Financial Management Improvement Program, 4201 Wilson Blvd., #575, Arlington, VA 22230

DESCRIPTION

The following is from a press release provided by NSF:
"FinanceNet—a terrific opportunity for you to participate in reinventing government financial management.

We invite you to join with thousands of accountants, auditors, financial managers, and others to share your ideas and information. This is a vehicle that can help you do your job better. We encourage you to join and freely participate in this project. Its free and available to anyone having Internet access and the desire to improve government financial management. Coordination and support are provided by Vice President Gore's National Performance Review (NPR) and the National Science Foundation.

Your participation and ideas are the most important ingredients in FinanceNet!

This ambitious Internet initiative links people in all Federal agencies; State, local and international communities; professional financial management organizations, and private sector support organizations. It provides a synergistic medium for sharing ideas, information, successes, news, lessons learned, best practices and experience.

SERVICES

Electronic Mailing Lists devoted to a variety of subjects related to the accountability and stewardship of public financial assets—such as, Internal Controls, Audits, Financial Reporting and Policy, Payroll, Travel, Procurement, Financial Systems, Personnel and Training, Performance Measures, Audits, Accounting Standards, Cash Management, International, State and Local Issues, Government Asset Sales, and many others.

Internet Gopher (gopher.financenet.gov) and WWW Servers (http://www.financenet.gov/) carry libraries of important new electronic financial management documents, news announcements, employment openings, asset sales and much more from governments all around the world. FinanceNet servers offer a "one-stop-shop" navigation of all of the Internet's extensive worldwide resources.

Usenet Newsgroup Discussion Forums on financial management topics, open to all, and an electronic online, real-time conferencing capability rounds out the service list.

WOW!!! The only thing missing is YOU.

If you have an Internet accessible E-mail address, you can automatically receive complete information on the full spectrum of FinanceNet Internet services by return E-mail by simply sending a blank E-mail message to:

info@financenet.gov"

ANNOTATION

This is a resource-rich WWW server. The submenus will keep you interested for hours if you are interested in NSF-related topics and government online issues.

Science & Technology Information System

🖳N   Acronym for online service: STIS

🖳)   Online service number(s): 703-306-0212, 703-306-0213, FedWorld 703-321-8020

      Log on: varies depending on which STIS service you use.

🌐   Internet address(es): telnet fedworld.gov then gateway to STIS. ftp stis.nsf.gov.

🖳←   E-mail address(es): stis@nsf.gov

🏛   Government agency acronym: NSF

👥   Contact person & title: STET

🖳←   Contact person's E-mail address: stis@nsf.gov

☎   Contact person's voice phone number: 703-306-0214

✉   Mailing address: National Science Foundation, Information Office, 4201 Wilson Blvd., Arlington, VA 22230

DESCRIPTION

"STIS is an electronic dissemination system that provides fast, easy access to National Science Foundation (NSF) publications. There is no cost to you except for possible long-distance phone charges. The service is available 24 hours a day, except for brief weekly maintenance periods.

Publications currently available include:

- The NSF Bulletin
- Program announcements and "Dear Colleague" letters
- General publications and reports
- Press releases and other NSF news items
- NSF organization charts and alphabetical phone directories
- NSF vacancy announcements
- Award abstracts (1989–Present)

Our goal is for all printed publications to be available electronically.

Access Methods

There are many ways to access STIS. Choose the method that meets your needs and the communication facilities you have available.

Electronic Documents via E-Mail. If you have access to Internet, you can send a specially formatted message, and the document you request will be automatically returned to you via E-mail.

Anonymous FTP. Internet users who are familiar with this file transfer method can quickly and easily transfer STIS documents to their local system for browsing and printing.

Online STIS. If you have a VT100 emulator and an Internet connection or a modem, you can log on to the online system. The online system features full-text search and retrieval software to help you locate the documents and award abstracts that are of interest to you.

Once you locate a document, you can browse through it online or download it using the Kermit protocol or request that it be mailed to you.

Direct E-Mail. You can request that STIS keep you informed, via E-mail, of all new documents on STIS. You can elect to get either a summary or the full text of new documents.

Internet Gopher and WAIS. If your campus has access to these Internet information resources, you can use you local client software to search and download NSF publications. If you have the capability, it is the easiest way to access STIS.

Getting Started with Documents via E-Mail

Send a message to the Internet address stisserv@nsf.gov. The text of the message should be as follows (the Subject line is ignored):

get index

You will receive a list of all the documents on STIS and instructions for retrieving them. Please note that all requests for electronic documents should be sent to stisserv, as shown above. Requests for printed publications should be sent to pubs@nsf.gov.

Getting Started with Anonymous FTP

FTP to stis.nsf.gov. Enter anonymous for the username, and your E-mailaddress for the password. Retrieve the file 'index.' This contains a list of the files available on STIS and additional instructions.

Getting Started with the Online System

If you are on the Internet: telnet stis.nsf.gov. at the login prompt, enter 'public.'

If you are dialing in with a modem: Choose 1,200, 2,400, or 9,600 baud, 7-E-1. Dial 202-357-0359 or 202 357-0360. When connected, press Enter. At the login prompt, enter public.

The online system uses a powerful text search and retrieval system called TOPIC. If you are not familiar with TOPIC, you will want to obtain a copy of the STIS User's Guide, NSF 91-19. You can request an electronic copy

after you log on. For a printed copy send your mailing address to 'stis@nsf.gov' (Internet) or 'stis@nsf' (BITNET).

Getting Started with Direct E-Mail

Send an E-mailmessage to the Internet address stisserv@nsf.gov Put the following in the text:

get stisdirm

You will receive instructions for this service.

Getting Started with Gopher and WAIS

The NSF Gopher server is on port 70 of stis.nsf.gov. The WAIS server is also on stis.nsf.gov. You can get the '.src' file from the 'Directory of Servers' at quake.think.com. For further information contact your local computer support organization."

ANNOTATION

Depending on what telecommunications software you use, you may run into some problems accessing STIS. Less than perfect terminal emulators will not work well with STIS. Screen captures don't seem to work at all in Procomm for Windows, but it may not be Procomm's fault. STIS writes screens of information at a time, this may be why Procomm can't capture it. Although the STIS interface may be attractive to look at, many users will find that its unique features may be more of a hindrance than a help.

The following files were especially helpful for learning about STIS:

The following quote from the file "ACCESFAQ" is worth remembering when you access STIS:

"STIS contains very little scientific information. Rather, the information on STIS centers on how the NSF supports scientific research. Therefore, there is a lot of information about programs we fund, and general information on how to apply for grants. We *do* have abstracts

Title	File
FAQ—Accessing STIS and STIS Files	accesfaq (ASCII, 28887 bytes)
FAQ—Download Information from STIS	dwnldfaq (ASCII, 9289 bytes)
FAQ—Miscellaneous Information	miscfaq (ASCII, 10871 bytes)
FAQ—Publications Printed Information	pubsfaq (ASCII, 2693 bytes)
Getting STIS Documents Via Direct E-Mail	stisdirm (ASCII, 4393 bytes)
Locating a Specific Publication	stisfind (ASCII, 1821 bytes)
Downloading a Group of Documents	stisgrpd (ASCII, 2712 bytes)

on all the projects funded by NSF since 1989. Each abstract describes a project that has been funded, but does not have the results, since it is written before the project is started. Nonetheless, the abstracts can be valuable in identifying researchers and institutions that are active in a particular field."

NUCLEAR REGULATORY COMMISSION

Enhanced Participatory Rulemaking Bulletin Board System

🖳 Acronym for online service: EPRBBS

🖳 Online service number(s): 800-880-6091

🏛 Government agency acronym: NRC

👥 Contact person & title: Christine Daily, SYSOP

💻 Contact person's E-mail address: cxd@nrc.gov

☎ Contact person's voice phone number: 301-415-6026

🖷 Contact person's Fax phone number: 301-415-5385

✉ Mailing address: Nuclear Regulatory Commission, RES/DRA TWFN 9-C-24, Washington, DC 20555

DESCRIPTION

"The purpose of this bulletin board is to provide information to the public about the Nuclear Regulatory Commission's rulemaking process associated with decommissioning. If you would like some background information about this rulemaking, there are files available for review or downloading in file area 1 (type F at the main menu, then type L to list files, then type 1 to list files in area 1). If you would like to provide comments to the Nuclear Regulatory Commission on the decommissioning rulemaking, you can upload a file into file area 2. For questions about the rulemaking or comments about this BBS, please leave a message in the Message section.

There are several Nuclear Regulatory Commission publications that contain related information in greater detail. These publications are available from the Government Printing Office, which can be contacted at (202)783-3238. Documents can be ordered from the Superintendent of Documents, U.S. Government Printing Office, P.O. Box 37082, Washington DC.

Two publications that may be of particular interest with regard to decommissioning and residual radioactivity are NUREG/CR-5512, Volume 1 'Residual Radioactive Contamination from Decommissioning' and NUREG/CR-5849, 'Manual for Conducting Radiological Surveys in Support of License Termination' (Draft)."

ANNOTATION

The EPRBBS has an active message area with interesting subjects dealing with nuclear power issues. The file section has a large selection of documents also related to nuclear power.

Tech Specs Plus BBS

▭N Acronym for online service: TECH SPEC BBS

▭) Online service number(s): 800-679-5784, 301-504-1778, FedWorld 703-321-8020

⊕ Internet address(es): telnet fedworld.gov then gateway to TECH SPEC BBS.

🏛 Government agency acronym: NRC

👥 Contact person & title: Tom Dunning & Chris Hoxie SYSOPS

▭← Contact person's E-mail address: Dunning tgd@nrc.gov, Hoxie clh1@nrc.gov

☎ Contact person's voice phone number: Dunning 301-504-1189, Hoxie 301-504-3138

🖨 Contact person's Fax phone number: 301-504-3577

✉ Mailing address: Nuclear Regulatory Commission, OWFN MS 8H7, Washington, DC 20555-0001

DESCRIPTION

"The TECH SPECS BBS has WordPerfect 5.1 text files containing Improved Standard Technical Specifications for Babcock and Wilcox, Combustion Engineering, General Electric, and Westinghouse Plants; and Proposed Generic Communications on Line-Item Tech Spec Improvements (i.e., Generic Letters). The capability to download or upload information to the bulletin board is unrestricted within a framework of common courtesy type rules.

The Tech Specs Plus BBS also carries NRC Bulletins, Information Notices, Generic Letters, Daily Event Reports, and 2.2.06 petitions."

ANNOTATION

The "FILES" Bulletin is essential reading if you plan to decipher the file name descriptions used by Tech Specs BBS.

U.S. Nuclear Regulatory Commission Public Comments on the Decommissioning Rulemaking

▭N Acronym for online service: NRCDR

▭) Online service number(s): 800-880-6091, FedWorld 703-321-8020

⊕ Internet address(es): telnet fedworld.gov then gateway to NRCDR

🏛 Government agency acronym: NRC

👥 Contact person & title: Ms. Christin Daily, SYSOP

☎ Contact person's voice phone number: 301-492-3999

✉ Mailing address: Nuclear Regulatory Commission, Mail Stop 139, 2120 L Street, NW, Washington, DC 20555

DESCRIPTION

The description provided by the NRCDR BBS is the same as that provided by the EPRBBS.

ANNOTATION

The NRCDR is looking for your comments on decommissioning nuclear reactors, and this BBS provides one of the means for you to express yourself. Of course, you can also read the comments of others and download informational files on the NRC's rule-making process. When I logged on, the catalog of files was several months out of date and many of the files had cryptic titles. However, if you are a good researcher interested in nuclear reactor decommissioning, you will like what you find here.

OFFICE OF GOVERNMENT ETHICS

The Ethics Bulletin Board System

📞 Parent organization: Office of Information Resources Management

🖥N Acronym for online service: TEBBS

🖥) Online service number(s): 202-523-1186, FedWorld 703-321-8020

🌐 Internet address(es): telnet fedworld.gov then gateway to TEBBS

🏛 Government agency acronym: OGE

👥 Contact person & title: David E. Dorward, SYSOP

☎ Contact person's voice phone number: 202-523-5757

🖨 Contact person's Fax phone number: 202-523-6325, 202-523-1251, 202-523-1229.

✉ Mailing address: Office of Government Ethics, Suite 500. 1201 New York Avenue, NW, Washington, DC 20005-3917

DESCRIPTION

"The Ethics Bulletin Board System (TEBBS) is provided by the U.S. Office of Government Ethics, Office of Information Resources Management. OGE established this bulletin board in response to the departments' and agencies' desire to have another and more convenient method for obtaining information about ethics laws, regulations, policies, opinions, and other material relating to executive branch ethics activities.

Three main services are provided on TEBBS: reading bulletins, reading and downloading files, and sending and receiving messages to the OIRM bulletin board support staff. There is also a utilities section which controls 'housekeeping' tasks. TEBBS supports a free, limited-use service for users. Functions available on other electronic bulletin boards such as uploading files or sending messages to other users are not available on TEBBS.'

ANNOTATION

The file names and descriptions found on TEBBS read like bureaucratic jargon. For example, this a file name and description from REBBS: "CFR26CON.TXT, Title 5 Code of Fed. Regs Chap XVI Contents." There is, however, valuable information here for government employees, researchers, and journalists interested in ethics issues as they relate to the U.S. Government.

OFFICE OF PERSONNEL MANAGEMENT

Detroit Service Center BBS

🖳N Acronym for online service: DSC BBS

🖳) Online service number(s): 313-226-4423

🏛 Government agency acronym: OPM

👥 Contact person & title: Mike Makki, SYSOP

✉ Mailing address: Federal Job Information Center, 477 Michigan Avenue, Detroit, MI 48226

DESCRIPTION

"This bulletin board is operated by the Federal Job Information Center in Detroit, Michigan, on behalf of the Chicago Region.

The Bulletin Board Service (BBS) contains lists of jobs that cover every state in the country.

The Federal Job Information Center is an agency of the Federal Government. It exists to provide assistance to Federal agencies in recruiting to fill their vacancies in the civilian work force."

ANNOTATION

Although there is no guarantee that logging onto the Detroit Service Center BBS will lead to a new job with the Federal Government, it should not be overlooked as a job-search tool.

Federal Job Opportunity Board

🖳N Acronym for online service: FJOB

🖳) Online service number(s): 912-757-3100

🏛 Government agency acronym: OPM

👥 Contact person & title: Suzi Hamilton and Curtis Hooker, Co-SYSOPS

☎ Contact person's voice phone number: 912-744-2332 or 912-744-2121

✉ Mailing address: U.S. Office of Personnel Management, Staffing Service Center, Macon, GA 31298

DESCRIPTION

"The Federal Job Opportunities Board (FJOB) is an electronic bulletin board developed by the Office of Personnel Management, Staffing Service Center, Macon, Georgia. The FJOB provides up-to-date FEDERAL JOB INFORMATION as well as bulletins, notices, electronic messaging, and processing help. It is available free of charge from 4:30 A.M. to 2:00 A.M. EST, seven (7) days a week.

WHAT IS OPM?
The United States Office of Personnel Management (OPM) is the central personnel agency of the U.S. Government. As such, it administers a merit system for Federal employment, which includes recruiting, examining,

training, and promoting people on the basis of their knowledge and skills, regardless of their race, religion, sex, political influence, or other nonmerit factors.

OPM's role is to ensure that the Federal government provides an array of personnel services to applicants and employees. Through a range of programs designed to develop and encourage the effectiveness of the Government employee, OPM supports program managers in their personnel management responsibilities and provides benefits to employees directly.

OPM's activities include Recruiting and Examining, Personnel Investigations, Affirmative Employment, Employee Development and Training, Incentive Awards, Personnel Management, Employee Benefits, and other personnel programs."

ANNOTATION

FJOB provides an impressive, self-running demonstration of their BBS. It is available as a file FJOBDEMO.ZIP for downloading to MS-DOS™–compatible computers. FJOB also provides the telephone numbers and Internet addresses of other online sources of employment information.

Federal Pay & Performance Management BBS

☐N   Acronym for online service: PayPerNet BBS

☐)   Online service number(s): 202-606-2675, FedWorld BBS 703-321-8020.

⊕   Internet address(es): telnet fedworld.gov gateway to PayPerNet

🏛   Government agency acronym: OPM

👥   Contact person & title: Denise Jenkins, Program Analyst

☎   Contact person's voice phone number: 202-606-2092

🖷   Contact person's Fax phone number: 202-606-1349

✉   Mailing address: U.S. Office of Personnel Management, Office of Compensation Policy, 1900 E Street, NW, Washington, DC 20415

DESCRIPTION

"The PayPerNet Information System is a public Bulletin Board which provides information to Federal agencies in the areas of concern to the Federal Personnel community and other interested persons and organizations. We have information/programs relating to Title 5 Special Rates, Position Classification, Pay Administration, Total Quality Management, Employee and Labor Relations, Senior Executive Service, Federal Employees Pay Comparability Act of 1990 (FEPCA), Federal Wage System, Federal Personnel Processing, Performance Management and Incentive Awards.

Initially, the system did concentrate on the dissemination of information about Title 5 Special Rate authorizations in the form of reports from the Special Rates Tracking/Information System (SRTIS).

This BBS is organized as a Main Board with conferences. Conferences are sort of analogous to subdirectories. Using this analogy, the Main Board is the root directory and *HAS NO FILES FOR DOWNLOADING*. All files available for downloading and the directories of those files are only accessible from the appropriate conference. Use the J command to 'Join' a conference. The conferences are organized by subject and will be shown in a Conference Menu when you enter the J command. Select the conference you want by entering its NUMBER as shown on the menu.

On joining a conference, you are given an additional 30 minutes on the BBS (Total time = 1 hour)."

PayPerNet is also accessible through the Mainstreet BBS of OPM.

Los Angeles Federal JobLine

💻) Online service number(s): 818-575-6521

🏛 Government agency acronym: OPM

👥 Contact person & title: Jim Christopher, SYSOP

☎ Contact person's voice phone number: 818-575-6503

✉ Mailing address: U.S. Office of Personnel Management, 9650 Flair Drive, Room 100A, El Monte, CA 91731

DESCRIPTION

"Content: Focuses on job opportunities in the Western United States and Pacific Overseas areas, but also provides data on job opportunities nationwide. Agency personnel office staff and college placement office staff may request upgraded access to the agency and college conferences, respectively, by contacting the SYSOP through the online page, message to the SYSOP, or voice telephone. These conferences provide forums for interchange of Federal personnel and recruiting information among conference members. The BBS also contains information on personnel processing and record keeping."

ANNOTATION

Los Angeles Federal JobLine is also accessible through the Mainstreet BBS of OPM. If you are calling from the East Coast, you may want to use the Mainstreet gateway to this BBS to save the long-distance charges.

Office of Personnel Management Mainstreet BBS

💻N Acronym for online service: OPM Mainstreet

💻) Online service number(s): 202-606-4800, FedWorld BBS 703-321-8020.

🌐 Internet address(es): telnet fedworld.gov and gateway to OPM Mainstreet

🏛 Government agency acronym: OPM

👥 Contact person & title: Laurel Burcham, SYSOP

☎ Contact person's voice phone number: 202-606-1396

✉ Mailing address: Office of Personnel Management, 1900 E Street NW, Washington, DC 20415

DESCRIPTION

"Content: Supporting agencies and the public with online Federal personnel guidance and job information exchange."

ANNOTATION

From Mainstreet BBS you can connect with other Office of Personnel Management BBSs through a gateway. From the main menu select "Connect to OPM's Other BBSs" and select the BBS you want to connect to.

OPM Express

⌨N Acronym for online service: OPM Express

🖥) Online service number(s): 214-767-0565

🏛 Government agency acronym: OPM

👥 Contact person & title: The SYSOP requested not to have their name mentioned.

☎ Contact person's voice phone number: 214-767-8245

📠 Contact person's Fax phone number: 214-767-8205

✉ Mailing address: Dallas Regional Training Center, Human Resources Development Division, U.S. Office of Personnel Management, 1100 Commercial Street, Room 4B25, Dallas, TX 75242-0495

DESCRIPTION

"This system offers you free national E-mail with other government employees. The system also allows employees to exchange public domain computer programs, templates, and formats useful in their work.

This system is intended for use by any Government employee or office as a means for employees and offices to get and share information useful in their work. 'Government' means ANY Federal, City, State, local, tribal, public college or university, or governmental entity of any kind."

ANNOTATION

According to the SYSOP of OPM Express who requested anonymity, "The OPM Express is one of many bulletin boards in the U.S. Office of Personnel Management. The 'main' bulletin board is located in Washington, DC. It is called Mainstreet..." The Mainstreet BBS provided additional information about the OPM Express which included the following:

Content: Information on all aspects of Federal personnel management, but with a strong emphasis on training and development of employees. Includes the most recent OPM position on many issues. Provides listings of software of interest to personnel lists and has a strong emphasis on training and development. The BBS also contains information on personnel processing and record keeping. HRD Info, the Human Resources Development Conference, promotes and facilitates human resources development throughout the Federal Government by providing users the following: HRD News and Bulletins, E-mail, and Utilities. The News and Bulletins feature contains text items on OPM policy and HRD initiatives, national training and development issues, HRD management, training courses and programs, and system use. Information about OPM-sponsored HRD research, executive summaries of Federal studies and reports, and training publications are also included. Users may copy wordprocessed documents from and to HRD Info. The E-mail feature permits users to share material on employee development programs, policies, practices; to ask for and receive technical assistance on specific HRD matters; and to exchange HRD career development information including details on upcoming showcases and conferences. The Utilities feature allows users to search specific data bases including the training schedules of government agencies. This can be particularly helpful for those needing to select or recommend training courses for others."

If you need the name of the OPM Express SYSOPs you can find that information on the

Mainstreet BBS Description for OPM Express.

Philadelphia Region BBS

💻) Online service number(s): 215-580-2216

🏛 Government agency acronym: OPM

👥 Contact person & title: Glenn Catlin

☎ Contact person's voice phone number: 215-597-4508, 215-597-3804

✉ Mailing address: U.S. Office of Personnel Management, Philadelphia Regional Office, Federal Building, 600 Arch Street, Philadelphia, PA 19106

DESCRIPTION

"Content: Among the information available are files about Federal job opportunities, locally and nationwide. There are also OPM and Government text files. After logging on and reading the 'news,' callers will move to the main menu with its alphabetical listings. Help on moving around on the BBS is always available from any screen. Callers can request 'job applications' on line by completing the appropriate questionnaire. There are a number of 'conference' areas with topics like CAREER AMERICA, COLLEGES, OPM EXAMS, BEYOND THE BA, SENIOR EXECUTIVE SERVICE, AND AGENCIES. The BBS has the capability of exchanging message 'mail' with other BBS."

ANNOTATION

The OPM Philadelphia Region BBS is also accessible through the Mainstreet BBS of OPM. There is a rich assortment of government and nongovernment files on this BBS.

PANAMA CANAL COMMISSION

Panama Canal Commission

ANNOTATION

Panama Canal Commission information is available through the Office of Personnel Management's Main Street BBS.

POSTAL RATE COMMISSION

Office of the Consumer Advocate BBS

💻N Acronym for online service: OCA BBS

💻) Online service number(s): 202-788-6891, FedWorld 703-321-8020

🌐 Internet address(es): telnet fedworld.gov then gateway to OCA BBS

🏛 Government agency acronym: PRC

👥 Contact person & title: Mark. F. Ramage, SYSOP

✉ Mailing address: U. S. Postal Rate Commission, Office of the Consumer Advocate, 1333 H St., N.W., Washington, DC 20268-0001

DESCRIPTION

"The purpose of this BBS is to make documents, spreadsheets, or other files that are already in electronic form, available to persons with an interest in Commission proceedings. Although this BBS is open to the general public, much of the data available for downloading is somewhat specialized and would be of value only to persons who closely follow or actively participate in Commission proceedings.

The goal of OCA's BBS is to make documents, library references, work papers, etc., more readily accessible to all persons who rely on them.

Initially, the files on this BBS will consist mainly of the diskette files that accompany library references filed in the dockets section of the PRC. In addition, other documents made available to the OCA in electronic form will be available on this BBS (this would include Commission Orders, Opinions, etc.)."

ANNOTATION

Have you ever been puzzled why first class postage is 32 cents rather than 30 cents? Do you find it odd that a Priority Mail rate is often almost the same rate as First Class? If you are willing to dig through the files found on the OCA BBS, you may come away with a greater insight as to how postal rates are decided, or you may not. I couldn't decode the file descriptions, so I had little success finding answers to my questions. The following is sampling of file descriptions found on the OCA BBS:

- DJ-LR-2 files—diskette 1 of 3.
- DJ-LR-2 files—diskette 2 of 3.
- DJ-LR-2 files—diskette 3 of 3.
- DJ-LR-3. Diskette containing wp's wrt int. OCA/DJ-T1-2.
- MC91-3 Commission Docket Sheets—chron. list of filings
- List of all librefs filed for MC91-3 as of 2/5/92
- Libref USPS-PD-1 diskette files

RESOLUTION TRUST CORPORATION

Resolution Trust Corporation

ANNOTATION

The Resolution Trust Corporation's data may be available through the Federal Deposit Insurance Corporation by the time you read this. If not, call 800-366-9246 and ask for information about RTCNET.

SMALL BUSINESS ADMINISTRATION

Small Business Administration Online

🖳N Acronym for online service: SBA Online

🖳) Online service number(s): 800-697-4636, 202-401-9600, 900-463-4636, FedWorld BBS 703-321-8020.

Log on: Standard BBS for free service. The 900 number requires call-back verification.

🌐 Internet address(es): URL http://www.sbaonline.gov, telnet fedworld.gov then gateway to SBA Online

🏛 Government agency acronym: SBA

👥 Contact person & title: Ms. Diane Gannon, Mark Rorabaugh

🖳← Contact person's E-mail address: Rorabuagh mark@www.sbaonline.sba.gov

☎ Contact person's voice phone number: Gannon 202-205-7009

✉ Mailing address: Small Business Administration, 409 Third Street, SW, Washington, DC 20416

DESCRIPTION

"The SBA Online is a pilot bulletin board system developed and maintained by the Small Business Administration. Its purpose is to provide the Small Business Community immediate access to SBA information, services and publications. Specific topic areas are provided to the public for the exchange of information related to the Start-up, Development, and Management of small business. These areas or mailboxes furnish a means by which callers can network with each other for the sharing of ideas, techniques, and resources that will contribute to improved operations. We appreciate your cooperation and support in helping us serve the small business community."

ANNOTATION

Are you thinking about starting your own small business? Are you seeking advice about operating your existing small business? Do you have questions specific to women or minorities starting their own business? Do you live in an isolated area and need to network with others operating a similar kind of business? Are you pursuing a career in the Small Business Administration? Are you looking for free or shareware business software for your computer? Are you a woman seeking business contacts in your geographic area? Would you like to learn more about the Small Business Administration and what it has to offer you? If your answer to any of these questions was yes, SBA Online has help files, message areas, and software programs that you may find valuable and it's free and easy to use.

SBA Online provides a toll-free number and basic access to the BBS is free, but to get full access you have to use a 900 number. The toll number provides users with full messaging, Internet, and gateway services.

The bulletin board software is menu driven, so all you have to do is select a number or character to enter a command. They maintain 48 phone lines, so busy signals are uncommon. The SBA Online WWW server allows connection to the SBA Online BBS through telnet.

I was able to put SBA Online to immediate use. Two women I know are moving to Maine to set up small businesses as artists. I knew they were looking for business contacts, so I downloaded a file containing WBO Contacts, WBR1.TXT, from File Area 1, WOMEN. The file contained ASCII text listing the names, addresses, and telephone numbers of contacts that I printed out and gave to the artists. I also found several business contact programs worth downloading in the Files section.

SBA Online fulfills its objective completely. All of the services described in their purpose statement exist and function properly.

Small Business Administration Software Clearinghouse Bulletin Board System

🖥 Acronym for online service: SBAI-BBS

🖥 Online service number(s): FedWorld 703-321-8020

🌐 Internet address(es): telnet fed-world.gov then gateway to SBAI-BBS

🏛 Government agency acronym: SBA

"This BBS is for internal use by all Federal or State Government Employees or contractors working for the SBA."

ANNOTATION

If you do not belong to one of the above mentioned categories, you will be bumped off the system. I was. The contact information was omitted at the request of the contact.

TENNESSEE VALLEY AUTHORITY

Tennessee Valley Authority FTP Server

🌐 Internet address(es): ftp 152.85.3.3

Log on: Use anonymous as your I.D. and your E-mail address as your password.

🏛 Government agency acronym: TVA

👥 Contact person & title: Lee Workman

☎ Contact person's voice phone number: 615-751-2399

📠 Contact person's Fax phone number: 615-751-3163

✉ Mailing address: Tennessee Valley Authority, 150 W 11th Street, Chattanooga, TN 37402

DESCRIPTION

Provides information on river water levels, surplus equipment, blueprints, and graphic images.

ANNOTATION

TVA's ftp server is a "test and demonstration facility," says the opening welcome statement. There are some interesting files available through this server, but you will have to navigate the directories to find them and the "README" files are not much help. I downloaded a photograph of a dam and an out-of-date graphic from 1992 on the water quality of the Blue Ridge Dam area.

UNITED STATES AGENCY FOR INTERNATIONAL DEVELOPMENT

United States Agency for International Development

🖥 Acronym for online service: USAID Gopher

🌐 Internet address(es): Gopher gopher.info.usaid.gov

🏛 Government agency acronym: USAID

✉ Mailing address: United States Agency for International Development Agency, 320 Twenty-First St., NW, Washington, DC 20523

DESCRIPTION

"This is a new Gopher Server intended to facilitate the distribution of USAID information to the public. It is administered by the USAID Bureau for Management, Office of Information Resource Management (M/IRM), and is open to the general public at no charge. All material on this Gopher server is non-classified.

The U.S. Agency for International Development is the branch of the U.S. Government responsible for administering programs designed to promote broad-based economic growth, stabilize population growth, promote health, protect the environment, promote democracy, and provide humanitarian assistance—in the developing world.

You will find the following types of information on this Gopher server:

- Administrative information about USAID
- Information on USAID development efforts
- Congressional presentations
- USAID procurement and business resources
- USAID documents and publications
- Other development-related Internet resources."

USAID has a Listserv for distribution of its press releases. Send an E-mail message to "listproc@inof.usaid.gov" and in the message body include the following statement "sub usaid_press_release" and your full name.

UNITED STATES INFORMATION AGENCY

VOA Worldnet Server

🌐 Internet address(es): ftp ftp.voa.gov, Gopher gopher.voa.gov.

Log on: Use "anonymous" for user name and your E-mail address as your password.

🏛 Government agency acronym: USIA

👥 Contact person & title: Chris Kern

💻 Contact person's E-mail address: ck@voa.gov

✉ Mailing address: United States Information Agency-Worldnet, 301 Fourth Street, SW., Washington, DC 20547

"The Voice of America is the international broadcast service of the U.S. Information Agency. USIA was established in 1953 to carry out the overseas information and cultural exchange programs of the U.S. government. USIA maintains a global radio and television broadcast operation through its Bureau of Broadcasting. The Bureau includes the Voice of America, WORLDNET Television and Film Service, and the office of Cuba Broadcasting (Radio and TV Marti).

Some Information with a long 'shelf life,' such as VOA and Worldnet program schedules—but, significantly, not the VOA News and English Broadcasts newswire or VOA Internet Audio—is available by E-mail. Send an E-mail message with the contents "send index" to the address info@voa for instructions on how to retrieve information from the VOA/Worldnet server via E-mail."

Being a long-time fan of Voice of America English-language shortwave radio broadcasts, I was pleased to see that the VOA now provides online information as well.

Shortwave radio fans, request a copy of the schedules for broadcasts by electronic mail. An E-mail address directory for VOA is available in the radio/info directory. The file name for the directory is voa-worldnet-e-mail-addresses.

Arms Control and Disarmament Agency BBS

🖥 Acronym for online service: ACDA BBS

💻 Online service number(s): 202-736-4436

🏛 Government agency acronym: ACDA

👥 Contact person & title: Roberta Jackson

☎ Contact person's voice phone number: 202-736-4436

📠 Contact person's Fax phone number: 202-647-6928

✉ Mailing address: Arms Control and Disarmament Agency, 320 Twenty-First St., NW., Washington, DC 20451

DESCRIPTION

"The publications on this electronic bulletin board are prepared by the U.S. Arms Control and Disarmament Agency Public Information Office (ACDA/PI) to bring to your attention items of interest. They are not intended to substitute for newspapers, periodicals, and documents as a means of keeping informed about the meaning and impact of developments on arms control and non-proliferation matters. Further reproduction for private use or gain is subject to original copyright restrictions."

ANNOTATION

When I logged onto the ACDA BBS, the file ALLFILES.ZIP hadn't been updated in some time and it would not download. To obtain a full listing of the files available, set your software to capture what is displayed on the monitor. Next, use the search file-name using the wild card "*.*" command. This will result in all files being displayed and captured to file on your computer.

The following are typical of files you will find on the ACDA BBS:

NUCLEARW.TXT   12920   10-14-94
Signatories and Parties to the Treaty on Nonproliferation of Nuclear Weapons.

CSCINEUR.TXT   6327   10-13-94
Conference on Security and Cooperation In Europe.

CWSIG.TXT   4835   10-11-94
Chemical Weapons Convention Signatories/Parties.

MLDVANPT.TXT   1681   10-13-94
Moldova Accedes to the Non-Proliferation Treaty.

48SESSCC.TXT   1075   10-12-94
Forty-Eighth Session of the Standing Commission Opens in Geneva.

FYI.TXT   3382   10-13-94
Arms Control and Non-Proliferation Calendar.

UNITED STATES POSTAL SERVICE

Rapid Information BBS

🖥 Acronym for online service: RIBBS

💻 Online service number(s): 800-262-9541

🏛 Government agency acronym: USPS

👥 Contact person & title: Matt Linxwiler, SYSOP

☎ Contact person's voice phone number: 800-238-3150

✉ Mailing address: U.S. Postal Service, National Customer Support Center, 6060 Primacy Parkway, STE 101, Memphis, TN 38188-0001

DESCRIPTION

"The Rapid Information Bulletin Board System (RIBBS), developed by the U.S. Postal Service to address mailing questions and issues in an electronic medium, is an excellent informational source that allows postal customers and mailers to

- access postal information
- ask and receive answers to questions on products and services offered by the USPS
- better utilize the customer support offered by the USPS

RIBBS is open to the general public with special interest toward the mailing community. Individuals or mailing organizations needing additional information on postal programs, policies, or other information can use RIBBS to ask questions and receive answers from the USPS National Customer Support Center or other participating postal organizations. Users also can benefit by reading questions and answers left by other users and conference SYSOPs. File areas are also provided to allow distribution of various utilities and postal products."

ANNOTATION

RIBBS is a well-thought-out BBS. The often incomprehensible acronyms used by the U. S. Postal Services (USPS) and RIBBS are deciphered in the bulletin "Conference Descriptions." The structure of RIBBS is logical and easy to navigate. The well-written user's guide (RIBBUSER.TXT) will be useful to new users. However, the file descriptions are not as informative as they should be. The message section is also easy to use and offers off-line message reading. Messages posted on RIBBS get quick responses from the SYSOP or from other users.

PART

III

NONGOVERNMENT ONLINE SOURCES OF GOVERNMENT INFORMATION

Chapter 12
C-SPAN ONLINE

C-SPAN ONLINE

- Internet address(es): Gopher c-span.org

  AOL users can reach the C-SPAN area on America Online by using keyword: CSPAN

  X*CHANGE: Teachers and other Ingenious subscribers will find C-SPAN's schedules, lesson plans, and other data listed in the Cable in the Classroom services area.

  C-SPAN on Internet (To access, type: gopher c-span.org)

- E-mail addresses: The following are mail addresses viewers can use to reach C-SPAN via Internet or America Online.

  viewer@c-span.org (comments and questions)

  audio@c-span.org (comments and questions about audio networks)

  cspanprogm@aol.com (program suggestions)

  cspanviewr@aol.com (comments and questions about the networks)

  cspanguest@aol.com (questions to guests during call-in programs)

  cspanaudio@aol.com (comments and questions about audio networks)

  cspanbus@aol.com (comments and questions about the C-SPAN Bus)

  cspaneduc@aol.com (comments and questions to C-SPAN's Education

- ✉ Mailing address: C-SPAN, 400 N. Capitol St., NW, Washington, DC 20001

DESCRIPTION

"The cable television industry created C-SPAN (Cable-Satellite Public Affairs Network) in 1977 to provide live, gavel-to-gavel coverage of the U.S. House of Representatives. Since those early days of covering the House, C-SPAN has grown into a combination of networks that provide diverse public affairs programming 24 hours a day. The cable industry continues to carry and fund all of the C-SPAN networks as a public service for cable television viewers across America.

Throughout C-SPAN's development, the people behind the network have never strayed from its mission: to present an unedited, balanced view of government and public policy forums at work and to provide viewers with direct access to elected officials, decision-makers, and journalists.

Through our electronic services, computer users can:

- learn about C-SPAN, how the network was founded, and its relationship to the cable television industry;
- receive continually updated schedule information and background information on political events and issues the network covers;
- send questions and comments by mail to C-SPAN and communicate with other viewers about issues discussed on the network; and
- teachers can get information about C-SPAN in the Classroom and lesson plans for using the network's programming in their classrooms."

Chapter 13
FREE-NET

E-mail addresses: info@nptn.org

Voice phone number: 216-247-5800

Fax phone number: 216-247-3328

Mailing address: National Public
Telecomputing Network, P.O. Box
1987, Cleveland, OH 44106

DESCRIPTION

Imagine individuals joining together by volunteering to form organizations with the objective of providing free electronic access to local and national government and the Internet. Imagine the technical jargon of electronic bulletin board being replaced with words like city hall, library, medical center, soap box, and so on. Imagine these organizations starting up all over the United States and around the world. Imagine these organizations operating similarly to National Public Radio or National Public Television where financial support comes from contributions. Imagine no more, Free-Net is here. The reason that Free-Nets are included in *Government Online* is that they provide free access to government at the community, state, and national levels.

The history of Free-Net goes back to 1984 when Dr. Tom Grundner, then working at Case Western Reserve's Department of Family Medicine, set up a very simple BBS as means of distributing health information to the public. It was a success. Grundner expanded and enlarged the concept into a community-oriented BBS known as Free-Net. Grundner expanded the Free-Net concept by creating the National Public Telecomputing Network (NPTN) to function as a parent organization to the Free-Net organizations. Grundner's concept for integrating computers with communities works. Look for a Free-Net to open in your community soon. Better still, if your community doesn't have a Free-Net, start one. NPTN will show you how.

The Free-Net according to NPTN

"Community computers provide citizens with an inexpensive and rapid way to make contact with their elected representatives at the city, county, state, and national levels—contacts which include everything from obtaining information on governmental services to providing access to taxpayer-supported, governmentally produced databases. It should also be pointed out that these communications are not one way. Elected representatives and other officials also have the ability to electronically communicate with their constituents."

For information about Free-Nets in your state refer to the section of this book on State and Local Online Services.

FREE-NET ORGANIZING COMMITTEES AND AFFILIATES

Free-Net organizations are organized under a parent organization. The parent organization is National Public Telecomputing Network. Affiliate Systems (as existing Free-Nets are referred to) and Organizing Committees (future Free-Nets) are listed below.

(This list was originally obtained from NPTN and then verified by phone and E-mail.)

United States

Alabama

Organizing Committees

Tennessee Valley Free-Net—Huntsville
Billy Ray Wilson
Voice phone number: 205-544-3849

Mobile Free-Net—Mobile
Geoff Peacock
Voice phone number: 205-344-7243
E-mail: geoffp@netcom.com

Tuscaloosa Free-Net—Tuscaloosa
Dr. Ron Doctor
Voice phone number: 205-348-2398
E-mail: rdoctor@ua1vm.ua.edu

Alaska

Organizing Committees

AnchorNet—Anchorage
Peg Thompson
Voice phone number: 907-261-2891
E-mail: pegt@muskox.alaska.edu

FairNet—Fairbanks
Mark O. Badger
Voice phone number: 907-474-7508
E-mail: ffmob@aurora.alaska.edu

Arizona

Organizing Committees

AzTeC Computing—Tempe
Joseph A. Askins
Voice phone number: 602-965-5985
E-mail: joe.askins@asu.edu

Arkansas

Organizing Committees

Greater Pulaski County Free-Net—Little Rock
John Eichler
Voice phone number: 501-666-2222
E-mail: john.eichler@grapevine.lrk.ar.us

California

Affiliates

Los Angeles Free-Net—
Los Angeles
Avrum Z. Bluming, M.D.
>Voice phone number: 818-981-3818
>E-mail: ablumin@eis.calstate.edu

Modem: 818-776-5000

Internet: lafn.org
>Visitor login: Select #2 at first menu

Educational Affiliates

California Online Resources for
Education—Seal Beach
Keith Vogt
>Voice phone number: 1-800-272-8743
>E-mail: kvogt@eis.calstate.edu

Internet: eis.calstate.edu

Organizing Committees

Northern California Regional
Computing Network—Chico
Beverly Taylor
>Voice phone number: 916-898-4394
>E-mail: btaylor@macgate.csuchico.edu

Davis Free-Net—Davis
Ann Mansker
>Voice phone number: 916-752-7764
>E-mail: acmansker@ucdavis.edu

Sacramento Free-Net—
Sacramento
Cynthia Mulit
>Voice phone number: 916-484-6789
>E-mail: sacrapar@class.org

Silicon Valley Public Access
Link—San Jose
Marc Siegel
>Voice phone number: 408-448-3071
>E-mail: info@svpal.org

SLONET—San Luis Obispo
Phil Wagner
>Voice phone number: 805-544-7328
>E-mail: pwagner@oboe.calpoly.edu

Santa Barbara RAIN—Santa
Barbara
Timothy Tyndall
>Voice phone number: 805-967-7246
>E-mail: rain%engrhub@hub.ucsb.edu

Colorado

Affiliates

Denver Free-Net—Denver
Drew Mirque
>Voice phone number: 303-270-4300
>E-mail: drew@freenet.hsc.colorado.edu

Modem: 303-270-4865

Internet: freenet.hsc.colorado.edu
>Visitor login: guest

Connecticut

Organizing Committees

CPBI—Free-Net—Hartford
Alfred Steel
>Voice phone number: 203-278-5310
>ext 1230
>E-mail: steela@csusys.ctstateu.edu

Danbury Area Free-Net—Danbury

Diane Greenwald
   Voice phone number: 203-797-4512
   E-mail: dmg@pcnet.com

Florida

Affiliates

SEFLIN Free-Net— Broward County

Elizabeth Curry
   Voice phone number: 305-357-7318
   E-mail: currye@mail.seflin.lib.fl.us
Modem: 305-765-4332
Internet: bcfreenet.seflin.lib.fl.us
   Visitor login: visitor

Tallahassee Free-Net— Tallahassee

Hilbert Levitz
   Voice phone number: 904-644-1796
   E-mail: levitz@cs.fsu.edu
Modem: 904-488-5056
Internet: freenet.fsu.edu
   Visitor login: visitor

Organizing Committees

Alachua Free-Net—Gainesville

Bruce Brashear
   Voice phone number: 904-372-8401
   E-mail: 76314.352@compuserve.com

Miami Free-Net—Miami

Elizabeth Curry
   Voice phone number: 305-357-7318
   E-mail: currye@mail.seflin.lib.fl.us

Naples Free-Net—Naples

Dr. Melody Hainsworth
   Voice phone number: 1-800-466-8017
   E-mail: hainswm@firnvx.firn.edu

Orlando Free-Net—Orlando

C.A. Benoit
   Voice phone number: 407-833-9777
   E-mail: bruce@goliath.pbac.edu

Palm Beach Free-Net— Palm Beach

Elizabeth Curry
   Voice phone number: 305-357-7318
   E-mail: currye@mail.seflin.lib.fl.us

SMART—Sarasota

Sally Webb
   Voice phone number: 813-951-5502

MCNet—Stuart

Gretchen Hammerstein
   Voice phone number: 407-221-1410
   E-mail: hammerg@firnvx.firn.edu

Suncoast Free-Net—Tampa Bay

Marilyn Mulla
   Voice phone number: 813-273-3714
   E-mail: mullam@firnvx.firn.edu

Georgia

Organizing Committees

404 Free-Net—Atlanta

Mike Bernath
   E-mail: mike_bernath@solinet.net

Worth County-Sylvester Ga. Free-Net—Sylvester
Kent A. Guske
    Voice phone number: 912-776-8625
    E-mail: guske@freenet.fsu.edu

Hawaii

Organizing Committees

The Aloha Free-Net Project—Honolulu
Robert Mathews
    Voice phone number: 808-533-3969
    E-mail:
    mathews@gold.chem.hawaii.edu

Maui Free-Net—Maui
Donald Regalmuto
    Voice phone number: 808-572-0510
    E-mail: don.regal@tdp.org

Idaho

Organizing Committees

Sandpoint Free-Net—Sandpoint
Jason McMunn
    Voice phone number: 208-263-6105
    E-mail:
    mcmun911@crow.csru.uidaho.edu

Illinois

Affiliates

Prairienet—Champaign-Urbana
Ann P. Bishop
    Voice phone number: 217-244-1962
    E-mail: abishop@ uiuc.edu

Modem: 217-255-9000
Internet: prairienet.org (192.17.3.3)
    Visitor login: visitor

Educational Affiliates

Ameritech Extended Classroom—Chicago

Organizing Committees

Shawnee Free-Net—Carbondale
Robert A. Pauls
    Voice phone number: 618-549-1139
    E-mail:
    ad592@freenet.hsc.colorado.edu

SWIF-NET—Edgemont
Gary A. Ulery
    Voice phone number: 618-397-0968
    E-mail: gulery@minuet.siue.edu

Indiana

Educational Affiliates

Ameritech Extended Classroom—Indianapolis

Organizing Committees

Michiana Free-Net Society—Granger
Donald McLaughlin
    Voice phone number: 219-282-1574
    E-mail: dmclaugh@darwin.cc.nd.edu

Iowa

Organizing Committees

CedarNet—Cedar Falls
Robert Muffoletto
Voice phone number: 319-273-6282
E-mail: muffoletto@uni.edu

Iowa Knowledge Exchange—Des Moines
Gary Barrett
Voice phone number: 515-242-3556
E-mail: garyb@ins.infonet.net

Fairfield Free-Net—Fairfield
Steve Terry
Voice phone number: 515-472-7494
E-mail: sterry@ins.infonet.net

Kentucky

Organizing Committees

Pennyrile Area Free-Net—Hopkinsville
Mark Roseberry
Voice phone number: 502-886-2913
E-mail: mroseberry@delphi.com

On-Line Owensboro: The Western Kentucky Free-Net
Donna Treubig
Voice phone number: 502-686-4530
E-mail: donna@ndlc.occ.uky.edu

Louisiana

Organizing Committees

Baton Rouge Free-Net—Baton Rouge

Ann McMahon
Voice phone number: 504-346-0707
E-mail: anniemac@acm.org

Acadiana Free-Net—Lafayette
Bob Brantingham
Voice phone number: 318-837-9374
E-mail: bobbrant@delphi.com

Greater New Orleans Free-Net—New Orleans
Gordon H. Mueller
Voice phone number: 504-286-7187
E-mail: nrrmc@uno.edu

Maine

Organizing Committees

Maine Free-Net—Freeport
Elizabeth D. Frey
Voice phone number: 207-287-6615
E-mail: efrey@mmp.org

Maryland

Organizing Committees

Free State Free-Net—Baltimore
Andree Duggan
Voice phone number: 410-313-9259
E-mail: aduggan@well.sf.ca.us

Cheaspeake Free-Net—Easton
David M. Boan, Ph.D.
Voice phone number: 410-822-4132
E-mail: david_boan@martha.washcoll.edu

Garrett Communiversity Central—McHenry
Donald Storck
Voice phone number: 301-387-3035
E-mail: 71072.2304@compuserve.com

Massachusetts

Educational Affiliates

UMASSK12—Amherst, Massachusetts
Morton Sternheim
Voice phone number: 413-545-1908
E-mail: mms@k12.ucs.umass.edu
Modem: 413-572-5583 or 413-572-5268
Internet: k12.ucs.umass.edu
Visitor login: guest

Michigan

Affiliates

Great Lakes Free-Net—Battle Creek
Merritt W. Tumanis
Voice phone number: 616-961-4166
E-mail: merritt_tumanis@fc1.glfn.org
Modem: 616-969-4536
Visitor login: visitor

Educational Affiliates

Ameritech Extended Classroom—Detroit

Organizing Committees

Almont Expression—Almont
George Pratt
Voice phone number: 313-798-8171E
E-mail: gpratt@aol.com

Huron Valley Free-Net—Ann Arbor
Michael Todd Glazier
Voice phone number: 313-662-8374
E-mail: michael.todd.glazier@umich.edu

Greater Detroit Free-Net—Detroit
Paul Raine
Voice phone number: 810-574-8549
E-mail: info@detroit.freenet.org

Genesee Free-Net—Flint
David A. Cheslow
Voice phone number: 810-762-3309
E-mail: dcheslow@umich.edu

Grand Rapids Free-Net—Grand Rapids
Andrew Bass
Voice phone number: 616-459-6273
E-mail: andyb@bethany.org

Capitol City Free-Net—Lansing
Whitney M. Johnson
Voice phone number: 517-321-4972
E-mail: whit@jcn.com

Minnesota

Organizing Committees

Twin Cities Free-Net—Minneapolis
Scott Fritchie
Voice phone number: 507-646-3407
E-mail: fritchie@stolaf.edu

Northfield Free-Net—Northfield

Andrea Christianson
Voice phone number: 507-645-9301
E-mail: andreacris@aol.com

Mississippi

Organizing Committees

Meridian Area Free-Net—Meridian

Ric Rogers
Voice phone number: 601-482-2000
E-mail: ric4aardvark@delphi.com

Missouri

Affiliates

Columbia Online Information Network (COIN)—Columbia

Bill Mitchell
Voice phone number: 314-882-2000
E-mail: bill@more.net
Modem: 314-884-7000
Internet: bigcat.missouri.edu
Visitor login: guest

ORION—Springfield

Annie Linnemeyer
Voice phone number: 417-837-5050 ext 15
E-mail: annie@ozarks.sgcl.lib.mo.us
Modem: 417-864-6100
Internet: ozarks.sgcl.lib.mo.us
Visitor login: guest

Organizing Committees

Cape Girardeau Free-Net—Cape Girardeau

Larry Loos
Voice phone number: 314-334-9322
E-mail: LLoos@delphi.com

KC Free-Net—Kansas City

James E. Osbourn
Voice phone number: 816-340-4228
E-mail: josbourn@tyrell.net

Montana

Affiliates

Big Sky Telegraph—Dillon

Frank Odasz
Voice phone number: 406-683-7338
E-mail: franko@bigsky.dillon.mt.us
Modem: 406-683-7680
Internet: 192.231.192.1
Visitor login: bbs

Nebraska

Organizing Committees

Omaha Free-Net—Omaha

Howard Lowe
Voice phone number: 402-554-2516
E-mail: lowe@unomaha.edu

New Hampshire

Organizing Committees

The Granite State Oracle— Manchester
Quentin Lewis
   Voice phone number: 508-442-0279
   E-mail: quentin.lewis@sun.com

New Mexico

Organizing Committees

Santa Fe Metaverse—Santa Fe
John R. Grizz Deal
   Voice phone number: 505-989-7117
   E-mail: grizz@lanl.gov

New York

Affiliates

Buffalo Free-Net—Buffalo
James Finamore
   Voice phone number: 716-871-8855
   E-mail: finamore@ubvms.cc.buffalo.edu
   Modem: 716-645-3085
   Internet: freenet.buffalo.edu
   Visitor login: freeport

Organizing Committees

Capital Region Information Service—Albany
Norman D. Kurland
   Voice phone number: 518-442-3728
   E-mail: nkurland@albnyvms.bitnet

Southern Tier Free-Net— Endicott
Scott Cubic
   Voice phone number: 607-752-1201
   E-mail: cubicsr@vnet.ibm.com

Rochester Free-Net—Rochester
Jerry Seward
   Voice phone number: 716-594-0943
   E-mail: jerry@rochgte.fidonet.org

North Carolina

Organizing Committees

Triangle Free-Net—Chapel Hill
William R. Hutchins or
Judy Hallmann
   Voice phone number: 919-962-9107
   E-mail: hallman@gibbs.oit.unc.edu

Charlotte's Web—Charlotte
Stephen H. Snow
   Voice phone number: 704-358-5245
   E-mail: shsnow@vnet.net

Forsyth County Free-Net— Winston-Salem
John Annen
   Voice phone number: 919-727-2597
   ext 3023
   E-mail:
   annen@ledger.mis.co.forsyth.nc.us

North Dakota

Educational Affiliates

SENDIT—Fargo
Gleason Sackman
Voice phone number: 701-237-8109
E-mail: sackman@sendit.nodak.edu
Modem: 701-237-3283
Internet: sendit.nodak.edu
Visitor login: bbs (password: sendit2me)

Ohio

Affiliates

Tristate Online—Cincinnati
Michael King—TSO System
Administrator
Voice phone number: 513-397-1396
E-mail: sysadmin@cbos.uc.edu
Modem: 513-579-1990
Internet: tso.uc.edu
Visitor login: visitor

Cleveland Free-Net—Cleveland
Jeff Gumpf
Voice phone number: 216-368-2982
E-mail: jag@po.cwru.edu
Modem: 216-368-3888
Internet: freenet-in-a.cwru.edu
Visitor login: Select #2 at first menu

Greater Columbus Free-Net—Columbus
Steven I. Gordon
Voice phone number: 614-292-4132
E-mail: sgordon@freenet.columbus.oh.us
Modem: 614-292-7501
Internet: freenet.columbus.oh.us
Visitor login: guest

Dayton Free-Net—Dayton
Patricia Vendt
Voice phone number: 513-873-4035
E-mail: pvendt@desire.wright.edu
Modem: 513-229-4373
Internet: 130.108.128.174
Visitor login: visitor

Lorain County Free-Net—Elyria
Thom Gould
Voice phone number: 1-800-227-7113
ext. 2451 or 216-277-2451
E-mail: aa003@freenet.lorain.oberlin.edu
Modem: 216-366-9721
Internet: freenet.lorain.oberlin.edu
Visitor login: guest

Medina County Free-Net—Medina
Gary Linden—(Medina Gen. Hosp.)
Project Director
Voice phone number: 216-725-1000 ext 2550
E-mail: aa001@medina.freenet.edu
Modem: 216-723-6732
Internet: [Not receiving connections at this time]
Visitor login: visitor

Youngstown Free-Net—Youngstown
Lou Anschuetz
Voice phone number: 216-742-3075
E-mail: lou@yfn.ysu.edu
Modem: 216-742-3072
Internet: yfn2.ysu.edu
Visitor login: visitor

Educational Affiliates

SEORF—Athens

Damien O. Bawn
Voice phone number: 614-662-3211
E-mail: bawn@oucsace.cs.ohiou.edu
Internet: seorf.ohiou.edu
Visitor login: "guest"

Learning Village Cleveland—Cleveland

John Kurilec
Voice phone number: 216-247-5800
E-mail: jmk@nptn.org
Modem: 216-247-6196
Internet: nptn.org
Visitor login: visitor

Organizing Committees

Akron Regional Free-Net—Akron

Anne S. McFarland
Voice phone number: 216-972-6352
E-mail: r1asm@vm1.cc.uakron.edu

Canton Regional Free-Net—Canton

Maureen Kilcullen
Voice phone number: 216-499-9600 ext 322
E-mail: mkilcullen@ksuvxm.kent.edu

Lima Free-Net—Lima

Paul Monas
Voice phone number: 419-226-1218
E-mail: monus@clipo1.usachem.msnet.bp.com

Richland Free-Net—Mansfield

Ed Rebmann
Voice phone number: 419-521-3111/3110
E-mail: earmrcpl@class.org

Toledo Free-Net—Toledo

Rebecca Dent
Voice phone number: 419-537-3686
E-mail: rad@uoft02.utoledo.edu

Oklahoma

Organizing Committees

Oklahoma Public Information Network—Oklahoma City

David Drexler
Voice phone number: 405-947-8868
E-mail: fn-mail@okcforum.osrhe.edu

Ponca City/Pioneer Free-Net—Ponca City

Phil Abernathy
Voice phone number: 405-767-3461
E-mail: philber106@aol.com

Pennsylvania

Organizing Committees

Lehigh Valley Free-Net—Bethlehem

Timothy Lindgren
Voice phone number: 610-758-4998
E-mail: tpl2@lehigh.edu

Three Rivers Free-Net—Pittsburgh

Dan Iddings
> Voice phone number: 412-622-6502
> E-mail: iddings@clp2.clpgh.org

Chester County Free-Net—West Chester

Jordan Seidel
> Voice phone number: 610-431-2673
> E-mail: jseidel@locke.ccil.org

Rhode Island

Affiliates

Ocean State Free-Net—Providence

Howard Boksenbaum
> Voice phone number: 401-277-2726
> E-mail: howardbm@dsl.rhilinet.gov
> Modem: 401-831-4640
> Internet: 192.207.24.10

South Carolina

Organizing Committees

MidNet—Columbia

Stephen Bajjaly
> Voice phone number: 803-777-4825
> E-mail:
> bajjaly@univscvm.csd.scarolina.edu

Greenet—Greenville

Thompson R. Cummins
> Voice phone number: 803-242-5000 ext 231
> E-mail: sgr002@sol.solinet.net

GRINet—Greenwood

Kim Madden
> Voice phone number: 803-223-8431

Tennessee

Organizing Committees

Jackson Area Free-Net—Jackson

Donald Lewis
> Voice phone number: 901-425-2640
> E-mail: dlewis@jscc.cc.tn.us

Texas

Affiliates

Rio Grande Free-Net—El Paso

Don Furth
> Voice phone number: 915-775-6077
> E-mail: donf@laguna.epcc.edu
> Modem: 915-775-5600
> Internet: rgfn.epcc.edu
> Visitor login: visitor

Organizing Committees

Big Country Free-Net—Abilene

J. David Bavousett
> Voice phone number: 915-674-6964
> E-mail: davidb@alcon.acu.edu

Austin Free-Net—Austin

Jeff Evans
> Voice phone number: 512-288-5691
> E-mail: jeff_evans@capmac.org

North Texas Free-Net—Dallas
Ken Loss-Cutler
> Voice phone number: 214-942-2003
> E-mail: kenlc@tenet.edu

Tarrant County Free-Net—Fort Worth
Joseph Coles
> Voice phone number: 817-763-8437
> E-mail: jcoles@pubcon.com

Houston Civnet—Houston
Paul Hutmacher
> Voice phone number: 713-869-0521
> E-mail: paul@sugar.neosoft.com

West Texas Free-Net—San Angelo
Timothy R. Elwell
> Voice phone number: 915-655-7161
> E-mail: timelwell@delphi.com

San Antonio Free-Net—San Antonio
Michael S. Lotas
> Voice phone number: 210-561-9815
> E-mail: mlotas@espsun.space.swri.edu

Vermont

Organizing Committees

Lamoille Net—Morrisville
Balu Raman
> Voice phone number: 802-888-2606
> E-mail: braman@world.std.com

Virginia

Educational Affiliates

VaPEN—Richmond
Dr. Harold Cothern
> Voice phone number: 804-225-2921
> E-mail:
> hcothern@vdoe386.vak12ed.edu
> Internet: vdoe386.vak12ed.edu

Organizing Committees

Central Virginia's Free-Net—Richmond
Kenneth Guyre
> Voice phone number: 804-828-6650
> E-mail: kguyre@cabell.vcu.edu

Blue Ridge Free-Net—Roanoke
Cynthia Obrist
> Voice phone number: 703-981-1424
> E-mail: obrist@leo.vsla.edu

Washington

Affiliates

Seattle Community Network—Seattle
Randy Groves
> Voice phone number: 206-865-3424
> E-mail: randy@cpsr.org
> Modem: 206-386-4140
> Internet: scn.org
> Visitor login: visitor

Tri-Cities Free-Net—Tri-Cities

Bruce McComb

> Voice phone number: 509-586-6481
> E-mail: tcfn@delphi.com
> Modem: 509-375-1111

Organizing Committees

Kitsap Free-Net—Bremerton

Michael Schuyler

> Voice phone number: 206-405-9139
> E-mail: michael@kitsap.lib.wa.us

Inland Northwest Community Network—Spokane

Dr. Karen L. Michaelson

> Voice phone number: 509-359-6567
> E-mail: kmichaelson@ewu.edu

Clark County Free-Net—Vancouver

Thomas E. Ryan

> Voice phone number: 206-696-6846
> E-mail: tryan@netcom.com

Wisconsin

Educational Affiliates

Ameritech Extended Classroom—Milwaukee, Wisconsin

Organizing Committees

Cippewa Valley Free-Net—Eau Claire

Steve Marquardt

> Voice phone number: 715-836-3715
> E-mail: smarquar@uwec.edu

Chapter 14
PROJECT VOTE SMART

⌨N Acronym for online service: PVS

💻) Online service number(s): 503-737-3777 for BBS

Log on: BBS uses standard log on.

🌐 Internet address(es): Gopher gopher.neu.edu

👥 Contact person & title: Richard Kimball, president. (For online services contact Mike Krejci)

💻← Contact person's E-mail address: pvs.@neu.edu

☎ Contact person's voice phone number: Voter's Research Hotline 800-622-SMART, main office 503-754-2747

🖨 Contact person's Fax phone number: 503-754-2747

✉ Mailing address: Project Vote Smart, 129 NW 4th St., #204, Corvalis, OR 97330

DESCRIPTION

"Project Vote Smart is a national, nonpartisan organization that focuses on providing citizens with the most essential tool to members of a successful democracy: factual, unbiased information that is unfiltered by candidates and their campaigns. In recent years technology has been used to manipulate voters by confusing and distorting issue positions, sources of funding, and qualifications for office.... Project Vote Smart offers a Voter's Self-Defense System, available free and instantly."

ANNOTATION

Project Vote Smart is one of my favorite online services dealing with the government. Their honorary cofounders were Jimmy Carter and Gerald Ford. Nearly every name on their founders list was familiar to me, but reading that only convinced me that they had credibility. It was the act of actually looking at their files on the voting records of politicians running for office that convinced me that I was using an especially valuable and worthwhile resource.

Project Vote Smart provides information on candidates in the following areas:

• their voting records in over 20 key issues
• their past campaign position statements
• over 70 conservative to liberal organizations that have rated their performance
• who has paid for their campaigns
• their telephone numbers and mailing addresses

- biographical details of their service
- and more

They also provide two free manuals on request, the *Voter's Self-Defense Manual* and the *U.S. Government Owner's Manual*. Reporters can also obtain their *Reporter's Source Book*, which provides accuracy checks on candidate claims. And, teachers can obtain teaching materials, educational videotapes, and campaign games from Project Vote Smart.

My only criticism of Project Vote Smart concerns their electronic delivery of infor- mation. The structure of their Gopher was not as intuitive to use as it should be. Additionally, I would have liked to read more about Project Vote Smart online. I would have liked to have access to a guide to their online services. These criticisms are trivial considering the amount of work that went into compiling the data available.

If you vote and don't make use of Project Vote Smart's resources, you are voting with- out the benefit of full knowledge of the can- didates.

Chapter 15

UNIVERSITY OF CALIFORNIA AT IRVINE UNITED STATES GOVERNMENT GOPHERS

UNITED STATES GOVERNMENT GOPHERS

⊕   Internet addresse(s):

Type=1
Name=United States GOVERNMENT Gophers

Path=1/gopher.welcome/peg/GOPHERS/gov

Host=peg.cwis.uci.edu

Port=7000

URL:
gopher://peg.cwis.uci.edu:7000/11/gopher.w
elcome/peg/GOPHERS/gov

👥   Contact person Calvin J. Boyer

DESCRIPTION

Calvin J. Boyer has assembled a Gopher of U.S. Government gophers at the University of California at Irvine, Calif. Boyer's work enables users to easily locate and use U.S. Government gophers. Boyer says, "As far as we are aware, this gathering of U.S. Government Gopher servers is the most comprehensive yet available, and the quality of the file is of some measure due to those who bring to our attention new gophers, changed locations, etc."

ANNOTATION

Add this Gopher to your list of regularly visited gophers, and you will have the U.S. Government at your fingertips. Boyer's Gopher will save you time and money, especially if you are paying for Internet access by the minute.

PART

IV

STATE AND LOCAL
ONLINE SERVICES

Chapter 16

GOVERNMENT ONLINE SOURCES OF GOVERNMENT INFORMATION

The following is a list of state-, county-, city-, and community- government-related online services. The list is organized alphabetically by state, city, and by online service name. Only states with online services are listed. Free-Net online services are included because they have direct or indirect communication channels to local governments. Some of the Free-Nets listed did not have online service numbers when *Government Online* went to press. To find an online service number missing from a list, call or write to the contact person associated with the online service.

ALASKA (AK)

State Online Services
Alaska Legislative Information

🌐 Internet addresses: WWW gopher://info.alaska.edu:70/11/UA/Statewide/URelations/Leg/, gopher info.alaska.edu

DESCRIPTION

The information provided includes:
- House Roster
- Senate Roster
- Senate Bills
- Committee Hearings
- Teleconference Schedule
- Committee Assignments
- Election Information

ANNOTATION

This Gopher is provided by the University of Alaska. Finding the legislative information through their Gopher is more difficult than through the WWW server.

ARIZONA (AZ)

City Online Services

Tempe

AzTeC Computing

💻 Online service number(s): 602-965-4151

Log on: Use "guest" as your I.D. and "visitor" as your password

🌐 Internet addresses: telnet aztec.asu.edu.

👥 Contact person: Joseph A. Askins

💻 Contact person's E-mail address: joe.askins@asu.edu

☎ Contact person's voice phone number: 602-965-5985

✉ Mailing address: AzTeC Computing, P.O. Box 870201, Tempe, AZ 85287-0201

DESCRIPTION

"Arizona Telecommunication Community (AzTeC) Computing is Free-Net registered as an Operating Affiliate of the National Public Telecomputing Network (NPTN) for the Phoenix Metro area, but eventually planned to somehow service all of Arizona."

ANNOTATION

AzTeC is looking for volunteers to help them expand their coverage to all of Arizona.

Tucson

City of Tucson Information

🌐 Internet address: WWWgopher://econ.tucson.az.us:70/11/govpol/Tucson/mc, Gopher econ.tucson.az.us.

DESCRIPTION

This Gopher contains the following government-related sections:
• Who Are Your Elected Officials?
• Schedule of Mayor and Council Meetings
• Public Participation at the Meetings

ANNOTATION

By the time you read this, there may be other Arizona government-related sections available at this Gopher site.

CALIFORNIA (CA)

State Online Services

California Department of Fish and Game Home Page

🌐 Internet address: http://spock.dfg.ca.gov/

💻 Contact person's E-mail address: webmaster@spock.dfg.ca.gov

California Department of Fish and Game Home Page "...is part of the CERES project, an effort to provide information to all who are interested in California's larger environmental picture."

Among the resources available are:

• a mission statement
• DFG Organizational structure page
• Frequently Asked Questions

California Department of General Services Home Page

Internet address:
http://ois.dgs.ca.gov/dgs.html

California Department of General Services Home Page is a pathway to the California State Contracts Register.

There were no explanations available for what one is supposed to do with the data provided. The data displayed in the California State Contracts Register appears to be requests for bids.

California State Government (CSGnet) Home Page

Internet address: http://www.ca.gov

"The CSGnet Home Page leads to many Internet accessible applications. Although this is a home page for the California State Government, there are links to some other places of interest. This page is divided into the following sections:

I.   Special Interests
II. State of California Departments
     A. World Wide Webs 'WWW'
     B. Gopher Servers
     C. File Transfer Protocol 'FTP'
III. United States Federal Government
IV. California Local Governments
V.   Other Places of Interest"

This is *the* home page to explore if your are seeking information about California State Government. If you are interested in California local government information, move down the screen to "Other Places of Interest" then select "California Virtual Tourist WWW Server." The next menu you will see lists several pages of California WWW servers.

California State Senate Home Page

Internet address: WWW
http://www.sen.ca.gov/ Gopher
gopher.sen.ca.gov

Provides legislative information about the California State Senate including:
• Senate Bill Searching Tool
• Legislative Schedules
• Senator Finding Tool

The Gopher server has a greater variety of resources than the WWW server.

Governor's Office of Emergency Services

🌐 Internet address:
http://www.oes.ca.gov:8001/

👥 Contact person: Art Botterell

💻 Contact person's E-mail address:
acb@oes.ca.gov

DESCRIPTION

"The Governor's Office of Emergency Services (OES) coordinates overall state agency response to major disasters in support of local government."

ANNOTATION

OES's home page has an audio welcome message and photographs by Robert A. Eplett. However, the valuable content is in the OES Fact Sheet section.

City Online Services

Antioch

City of Antioch WWW Page

🌐 Internet address: http://solano.community.net/community/coco/government/Antioch.html

DESCRIPTION

Antioch's WWW page is a name and address directory of city government.

ANNOTATION

The information found here is a text document.

Berkeley

inBerkeley: City of Berkeley Home Page

🌐 Internet address:
http://www.ci.berkeley.ca.us/

👥 Contact person: Malcolm Humes

💻 Contact person's E-mail address:
mah2@ci.berkeley.ca.us

DESCRIPTION

inBerkeley's home page provides the following options:
• Internet E-mail addresses for city officials and departments
• Berkeley libraries
• Berkeley businesses and organizations
• Information about the city of Berkeley

ANNOTATION

In addition to the above options there are links to other Federal and California WWW servers.

Brentwood

City of Brentwood WWW Page

🌐 Internet address: http://solano.community.net/community/coco/government/Brentwood.html

DESCRIPTION

The City of Brentwood WWW page is a name and address directory of city government.

ANNOTATION

The information found here is a text document.

Brisbane

Brisbane Index WWW Page

🌐 Internet address:
http://tcomeng.com/cities/brisbane/index.html

👥 Contact person: Lee Panza

💻 Contact person's E-mail address:
panza@tcomeng.com

DESCRIPTION

The City of Brisbane WWW page is a name and address directory of city government.

ANNOTATION

This server is, according to Lee Panza, a demonstration project. However, it does provide access to useful local government information.

Carlsbad

Carlsbad California USA Home Page

🌐 Internet address: http://www.bluebird.com/carlsbad/

💻 Contact person's E-mail address: webmaster@bluebird.com

DESCRIPTION

The City of Carlsbad WWW page contents include:
• Background
• Local Information
• Places to Go
• City Government
• Neighbors

ANNOTATION

The City of Carlsbad WWW server is provided by a commercial service.

Clayton

City of Clayton WWW Page

🌐 Internet address: http://solano.community.net/community/coco/government/Clayton.html

DESCRIPTION

The City of Clayton's WWW page is a name and address directory of city government.

ANNOTATION

The information found here is a text document.

Concord

City of Concord WWW Page

🌐 Internet address: http://solano.community.net/community/coco/government/Concord.html

The City of Concord's WWW page is a name and address directory of city government.

The information found here is a text document.

Danville

Town of Danville WWW Page

🌐 Internet address: http://solano.community.net/community/coco/government/Danville.html

The Town of Danville's WWW page is a name and address directory of city government.

The information found here is a text document.

El Cerrito

City of El Cerrito WWW Page

🌐 Internet address: http://solano.community.net/community/coco/government/El_Cerrito.html

The City of El Cerrito's WWW page is a name and address directory of city government.

The information found here is a text document.

Hercules

City of Hercules WWW Page

🌐 Internet address: http://solano.community.net/community/coco/government/Hercules.html

The City of Hercules's WWW page is a name and address directory of city government.

The information found here is a text document.

Lafayette

City of Lafayette WWW Page

🌐 Internet address: http://solano.community.net/community/coco/government/Lafayette.html

The City of Lafayette's WWW page is a name and address directory of city government.

The information found here is a text document.

Los Angeles

Los Angeles Free-Net

💻) Online service number(s): 818-776-5000

Log on: Select Mailing address: 2 at first menu

🌐 Internet addresses: telnet lafn.org

👥 Contact person: Avrum Z. Bluming, M.D.

💻← Contact person's E-mail address: ablumin@eis.calstate.edu

☎ Contact person's voice phone number: 818-954-0080

✉ Mailing address: Los Angeles Free-Net Office (Mail only), 16161 Ventura Blvd. #597, Encino, CA 91436

DESCRIPTION

The Los Angeles Free-Net provides the usual Free-Net services and much more. It is larger than most other Free-Nets and has many areas to explore.

ANNOTATION

See Free-Net description.

Martinez

City of Martinez WWW Page

🌐 Internet address: http://solano.community.net/community/coco/government/Martinez.html

DESCRIPTION

The City of Martinez's WWW page is a name and address directory of city government.

ANNOTATION

The information found here is a text document.

Moraga

Town of Moraga WWW Page

🌐 Internet address: http://solano.community.net/community/coco/government/Moraga.html

DESCRIPTION

The Town of Moraga's WWW page is a name and address directory of city government.

ANNOTATION

The information found here is a text document.

Mountain View

Silicon Valley Public Access Link

🌐 Internet addresses: telnet svpal.org

☎ Contact person's voice phone number: 415-967-2873

✉ Mailing address: SV-PAL, 505 East Evelyn Avenue, Sunnyvale, CA 94041

DESCRIPTION

"SV-PAL provides full access to the existing information highway, the Internet, as well as access to information on local community activities. We do not support SLIP or PPP or Mosaic. SV-PAL is a nonprofit organization staffed by over 70 volunteers, including persons from major companies in the Santa Clara valley. SV-PAL is dedicated to making the world's information resources accessible to all citizens regardless of financial status and educational level. SV-PAL provides E-mail, bulletin board and Internet services and training for its members. This network provides immediate access to all realms of knowledge from literature, the arts and sciences, and current news and stock prices. Local information available will include nonprofit social services, local politics, business services, and other information of interest to the citizens of the Silicon Valley.

SV-PAL MISSION & VISION
- Provide Affordable Communications to the Community;
- Outreach & Training for Participation At All Income Levels, Particularly To Those Who Are Not Being Served Today;
- Provide Access To & For The Government At All Levels;
- Provide Access To The World's Information Resources;
- Provide Local Content & Access To Outside Information Providers.

SYSTEM AVAILABILITY
- 24 Hour access 7 Days/Week with no hourly charge from home users. In the future, public access terminals, in libraries and elsewhere.

SV-PAL SERVICES
- Local Menu Driven Information, Chat, Internet News (USENET), World Wide Web, Gopher, Veronica, Jughead, FTP, Archie, and telnet.

SV-PAL FEATURES
- Local, State, Federal Government Postings, Education Resources, Community Resources,
- Business Resources, Locally Managed &
- Operated, Focused on Local Community Content."

ANNOTATION

Like many other community online services SV-PAL was just getting started when I first logged on. By the time you read this many of the proposed services may be operational.

Orinda

City of Orinda WWW Page

Internet address: http://solano.community.net/community/coco/government/Orinda.html

DESCRIPTION

The City of Orinda's WWW page is a name and address directory of city government.

ANNOTATION

The information found here is a text document.

Pinole

City of Pinole WWW Page

Internet address: http://solano.community.net/community/coco/government/Pinole.html

DESCRIPTION

The City of Pinole's WWW page is a name and address directory of city government.

ANNOTATION

The information found here is a text document.

Pittsburg

City of Pittsburg WWW Page

🌐 Internet address: http://solano.community.net/community/coco/government/Pittsburg.html

DESCRIPTION

The City of Pittsburg's WWW page is a name and address directory of city government.

ANNOTATION

The information found here is a text document.

Pleasant Hill

City of Pleasant Hill WWW Page

🌐 Internet address: http://solano.community.net/community/coco/government/Pleasant_Hill.html

DESCRIPTION

The City of Pleasant Hill's WWW page is a name and address directory of city government.

ANNOTATION

The information found here is a text document.

Richmond

City of Richmond WWW Page

🌐 Internet address: http://solano.community.net/community/coco/government/Richmond.html

DESCRIPTION

The City of Richmond's WWW page is a name and address directory of city government.

ANNOTATION

The information found here is a text document.

San Jose

Silicon Valley Public Access Link (SV-PAL)

💻 Online service number(s): 408-366-0160

Log on: Log on as "guest"

🌐 Internet addresses: telnet, ftp, www, Gopher to svpal.org.

👥 Contact person: Marc Siegel

💻 Contact person's e-mail address: info@svpal.org

☎ Contact person's voice phone number: 408-448-3071

📠 Contact person's Fax phone number: 408-448-3073

✉ Mailing address: Silicon Valley Public Access Link (SV-PAL), 1777 Hamilton Ave., Suite 208A, San Jose, CA 95125

DESCRIPTION

"We are a community network and focus on helping people and organizations get on-line. Low cost access ($40/year for accounts, $150/year for information providers. Nonprofit, volunteer driven, member supported."

ANNOTATION

See Free-Net description.

San Luis Obispo

SLONET

💻) Online service number(s): 805-781-3666

Log on: Use "sloguest" as your ID and "slonet1" as your password

👥 Contact person: Phil Wagner

💻← Contact person's E-mail address: slonet@slonet.org

☎ Contact person's voice phone number: 805-545-5002

✉ Mailing address: SLONET, P.O. Box 15818, San Luis Obispo, CA 93406-5818

DESCRIPTION

"SLONET is a community information access system for the region (San Luis Obispo and northern Santa Barbara Counties). Information providers include government, nonprofits, and other organizations. All 'local' information is free to all users. Subscription services include Internet access for $10/month."

ANNOTATION

See Free-Net description.

San Pablo

City of San Pablo WWW Page

🌐 Internet address: http://solano.community.net/community/coco/government/San_Pablo.html

DESCRIPTION

The City of San Pablo's WWW page is a name and address directory of city government.

ANNOTATION

The information found here is a text document.

San Ramon

City of San Ramon WWW Page

🌐 Internet address: http://solano.community.net/community/coco/government/San_Ramon.html

DESCRIPTION

The City of San Ramon's WWW page is a name and address directory of city government.

ANNOTATION

The information found here is a text document.

Walnut Creek

City of Walnut Creek WWW Page

🌐 Internet address: http://solano.community.net/community/coco/government/Walnut_Creek.html

DESCRIPTION

The City of Walnut Creek's WWW page is a name and address directory of city government.

ANNOTATION

The information found here is a text document.

COLORADO (CO)

City Online Services

Denver

Denver Free-Net

🖥) Online service number(s): 303-270-4865

Log on: Visitors should log on as "guest"

🌐 Internet addresses: freenet.hsc.colorado.edu

👥 Contact person: Drew Mirque

💻 Contact person's E-mail address: drew@freenet.hsc.colorado.edu

☎ Contact person's voice phone number: 303-270-4300

DESCRIPTION

MISSION: "To promote the concept of community computing
  GOALS:
  1. To assist in the development of an information infrastructure within the state of Colorado.
  2. To provide citizens in the Denver metro area with free and open access to community information resources.
  3. To facilitate dissemination of information, particularly in the health and human services areas, to citizens of Colorado.
  4. To promote the use of an electronic medium for information exchange and communication.
  5. To provide access to a various electronic databases from a variety of institutions on a local, national, and international level."

ANNOTATION

See Free-Net description.

FLORIDA (FL)

State Online Services

Florida FishLINE

🏠 Parent organization: Florida Division of Fisheries

Government agency: Florida Game & Freshwater Fish Commission

🖥N Acronym for online service: GFC

🖥) Online service number(s) 904-488-3773

👥 Contact person & title: Scott Hardin

☎ Contact person's voice phone number: 904-488-4066

📠 Contact person's Fax phone number: 904-488-6988

✉ Mailing address: Florida Game & Fresh Water Fish Commission, 620 South Meridian St., Tallahassee, FL 32399-1600

"A BBS for anyone interested in fresh water fish, fisheries, and fishing. Some information is provided on the Division of Fisheries activities, along with user input on fishing areas, techniques, etc. There are file areas and message areas. This BBS contains information on freshwater fishing information—not saltwater."

Florida FishLINE was not operational when I attempted to log on.

County Online Services

Broward County

SEFLIN Free-Net

🖥) Online service number(s): 305-765-4332

Log on: Visitors should log on as "visitor"

🌐 Internet addresses: bcfreenet.seflin.lib.fl.us

👥 Contact person: Elizabeth Curry

💻 Contact person's E-mail address: currye@mail.seflin.lib.fl.us

☎ Contact person's voice phone number: 305-357-7318

📠 Contact person's Fax phone number: 305-357-6998

✉ Mailing address: SEFLIN Free-Net,

Registration Office, 100 South Andrews Avenue, Ft. Lauderdale, FL 33301

SEFLIN is the Southeast Florida Library Information Network which is a nonprofit membership organization founded in 1984 to promote cooperation, resource sharing, and innovation in libraries in Broward County, Palm Beach County and Dade County.

The Free-Net is our current project to extend access to information to the broadest possible community. The Broward County Public Library is an active partner in this pilot project, which we envision will grow to include Palm Beach and Dade County after testing.

See Free-Net description.

City Online Services

Tallahassee

Tallahassee Free-Net

🖥) Online service number(s): 904-488-5056

Log on: Visitors should log on as "visitor"

🌐 Internet addresses: telnet freenet.fsu.edu

👥 Contact person: Diane Wood

💻 Contact person's E-mail address: wood@scri.fsu.edu

☎ Contact person's voice phone number: 904-644-1010

✉ Mailing address: Supercomputer Computations Research Institute,

Florida State University, Tallahassee, FL 32306

DESCRIPTION

Free Public access community information system.

ANNOTATION

See Free-Net description.

HAWAII (HI)

State Online Services

Hawaii FYI

Parent organization: Department of Budget and Finance

Government agency: Information and Communication Services Division

Online service number(s): 808-536-7133

Government agency acronym: ISCD

Contact person & title: Al Fu, Hawaii FYI Coordinator

Contact person's voice phone number: 808-586-1940

Contact person's Fax phone number: 808-586-2337

Mailing address: Department of Budget and Finance, Information and Communication Services Division, 1151 Punchbowl Street, Room B-20, Honolulu, HI 96813

DESCRIPTION

"Hawaii FYI is an electronic gateway to more than 80 information services residing on a variety of platforms. Information services in ASCII and/or NAPLPS (graphics). NAPLPS requires the viewer to have special emulation software. Most services are free; some are fee-based. Set communication software to 8 data bits, no parity, 1 stop bit. Modem speeds: 1200/2400/9600 baud."

ANNOTATION

The following areas of Hawaii FYI are specifically government oriented:

- Boards and Commissions.
- Campaign Spending Data.
- Capitol Directory.
- Consumer Dial—"Consumer Dial is a service of the State Department of Commercet and Consumer Affairs (DCCA). It provides consumer tips on a wide range of products."
- Department of Labor and Industrial Relations—"Provides information on labor laws, helpful phone numbers and job tips."
- Government Forums 1994—"Ask the 1994 candidates for Governor of the State of Hawaii and Mayor of Honolulu your questions…"
- Honolulu City Council Information
- Legislative Information Service—"Allows users to access information on the legislative process and documents: bills, resolutions, committee reports and hearing notices."
- State Department of Business and Economic Development.

"The DBED BBS provides up-to-date data on Hawaii's economy including the State of Hawaii Data Book."

Annual Report—"Synopsis of the State's Department of Business and Economic Development and Tourism 1989 Annual Report."

After transacting your government business on Hawaii FYI, look up a good place to eat on one of the Hawaiian Islands. Search the Honolulu Magazine Annual List or the Hawaii Restaurant Guide. I recommend People's Cafe for real Hawaiian food and almost any cafe serving saimin.

ILLINOIS (IL)

City Online Services

Champaign-Urbana

Prairienet

💻) Online service number(s): 217-255-9000, 217-255-9033 if using a high speed modem.

Log on: Visitors should log on as "visitor"

🌐 Internet addresses: prairienet.org or 192.17.3.3

👥 Contact person: Ann P. Bishop

💻← Contact person's E-mail address: abishop@uiuc.edu

☎ Contact person's voice phone number: 217-244-1962

✉ Mailing address: Graduate School of Library and Information Science, University of Illinois, LIS Building, 501 East Daniel St., Champaign, IL 61820

Provides online guides to networked information by and about the Federal government. Local city governments post contact information and descriptions of various municipal services. County government posts meeting agendas and minutes in addition to contact and descriptive information.

See Free-Net description.

KENTUCKY (KY)

City Online Services

Hopkinsville

National Distance Learning Center

💻) Online service number(s): 2,400 bps 502-686-4555, 14,400 bps 502-686-4557

Log on: "ndlc" (no password required)

🌐 Internet addresses: telnet ndlc.occ.uky.edu, ftp ndlc.occ.uky.edu

👥 Contact person: Sue Cinnamond Mills

💻← Contact person's E-mail address: suec@ndlc.occ.uky.edu

☎ Contact person's voice phone number: 502-686-4530

🖨 Contact person's Fax phone number: 502-686-4558

✉ Mailing address: NDLC, 4800 New Hartford Road, Owensboro, KY 42378

"The National Distance Learning Center is an online database containing information on Distance Learning programs and resources. Professional development, post-secondary degrees and courses, K-12 DL courses, faculty/staff training, and supplemental resources for the classroom are listed, and can be searched by Provider, subject, or medium. The database is federally funded, and free to both users and providers. This national clearinghouse allows the public to access information on DL educational resources."

ANNOTATION

NDLC is at the edge of the subject matter covered by *Government Online*. Because it is a Federally funded operation and because it is worthy of mention, it is included here. To obtain a user's guide through the Internet, use the following commands:

ftp ndlc.occ.uky.edu

Enter "ndlc" at the login prompt.
At the password prompt enter your complete E-mail address and press". When you are finished type "quit."

MARYLAND (MD)

City Online Services

Easton

Chesapeake Free-Net

🖥) Online service number(s): 410-819-6860

Log on: Use real name

🌐 Internet addresses: telnet cfn.bluecrag

👥 Contact Person :David M. Boan, Ph.D.

💻← Contact person's E-mail address: david_boan@martha.washcoll.edu

☎ Contact person's voice phone number: 410-822-4132

🖨 Contact person's Fax phone number: 410-819-0303

✉ Mailing address: Chesapeake Free-Net, P.O. Box 2306, 300 Talbot St., Easton, MD 21601

DESCRIPTION

"Community computing system providing services to local residents, schools, organizations. Developing a Rural Health Care Archive."

ANNOTATION

See Free-Net description.

MASSACHUSETTS (MA)

State Online Services

Department of Environmental Protection, Office of Research and Standards Bulletin Board System

☎ Parent organization: Massachusetts Executive Office of Environmental Affairs

🏛 Government agency: Massachusetts Department of Environmental Protection, Office of Research and Standards

🖥N Acronym for online service: DEP/ORS BBS

🖥) Online service number(s): 617-292-5546

Government agency acronym: DEP/ORS

👥 Contact Person & Title: Michelle S. Bornstein, SYSOP

📞 Contact person's voice phone number: 617-556-1052, 617-292-5570

🖨 Contact person's Fax phone number: 617-556-1049

✉ Mailing address: Department of Environmental Protection, Office of Research and Standards, 1 Winter Street, 3rd Fl, Boston, MA 02108

DESCRIPTION

"A Computer bulletin board system that provides 24 hour access to selected D&P policies, regulations, and other documents of interest."

ANNOTATION

The office of Research and Standards (ORS) defines acceptable human exposure levels to toxic substances and provides information and guidance on public health issues.

Files are available online from the following agencies:
- Bureau of Waste Site Cleanup
- Bureau of Waste Prevention
- Office of Research and Standards

City Online Services

Amherst

UMASSK I 2

💻 Online service number(s): 413-572-5583 or 413-572-5268

Log on: Visitors should log on as "guest"

🌐 Internet addresses: k12.ucs.umass.edu

👥 Contact person: Morton Sternheim

💻 Contact person's E-mail address: mms@k12.ucs.umass.edu

📞 Contact person's voice phone number: 413-545-1908

✉ Mailing address: UMASSK12 c/o Helen Sternheim, Department of Physics and Astronomy, University of Massachusetts, Amherst, MA 01003

DESCRIPTION

UMassK12 is primarily for the use of Massachusetts K12 students and educators.

ANNOTATION

See Free-Net description.

Cambridge

Cambridge Web Pages

Acronym for online service: WWW

🌐 Internet addresses: http://www.ai.mit.edu/projects/iiip /Cambridge/homepage.html

👥 Contact person & title: Kennedy: Todd Marinoff, Technical Staff, Office of City Clerk, Cambridge, MA

💻 Contact person's E-mail address: Eric Loeb: loeb@ai.mit.edu or Cambridge: cambmis@ai.mit edu

📞 Contact person's voice phone number: (Loeb) 617-253-0771

✉ Mailing address: Eric Loeb, 3 Leonard Avenue, #1, Cambridge, MA 02139

DESCRIPTION

The Cambridge pages were built from May

to July of 1994 by a large team including Todd Marinoff, Eric Loeb, Suzanna Lisanti (MIT Information Systems, lisanti@mit.edu), and several MIT undergraduates working for summer credit. The long-term goal of this project is to use the web to provide useful information and interactive services for Cambridge citizens.

ANNOTATION

You will find information on the following topics on the Cambridge WWW page:
- The arts in Cambridge
- Educational Resources
  - —Libraries
  - —Universities (MIT and Harvard)
  - —Hugh Schools
  - —Grad Schools
- Cambridge Historical Background
- Tourist Information
- Cambridge Restaurant Guide
- Boston Area Restaurant Guide

Look for the Boston area map of WWW resources. It is a very impressive use of WWW technology.

MICHIGAN (MI)

City Online Services

Battle Creek

Great Lakes Free-Net

💻⟩ Online service number(s): 616-969-4536

Log on: Visitors should log on as "visitor"

👥 Contact person: Merritt W. Tumanis

💻 Contact person's E-mail address: merritt_tumanis@fc1.glfn.org

☎ Contact person's voice phone number: 616-961-4166

✉ Mailing address: GLFN c/o Willard Library, 7 W. VanBuren, Battle Creek, MI 49107

DESCRIPTION

"The Great Lakes Free-Net services users in Calhoun County Michigan. We have established areas for local city government, townships, and the county to exchange information with our 2800 + users. We also carry the White House press feeds and will be linking to our U.S. Congressman and Senator in the near future. We are currently providing space for incumbents and challengers for open debate on the GLFN"

ANNOTATION

See Free-Net description.

MISSOURI (MO)

City Online Services

Columbia

Columbia Online Information Network (COIN)

💻⟩ Online service number(s): 314-884-7000

Log on: Visitors should log on as "guest"

🌐 Internet addresses: bigcat.missouri.edu

👥 Contact person: Bill Mitchell

Contact person's E-mail address: bill@more.net

Contact person's voice phone number: 314-882-2000

Mailing address: COIN Help Desk, Daniel Boone Regional Library, P.O. Box 1267, Columbia, MO 65205

DESCRIPTION

"C(Columbia) O(Online) I(Information) N(Network) is jointly sponsored by the city of Columbia, the Columbia Public Schools, the Daniel Boone Regional Library, and the University of Missouri–Columbia. These organizations are providing this as a service to improve and expand access to community information. Other agencies are welcome to share items of interest. If you are interested in becoming involved in this project, check with the COIN help desk for information."

ANNOTATION

See Free-Net description.

Kansas City

KC Free-Net

Online service number(s): "Available 3rd Quarter, 1995"

Contact person: James E. Osbourn

Contact person's E-mail address: josourn@tyrell.net

Contact person's voice phone number: 816-340-4228

Contact person's Fax phone number: 816-340-4859

Mailing address: KC Free-Net, P.O. Box 22373, Kansas City, MO 64113-2373

DESCRIPTION

"KC Free-Net is the NPTN affiliate serving the Kansas City metropolitan area. The organizing committee is currently in the early planning stages."

ANNOTATION

See Free-Net description.

Springfield

ORION

Online service number(s): 417-864-6100

Log on: Visitors should log on as "guest"

Internet addresses: ozarks.sgcl.lib.mo.us

Contact person: Annie Linnemeyer

Contact person's E-mail address: annie@ozarks.sgcl.lib.mo.us

Contact person's voice phone number: 417-837-5050 ext 15

DESCRIPTION

"The City of Springfield is a charter member (financial supporter) of ORION. It has a seat on the ORION Board, and house information on the ORION system. The information it provides online is available to anyone who dials into ORION either with a user ID or as a guest.

At the county government level, we provide a location for them to place information, but to this point it has been restricted to a phone list.

At the State and Federal Government levels, we primarliy point to other locations that house information about Missouri and United States Government activities. The only exception to this is that the Social Security Administration houses information directly on ORION.

We are hoping to expand access to government information with an emphasis on local government information. This hopefully will ultimately include information about the local government activities in some of the smaller rural communities that are prevalent in this part of Missouri."

ANNOTATION

See Free-Net description.

MONTANA (MT)

State of Montana Electronic Bulletin Board System

💻) Online service number(s): 406-444-5648 or 800-962-1729 (within Montana only)

👥 Contact person & title: Forrest Christian, Information Service Specialist

☎ Contact person's voice phone number: 406-444-2921

📠 Contact person's Fax phone number: 406-444-2701

✉ Mailing address: P.O. Box 200113, Mitchel Bldg., Room 237, Helena, MT 59620-0113

DESCRIPTION

The following was captured from a bulletin posted on the BBS.

"HOUSE BILL NO. 520
2-17-322. Establishment.
1. The department of administration shall establish and maintain a centralized electronic bulletin board system for state agencies to use as a means of conveying information to the citizens of Montana. Agencies involved in communicating information to the public shall maintain appropriate information on the bulletin board system, including but not limited to:

   a. Environmental assessments
   b. Rulemaking notices
   c. Board vacancy notices
   d. Agency reports mandated by statute
   e. Parks reports required by 23-1-11
   f. Requests for bids or proposals; and
   g. Public meeting notices and agendas.
2. The purpose of the centralized electronic bulletin board system is to encourage the practice of providing for direct citizen access to the state computerized information."

ANNOTATION

The state of Montana's BBS is a big step in the right direction. It provides access to state government from the governor's office down. The file areas I explored didn't have many files. It is well designed, except for the fact that you have to go back to the main menu whenever you want to move into a different area.

NEW YORK (NY)

State Online Services

New York State Archives and Records Administration Gopher

🌐 Internet addresses: Gopher unix6.nysed.gov

📟 Contact person's E-mail address:
gosys@unix6.nysed.gov

✉ Mailing address: New York State
Archives and Records Administration,
State Government Records Programs,
Cultural Education Center, Room
9C71, Albany, NY 12230

DESCRIPTION

"This Gopher is operated by the New York
State Archives and Records Administration
(SARA) State Government Records
Programs. SARA identifies, preserves, and
makes available for research the perma-
nently valuable records created by New
York's colonial and state government agen-
cies, legislatures, and judiciary. SARA's
State Government Records Programs also
provides centralized records and informa-
tion management services for New York
State Government.

The SARA Gopher provides researchers
information on using State Archives records,
information on policies governing access to
records, access to descriptive information
about records in the Archives, information
on records available for specific research
interests, and access to finding aids for
records preserved by the Archives.

The SARA Gopher also provides information on records management services to
New York State government agencies. These
services include training and education programs, programs for managing electronic
records, and policies and procedures for
managing State government records.

For further information about SARA hold-
ings, finding aids, guide to records, etc.
please contact: Jim Folts, Reference Unit,
New York State Archives and Records
Administration, Room 11D40, Cultural
Education Center, Empire State Plaza,
Albany, NY 12230, (518) 474-8955; E-mail:
jfolts%sedofis@vm1.nysed.gov."

ANNOTATION

The opening menu is deceptively unpreten-
tious. Explore the Gopher and you will see
that this is an extensive resource. Take a
look at the "Women's History Records Fact
Sheet."

New York State Assembly Legislative Information System

🌐 Internet addresses: telnet or Gopher
assembly.state.ny.us

Log on: Use "guest" as user ID and
"pw" as a password.

DESCRIPTION

"NEW YORK STATE ASSEMBLY INFOR-
MATION ON THE INTERNET—WHAT'S
AVAILABLE

To help keep the public informed on its
activites, the New York State Assembly
maintains a Legislative Information System
on the Internet. This system is accessible to
anyone who can use the Internet's telnet
function.

Using the Legislative Information Service,
you can review detailed information in the
current two-year legislative session. You can
read the full text of a bill, check its current
status in the legislative process, and even
browse the sponsor's Memorandum in
Support.

You can also review Assembly committee
and floor calendars, find out when and
where public hearing are being held, and
explore the state constitution and laws of
New York State.

Additional Assembly information options
will be added on a regular basis."

New York State Assembly Legislative Information System is not user-friendly. Although it contains a wealth of information, the information is not easy to find. Better searching tools are needed in all areas. The telnet and Gopher addresses are the same. Using a Gopher results in a telnet connection.

The following is a list of options captured from the opening menu.

1. Bill Information
2. Assembly Calendar
3. Hearing Schedule
4. Committee Agenda
5. New York State Laws

New York State Department of Health (NYSDOH) Gopher

🖳N Acronym for online service: NYSDOH Gopher

🖳← Contact person's E-mail address: nyhealth@albnydh2.bitnet

🌐 Internet addresses: WWW gopher://gopher.health.state.ny.us:70/00/.topfiles/welcome, Gopher gopher.health.state.ny.us

DESCRIPTION

"The NYSDOH Gopher is your electronic guide to public information, data, and services provided by the Department. Looking for a facility near you that does screening for breast cancer? Check under 'Consumer Health Information.' Doing research on breast cancer rates in New York State? If it's numbers you are after, the 'Statistical Reports/Data' menu is a good place to start. If you are interested in a toll free '800' number for health information or services, check the 'Directory Services' listing. So whether you're a consumer of health care, a health care provider, or someone doing health-related research, the NYSDOH Gopher is for you. There's something for everyone!"

ANNOTATION

Look beneath the surface and you will find a wealth of health information on the NYSDOH Gopher and it is growing.

New York State Office of Telecommunications Policy Analysis and Development

🌐 Internet addresses: Gopher unix5.nysed.gov

🖳← Contact person's E-mail address: gcasler@unix5.nysed.gov

DESCRIPTION

"This gopher is run by the Office of Telecommunications Policy Analysis and Development, at the New York State Education Department in Albany, NY. OTPAD is an office created from people of various other parts of the department. The gopher administrator, for example, is officially a member of the Office of Elementary, Middle and Secondary Education. The machine on which this gopher runs is owned by the Office of Higher and Professional Education. The deputy commissioner responsible for this office, however, is the Deputy Commissioner for Cultural Education. What we have set out to do here is serve two purposes: to collect and distribute information relating to telecommunications and telecommunications policy, so our advisor committee (ACT—Advisor Committee on Telecommunications) can look at one place and collect a great deal of information easily; and also to provide a gathering and organizing place for resources which may be of use to the classroom teacher."

County Online Services

Monroe County

Monroe County Library System Public Access Catalog

⌨N Acronym for online service: PAC

💻) Online service number(s): 716-428-7777

Log on: No ID or password required

👥 Contact person & title: Carole Joyce, Library Systems Analyst

💻← Contact person's E-mail address: joyce_carole#csi@csi.carl.org

☎ Contact person's voice phone number: 716-428-7166

🖨 Contact person's fax phone number: 716-428-7313

✉ Mailing address: Rochester Public Library, 115 South Clinton Avenue, Rochester, NY 14604

DESCRIPTION

The Public Access Catalog (PAC) provides access to the card catalog of the Rochester Public Library, the MCLS Online catalog, magazine indexes, and other library catalogs.

ANNOTATION

By the time you read this, PAC may also have other community services available.

City Online Services

Buffalo

Buffalo Free-Net

💻) Online service number(s): 716-645-3085

Log on: Visitors should log on as "freeport"

🌐 Internet addresses: telnet freenet. buffalo.edu

👥 Contact person:James Finamore

💻← Contact person's E-mail address: finamore@ubvms.cc.buffalo.edu

☎ Contact person's voice phone number: 716-877-8800 ext 451

🖨 Contact person's fax phone number: 716-876-4255

✉ Mailing address: Town of Tonawanda Job Training Department, 1835 Sheridan Drive, Buffalo, NY 14223

DESCRIPTION

"A free, open access community computer system for information and education."

ANNOTATION

See Free-Net description.

NORTH CAROLINA (NC)

City Online Services

Chapel Hill

Triangle Free-Net

🌐 Internet addresses: Gopher

tfnet.ils.unc, telnet tfnet.ils.unc.edu,
URL: //tfnet.ils.unc.edu/

Log on: Using telnet, log on as freenet.

👥 Contact person: William R Hutchins or
Judy Hallman

💻 Contact person's E-mail address:
hallman @gibbs.oit.unc.edu

☎ Contact person's voice phone number:
919-962-9107

🖨 Contact person's Fax phone number:
919-966-4909

✉ Mailing address: Triangle Free-Net,
CB# 3460, University of North
Carolina, Chapel Hill, NC 27599-
3460

DESCRIPTION

"Triangle Free-Net has a broad range of
community information. It also gives you
access to electronic information services
world-wide, through the menu choice
'Beyond the Triangle Free-Net.'

Our first major project will be to try to set
up a server for county information—probably a WWW server on their PC, so we can
get data from them."

ANNOTATION

The Triangle Free-Net is well organized
and offers many resources dealing with
government at the local, state, and national
level. The description Triangle Free-Net
provided for their Free-Net is overly modest. This is a terrific resource and it is getting better.

NORTH DAKOTA (ND)

City Online Services

Fargo

SENDIT

💻 Online service number(s): 701-237-3283

Log on: Visitors logging onto bbs
should use the password "sendit2me"

🌐 Internet addresses: sendit.nodak.edu

👥 Contact person: Gleason Sackman

💻 Contact person's E-mail address:
sackman@sendit.nodak.edu

☎ Contact person's voice phone number:
701-237-8109

DESCRIPTION

SENDIT is mostly educationally-oriented.

ANNOTATION

See Free-Net description.

OHIO (OH)

City Online Services

Cincinnati

Tristate Online

💻 Online service number(s): 606-781-
5575 (Subject to change)

Log on: Visitors should log on as "visitor"

Internet addresses: telnet tso.uc.edu

Contact person: Steve Shoemaker–TSO Interim System Adminstrator

Contact person's E-mail address: sysadmin@tso,uc.edu

Mailing address: Tristate Online, P.O. Box 54067, Cincinnati, OH 45254-0067

DESCRIPTION

According to Steve Shoemaker, Tristate Online is similar to other Free-Nets.

ANNOTATION

See Free-Net description.

Cleveland

Cleveland Free-Net

Online service number(s): 216-368-3888

Log on: "Select Mailing address:2 at first menu"

Internet addresses: freenet-in-a.cwru.edu

Contact person: Jeff Gumpf

Contact person's E-mail address: jag@po.cwru.edu

Contact person's voice phone number: 216-368-2982

DESCRIPTION

"Since 1985, Case Western Reserve University has been experimenting with free, open-access, community computer systems as a new communications and information medium.

In effect, these systems represent a new application in computing. A multi-user computer is established at a central location in a given area and the machine is connected to the telephone system through a series of devices called modems. Running on the machine is a computer program that provides its users with everything from electronic mail services to information about health care, education, technology, government, recreation, or just about anything else the host operators would like to place on the machine.

Anyone in the community with access to a home, office, or school computer and a modem can contact the system anytime, 24 hours a day. They simply dial a central phone number, make connection, and a series of menus appears on the screen which allows them to select the information or communication services they would like. All of it is free and all of it can be easily accomplished by a first-time user.

The key to the economics of operating a community computer system is the fact that the system is literally run by the community itself. Everything that appears on one of these machines is there because there are individuals or organizations in the community who are prepared to contribute their time, effort, and expertise to place it there and operate it over time. This, of course, is in contrast to the commercial services which have very high personnel and information-acquisition costs and must pass those costs on to the consumer

Couple this volunteerism with the rapidly-dropping costs of computing power, the use of inexpensive transmission technology, and the fact that the necessary software to operate theses systems is avaible for low cost—and public access computing becomes an economically-viable entity."

ANNOTATION

See Free-Net description.

Learning Village Cleveland

⌨) Online service number(s): 216-247-6196

Log on: Visitors should log on as "Visitor"

🌐 Internet addresses: nptn.org

👥 Contact person: John Kurilec

💻 Contact person's E-mail address: jmk@nptn.org

☎ Contact person's voice phone number: 216-247-5800

DESCRIPTION

"About the Learning Village.

The National Public Telecomputing Network (NPTN) and Ameritech Services have signed a two-year agreement for the development of the Learning Village based upon NPTN's highly successful Academy One program. The Learning Village is a combination of projects, information, and special events that are centered on the core curriculum. It is being developed in partnership with the governor's offices in Illinois, Indiana, Michigan, Ohio and Wisconsin.

The Learning Village is built around an 'electronic schoolhouse' motif. There are areas specifically designed for use by teachers and students. There is a wealth of information in the Learning Village and you are encouraged to browse and find that which interests you the most.

This program is one of many organized by the Great Lakes/Ameritech Partnership, a cooperative effort of Ameritech and the governors of the five states it serves. The partnership is designed to bring new jobs, better educational opportunities and improvements in quality of life to the Midwest.

Please send all messages indicating things that you discover are not working to a-l@nptn.org. Feel free to send us suggestions for what you'd like to see developed, as well. The growth of the Learning Village is limited only by your creativity and time. We want to assist you in developing this educational and communication tool. It is a reflection of what you need, want, and do in the Learning Village."

ANNOTATION

See Free-Net description.

Columbus

Greater Columbus Free-Net

⌨) Online service number(s): 614-292-7501

Log on: Local non-telnet visitors should log on as "guest"

🌐 Internet addresses: telnet freenet.columbus.oh.us, Gopher gopher.freenet.columbus.oh.us

👥 Contact person: Steven I. Gordon

💻 Contact person's E-mail address: sgordon@freenet.columbus.oh.us

☎ Contact person's voice phone number: 614-292-4132

✉ Mailing address: Greater Columbus Free-Net, 1224 Kinnear Road, Columbus, OH 43212

"We have a number of communities that have been allocated space on our Free-Net and use it to post notices of meetings, contacts for information, selected datasheets, etc. Currently, the agencies involved are:

- City of Columbus—12 major departments/divisions
- Franklin County—8 departments
- City of Worthington
- City of Westerville
- City of Dublin
- Mid-Ohio Regional Planning Commission

We also have a number of State agencies who are using us to post information of state-wide interest. This is then being carried by any other Free-Nets around the State of Ohio. These agences are:

- Ohio Department of Development
- Ohio Department of Commerce
- Ohio Department of Adminstrative Services (have state jobs information posted)
- Ohio Dispute Resolution Commission

Several others should be added soon.

We also have a number of neighborhood and civic groups that post information to the Free-Net.

Our information can be viewed worldwide through Gopher: gopher.freenet.columbus.og.us."

ANNOTATION

"Guest logins are for local people only." telnet guest logins are not allowed. Locals are defined as "...residents of Franklin and surrounding counties in Ohio." However, you can use Gopher to tour the Greater Columbus Free-Net.

Dayton

Dayton Free-Net

🖥) Online service number(s): 513-229-4373

Log on: Visitors should log on as "visitor"

🌐 Internet addresses: 130.108.128.174

👥 Contact person: Patricia Vendt

💻 Contact person's E-mail address: pvendt@desire.wright.edu

☎ Contact person's voice phone number: 513-873-4035

DESCRIPTION

The Dayton Free-Net was just coming online when I logged on. Many of the Free-Net areas were "under construction." However, the Dayton Free-Net appears to be very similar in design and layout to other Free-Nets.

ANNOTATION

See Free-Net description.

Elyria

Lorain County Free-Net

🖥) Online service number(s): 216-366-9721

Log on: Visitors should log on as "guest"

🌐 Internet addresses: freenet.lorain.oberlin.edu

👥 Contact person: Thom Gould

💻 Contact person's E-mail address: aa003@freenet.lorain.oberlin.edu

☎ Contact person's voice phone number: 1-800-227-7113 ext. 2451 or 216-277-2451

✉ Mailing adrress: Lorain County Free-Net, Inc., P.O. Box 144, Lorain, OH 44052

DESCRIPTION

"Lorain County Free-Net, Inc., is an open access community information network made possible by the yeoman efforts of a dedicated group of community volunteers who comprised the Class of 1990—Leadership Lorain County. The Network is governed by a 13 member Board of Trustees who represent a cross section of Lorain County residents. Lorain County Free-Net, Inc., is funded entirely through the largesse of foundations, corporations and individuals."

ANNOTATION

See Free-Net description.

Medina

Medina County Free-Net

💻 Online service number(s): 216-723-6732, 216-225-6732, 216-335-6732

Log on: Visitors should log on as "visitor" and use "visitor" as a password

👥 Contact person: Tony Carmack –System Administrator

💻 Contact person's E-mail address: administrator@freenet.medina.org

☎ Contact person's voice phone number: 216-725-0588

📠 Contact person's fax phone number: 216-725-2053

✉ Mailing Address: Medina County District Library, 210 South Broadway, Medina, OH 44256

DESCRIPTION

The Medina Free-Net is organized into the following sections:
- MailBox
- HelpFolder
- Library
- Club House
- Administration Building
- Government House
- News Stand
- Community Center
- School House
- The Clinic
- Agricultural Center
- Science Center

ANNOTATION

See Free-Net description.

Youngstown

Youngstown Free-Net

💻 Online service number(s): 216-742-7035

Log on: Visitors should log on as "visitor"

🌐 Internet addresses: telnet yfn2.ysu.edu, Gopher or WWW yfn.ysu.edu

👥 Contact person: Lou Anschuetz

💻 Contact person's E-mail address: lou@yfn.ysu.edu

☎ Contact person's voice phone number: 216-742-3075

✉ Mailing Address: Youngstown Free-Net, c/o Lou Anschuetz, Computer Center, Youngstown State University, Youngstown, OH 455-3036

"Youngstown Free-Net has been in existence since 1987 as a fully fledged Free-Net system. It provides access to dozens of local services, the SA/TODAY, USENet, News, telnet, Gopher, etc. One time registration fee of $10 for those over 17. Free otherwise."

See Free-Net description.

PENNSYLVANIA (PA)

City Online Services

West Chester

Chester County InterLink (CCIL)

💻 Online service number(s): 610-431-2839

Log on: Use "tourist" as ID

🌐 Internet addresses: telnet locke.ccil.org, Gopher locke.ccil.org

👥 Contact person: Jordan Seidel

💻 Contact person's E-mail address: jseidel@locke.ccil.org

☎ Contact person's voice phone number: 610-431-2673

✉ Mailing address: CCIL c/o Chester County Hospital, 710 E. Marshall Str., West Chester, PA 19380

"Online community computer system, providing the residents and employees in Chester County with local info and connectivity to the global Internet."

See Free-Net description.

RHODE ISLAND (RI)

City Online Services

Providence

Ocean State Free-Net

💻 Online service number(s): 401-831-4640

🌐 Internet addresses: 192.207.24.10

👥 Contact person: Howard Boksenbaum

💻 Contact person's E-mail address: howardbm@dsl.rhilinet.gov

☎ Contact person's voice phone number: 401-277-2726

✉ Mailing address: Ocean State Free-Net, c/o RI Department of State Library Services, 300 Richmond Street, Providence, RI 02903-4222

The Ocean State Free-Net is organized into the following sections:
- Administration
- Post Office
- Libraries

- Learning Center
- Health Center
- Gopher Center
- Challenges
- Government Center
- Jobs and Training Center
- Communications Center (SIGS, NPTN, Teleport)
- Science, Technology & Computing Center
- Business Center
- Arts Center (Under Construction)

See Free-Net description.

TEXAS (TX)

City Online Services

El Paso

Rio Grande Free-Net

💻) Online service number(s): 915-775-5600

Log on: Visitors should log on as "visitor"

🌐 Internet addresses: rgfn.epcc.edu
rgfn.epcc.edu

👥 Contact person: Don Furth

💻← Contact person's E-mail address: donf@laguna.epcc.edu

☎ Contact person's voice phone number: 915-775-6077

✉ Mailing address: EPCC-Rio Grande Free-Net, ATTN: CSC/Room 208, PO Box 20500, El Paso, TX 79998

"A Free-Net represents the community computing concept and consists of a multi-user computer established at a central location which is connected to the telephone system through modems. This computer contains programs that provide its users with everything from electronic mail services to information about health care, education, technology, government, recreation, news, weather, sports, or just about anything else of significant interest. The Rio Grande Free-Net was established in El Paso, TX, went online in September 1993, and is the first of its kind in Texas."

See Free-Net description.

VIRGINIA (VA)

City Online Services

Richmond

VaPEN

👥 Contact person: Dr. Harold Cothern

💻← Contact person's E-mail address: hcothern@vdoe386.vak12ed.edu

☎ Contact person's voice phone number: 804-225-2921

See Free-Net description. The Internet address requires an ID and password for accessing the system.

City Online Services

Bremerton

Kitsap LinkNet

🖥) Online service number(s): 206-698-4737

Log on: Use "guest" if you are a guest, or your assigned ID

🌐 Internet addresses: telnet 198.187.135.22

👥 Contact person: Michael Schuyler

💻← Contact person's E-mail address: michael@linknet.kitsap.lib.wa.us

☎ Contact person's voice phone number: 360-405-9139

🖨 Contact person's fax phone number: 360-405-9128

✉ Mailing address: Kitsap Regional Library, 1301 Sylvan Way, Bremerton, WA 98310

DESCRIPTION

"Online Dec. 19, 1994."

ANNOTATION

See Free-Net description.

Seattle

Seattle Community Network

🖥) Online service number(s): 206-386-4140

Log on: Visitors should log on as "visitor"

🌐 Internet addresses: telnet scn.org

👥 Contact person: Randy Groves

💻← Contact person's E-mail address: randy@cpsr.org

☎ Contact person's voice phone number: 206-865-3424

✉ Mailing address: Seattle Community Network c/o CPSR/Seattle, P.O. Box 85481, Seattle, WA 98145-1481

DESCRIPTION

"Seattle Community Network is an information resource for the greater Seattle area. People can access SCN via dial-up, telnet, and terminals in both the Seattle Public Library and the King County Library System. Our emphasis is on information that is of import to the citizens of the Seattle community."

ANNOTATION

See Free-Net description.

Tri-Cities

Tri-Cities Free-Net

🖥) Online service number(s): 509-375-1111

👥 Contact person: Bruce McComb

💻← Contact person's E-mail address: tcfn@delphi.com

☎ Contact person's voice phone number: 509-586-6481

DESCRIPTION

Tri-Cities Free-Net is operated by the RECA FOUNDATION which is a non-profit organization. They state that they are "...working toward networking all the Tri-Cities Library assets together (including public schools) and providing a community Internet connection. Additional information (inlcuding annual reports) are available online."

ANNOTATION

See Free-Net description.

PART

V

Appendixes

Appendix A
ONLINE DIRECTORIES

Following is a list of online directories providing additional, well-researched information on government online services. Online lists have the advantage that they can be updated instantly while a book like this takes a year to go through the data compilation and publishing process. However, *Government Online* strives to provide more information about government online services that is organized in an easy-to-use format.

GODORT Handout Exchange
Larry Romans, administrator

DESCRIPTION

"The GODORT Handout Exchange is a collection of guides to government information sources written by library staffs across the United States and distributed by the Education Committee of the American Library Association's Government Documents Round Table."

To connect to the GODORT Gopher, use the following Gopher address:

Host=una.hh.lib.umich.edu

Path=1/socsci/poliscilaw/godort/guides

ANNOTATION

Gumprecht's and Parhamovich's guides are available from this Gopher server.

Federal Information on the Internet
compiled by Maggie Parhamovich

DESCRIPTION

Parhamovich describes her document as being "compiled primarily for librarians." However, anyone interested in government online sources will find it a valuable resource. The document is well organized and has a table of contents. It is about 35 pages long in 10 point type.

ANNOTATION

You can obtain *Federal Information on the Internet* through ftp from: nevada.edu directory /liaison. (You may experience difficulty getting into this ftp site during working hours.) You can also find this document by using Gopher. Search for the terms "federal" and "government" using Veronica.

Internet Sources of Government Information
compiled by Blake Gumprecht

DESCRIPTION

"*Internet Sources of Government Information,* compiled by Blake Gumprecht, a former government documents librarian at Temple University, is a comprehensive guide to hundreds of network sources of current government information available worldwide. Internet users can access Census data, Supreme Court decisions, world health statistics, company financial reports, weather forecasts, United Nations information, daily White House press briefings and much more.

The second edition of Gumprecht's guide, produced in February 1994, includes more than 325 sources and is widely available on the network. It can be retrieved from the University of Michigan Clearinghouse of Subject-Oriented Internet Resource Guides: gopher una.hh.lib.umich.edu/inetdirs/all guides/government information

telnet una.hh.lib.umich.edu/login:gopher /social sciences resources/information and library studies/clearinghouse of subject-oriented Internet resource guides/all guides/ government information

ftp una.hh.lib.umich.edu/user:anonymous /password:e-mail address/cd inetdirsstacks /get government:gumprecht

http://www.lib.umich.edu/chhome.html

The guide is also available via E-mail. Send a message to mail-server@rtfm.mit. edu. The message should read:

send usenet/news.answers/us-govt-net-pointers/part1

send usenet/news.answers/us-govt-net-pointers/part2"

Special Internet Connections
Compiled By: Scott Yanoff— yanoff@alpha2.csd.uwm.edu

DESCRIPTION

Scott Yanoff's list of Internet connections is legendary on the Net and in the press. Although his list is not specifically government related, it does contain a number of interesting government online services. Open Yanoff's list as a word-processing document, and search for the word "gov" to find online services containing the word gov or gov as part of another word. This will point you toward most of the government line services listed. The list is about 30 pages long.

ANNOTATION

There are several ways to obtain Yanoff's list. To obtain the latest list send an E-mail message to "inetlist@uag3.augsburg.edu" with or without a message. You can also find Yanoff's list on gophers by using Veronica to search for Yanoff. Yanoff's list can also be seen through WWW at the following address:

http://slacvx.slac.stanford.edu/misc/internet-services.html

The WWW list allows you to immediately connect to any online service listed.

Appendix B

U.S. GOVERNMENT AGENCIES AND ONLINE SERVICES ACRONYM AND ABBREVIATION DIRECTORY

The following data incorporates data from the *United States Government Manual* and from online services research. The data is sorted alphabetically by agency or online service acronym or abbreviation.

1040 BBS	Electronic Filing Service Bulletin Board, Department of the Treasury
ABLEDATA	ABLEDATA Database of Assistive Technology and National Rehabilitation Information Center, Department of Education
ABMC	American Battle Monuments Commission
ACDA	United States Arms Control and Disarmament Agency
ACF	Administration for Children and Families
ACS	Agricultural Cooperative Service
ACUS	Administrative Conference of the United States
ACYF	Administration for Children, Youth, and Families
ADA	Americans with Disabilities Act of 1990
ADABBS	Ada Technical Support Bulletin Board System, Department of the Navy
ADB	Asian Development Bank
ADD	Administration on Developmental Disabilities

AEDS	Atomic Energy Detection System
AFAA	Air Force Audit Agency
AFBCMR	Air Force Review Board for Correction of Military Records
AFCARA	Air Force Civilian Appellate Review Agency
AFDB	African Development Bank
AFDC	Aid to Families with Dependent Children
AFDF	African Development Fund
AFIS	American Forces Information Service
AFPC	Armed Forces Policy Council
AFPEO	Air Force Program Executive Offices
AFPPS	American Forces Press and Publications Service
AFRRI	Armed Forces Radiobiology Research Institute
AFRTS	Armed Forces Radio and Television Service
AFSC	Armed Forces Staff College Agency
AGRICLA	Agricultural OnLine Access
AID	Agency for International Development
AIDS	Acquired Immune Deficiency Syndrome
ALF	Agricultural Library Forum, Department of Agriculture
ALIX	Automated Library Information Exchange, Library of Congress
AMS	Agricultural Marketing Service
Amtrak	National Railroad Passenger Corporation
ANA	Administration for Native Americans
AOA	Administration on Aging
APHIS	Animal and Plant Health Inspection Service
ARC	Appalachian Regional Commission
ARPA	Advanced Research Projects Agency
ARS	Agricultural Research Service
ASCS	Agricultural Stabilization and Conservation Service
ATSDR	Agency for Toxic Substances and Disease Registry
BEA	Bureau of Economic Analysis
BEA BBS	Census-BEA Electronic Forum, Department of Commerce
BIA	Bureau of Indian Affairs
BIB	Board for International Broadcasting
BJA	Bureau of Justice Assistance

BJS	Bureau of Justice Statistics
BLM	Bureau of Land Management
BLMRCP	Bureau of Labor- Management Relations and Cooperative Programs
BLS	Bureau of Labor Statistics
BOM-BBN	Bureau of Mines Electronic Bulletin Board, Department of the Interior
BPA	Bonneville Power Administration
BSC's	Business Service Centers
BTS	Bureau of Transportation Statistics
BVA	Board of Veterans Appeals
C^4	Command, Control, Communication, and Computer Systems
C41	Communication, Command, Control, Computer, and Intelligence
CALS/C	Computer-Aided Acquisition and Logistic Support/Concurrent Engineering Program
CBO	Congressional Budget Office
CCC	Commodity Credit Corporation; Customs Cooperation Council
CCEA	Cabinet Council on Economic Affairs
CCR	Commission on Civil Rights
CDBG	Community Development Block Grants
CDC	Centers for Disease Control
CEA	Council of Economic Advisers
CEBB	Customs Electronic Bulletin Board, Department of the Treasury
CEQ	Council on Environmental Quality
CFA	Commission of Fine Arts
CFR	Code of Federal Regulations
CFTC	Commodity Futures Trading Commission
CG	Commanding General
CHAMP	A Civilian Health and Medical Program of the Veterans Administration
CIA	Central Intelligence
CIC	Consumer Information Center
CIC-BBS	Consumer Information Center BBS, General Services Administration
CIDS	Computer Information Delivery Service

CIDS	Computerized Information Delivery Service, Department of Agriculture
CIO	Central Imagery Office
CIO	Command, Control, Communications, and Intelligence
CIPS	Commission Issuance Posting System, Department of Energy
CLU-INBBS	The Cleanup Information Bulletin Board, Environmental Protection Agency
CMHS	Center for Mental Health Services
CNO	Chief of Naval Operations
Conrail	Consolidated Rail Corporation
CPSC	Consumer Product Safety Commission
CRS	Congressional Research Service; Community Relations Service
CRS-BB	Americans with Disabilities Electronic BBS, Department of Justice
CSA	Community Services Administration
CSAP	Center for Substance Abuse Prevention
CSAT	Center for Substance Abuse Treatment
CSRS	Cooperative State Research Service
CUFT	Center for the Utilization of Federal Technology
CV BBS	Census Vacancy BBS, Department of Commerce
DA	Department of the Army
DAU	Defense Acquisition University
DCAA	Defense Contract Audit Agency
DCASR's	Defense Contract Administration Services Regions
DCS	Defense Communications System
DEA	Drug Enforcement Administration
DIA	Defense Intelligence—Agency
DINFOS	Defense Information School
DIPEC	Defense Industrial Plant Equipment Center
DIS	Defense Investigative Service
DISA	Defense Information Services Activity; Defense Information Systems Agency
DISAM	Defense Institute of Security Assistance Management
DLA	Defense Logistics Agency
DLSA	Defense Legal Services Agency

DMA	Defense Mapping Agency
DMFO	Defense Medical Facilities Office
DMS	Defense Mapping School
DMSA	Defense Medical Support Activity
DMSSC	Defense Medical Systems Support Center
DNA	Defense Nuclear Agency
DOC	Department of Commerce
DOD	Department of Defense
DODDS	Department of Defense Dependents Schools
DOE	Department of Energy
DOL	Department of Labor
DOT	Department of Transportation
DSAA	Defense Security Assistance Agency
DSC BB	Detroit Service Center BBS, Office of Personnel Management
DTSA	Defense Technology Security Administration
EBB	Economic Bulletin Board, Department of Commerce
EDA	Economic Development Administration
EEOC	Equal Employment Opportunity Commission
EHSC-BS	U.S. Army Engineering and Housing Support Center Data Distribution BBS, Department of the Army
EIA	Energy Information Administration
ELISA	Export License Status Advisor, Department of Defense
EO	Executive Order
EOUSA	Executive Office for United States Attorneys
EPA	Environmental Protection Agency
EPUB	EIA Electronic Publishing System, Department of Energy
ERA	Economic Regulatory Administration
EREN	Energy Efficiency and Renewable Energy Network
ERS	Economic Research Service
ES	Extension Service
ESA	Employment Standards Administration
ETA	Employment and Training Administration
Eximbank	Export-Import Bank of the United States
Eximbank BBS	Eximbank Bulletin Board, Export-Import Bank of the United States

FAA	Federal Aviation Administration
Farmer Mac	Federal Agricultural Mortgage Corporation
FAS	Foreign Agricultural Service
FBI	Federal Bureau of Investigation
FCA	Farm Credit Administration
FCC	Federal Communications Commission
FCIA	Foreign Credit Insurance Association
FCIC	Federal Crop Insurance Corporation
FDA	Food and Drug Administration
FDA BB	The FD Electronic Bulletin Board, Department of Health and Human Services
FDIC	Federal Deposit Insurance Corporation
FEB's	Federal Executive Boards
FEBBS	Federal Highway Electronic Bulletin Board System, Department of Transportation
FEC	Federal Election Commission
Federal BBS	The Federal Bulletin Board, Government Printing Office
FEDRIP	Federal Research in Progress Database
FedWorld BBS	FedWorld BBS, Department of Commerce
FEMA	Federal Emergency Management Agency
FERC	Federal Energy Regulatory Commission
FFB	Federal Financing Bank
FGIS	Federal Grain Inspection Service
FHA	Federal Housing Administration
FHFB	Federal Housing Finance Board
FHWA	Federal Highway Administration
FIA	Federal Insurance Administration
FIC	Federal Information Centers
FICO	Financing Corporation
FIE	Federal Information Exchange, Department of Energy
FIRS	Federal Information Relay Service
FJOB	Federal Job Opportunity Board, Office of Personnel Management
FLETC	Federal Law Enforcement Training Center
FLRA	Federal Labor Relations Authority

FMC	Federal Maritime Commission
FMCS	Federal Mediation and Conciliation Service
FmHA	Farmers Home Administration
FMS	Financial Management Service
FNMA	Federal National Mortgage Association
FNS	Food and Nutrition Service
FOIA	Freedom of Information Act
FOMC	Federal Open Market Committee
FPRS	Federal Property Resources Service
FR	Federal Register
FRA	Federal Railroad Administration
FRED	Federal Reserve Economic Data
FRS	Federal Reserve System
FSA/IRM BBS	Federal Information Resources Management Electronic Bulletin Board, General Services Administration
FSIS	Food Safety and Inspection Service
FSLIC	Federal Savings and Loan Insurance Corporation
FSS	Federal Supply Service
FST5	Federal Secure Telephone Service
FTC	Federal Trade Commission
FTS	Federal Telecommunications System
FWS	Fish and Wildlife Service
GAO	General Accounting Office
GATT	General Agreement on Tariffs and Trade
GNMA	Government National Mortgage Association
GPO	Government Printing Office
GSA	General Services Administration
HCFA	Health Care Financing Administration
HDS	Office of Human Development Services
HHS	Department of Health and Human Services
HIRA	Health Resources Administration
HIV	Human Immunodeficiency Virus
HNIS	Human Nutrition Information Service
HUD	Department of Housing and Urban Development

IAEA	International Atomic Energy Agency
IAF	Inter-American Foundation
IBRD	International Bank for Reconstruction and Development
ICAF	Industrial College of the Armed Forces
ICAO	International Civil Aviation Organization
ICC	Interstate Commerce Commission
ICO	International Coffee Organization
IDA	International Development Association; Institute for Defense Analyses
IDB	Inter-American Development Bank
IDCA	United States International Development Cooperation Agency
IEVS	Income Eligibility Verification Systems
IFAD	International Fund for Agricultural Development
IFC	International Finance Corporation
IGDOD	Inspector General, Department of Defense
IHA's	Indian Housing Authorities
IHS	Indian Health Service
ILO	International Labor Organization
IMF	International Monetary Fund
IMS	Institute of Museum Services
INF	Intermediate-range Nuclear Forces
INS	Immigration and Naturalization Service
INTERPL	International Criminal Police Organization
IOM	International Organization for Migration
IRMC	Information Resources Management College
IRMS	Information Resources Management Service
IRS	Internal Revenue Service
ISDN	North American ISDN Users Forum, Department of Commerce
ITA	International Trade Administration
ITAR	International Traffic in Arms Regulations
ITU	International Telecommunication Union
IVHS	Intelligent Vehicle-Highway System
JAG	Judge Advocate General
JAGNE	Judge Avocate General's Office BBS, Department of the Navy

JCEWS	Joint Command, Control, and Electronic Warfare School
JCS	Joint Chiefs of Staff
JCSOS	Joint and Combined Staff Officer School
JICST	Japan International Center of Science and Technology
JPL Info	BBS
JPL Info	BBS, National Aeronautics and Space Administration
JSC BBS	Johnson Space Center BBS, National Aeronautics and Space Administration
JTC3A	Joint Tactical Command, Control, and Communications Agency
Labor News BBS	Labor News BBS, Department of Labor
MA	Maritime Administration
MBDA	Minority Business Development Agency
MBFR	Mutual and Balanced Force Reduction
MED	Office of Medical Services (State)
Megawatts	Megawatts BBS, Department of Energy
MHSS	Military Health Services System
MIGA	Multilateral Investment Guarantee Agency
MMS	Minerals Management Service
MSHA	Mine Safety and Health Administration
MSPB	Merit Systems Protection Board
MSSD	Model Secondary School for the Deaf
MTB	Materials Transportation Bureau
NADAPBBS	Navy Drug and Alcohol Abuse Prevention BBS, Department of the Navy
NARA	National Archives and Records Administration
NASA	National Aeronautics and Space Administration
NASS	National Agricultural Statistics Service
NATO	Noah Atlantic Treaty Organization
NATSG	National Soil Survey Database
NBIAP	The National Biological Impact Assessment Program Bulletin Board, United States Department of Agriculture
NBS	National Bureau of Standards
NCC	National Coordinating Committee
NCI	National Cancer Institute

NCIC	National Cartographic Information Center
NCJRS	National Criminal Justice Reference Service
NCPC	National Capital Planning Commission
NCS	National Cemetery System
NCSLC BS	National Computer Systems Laboratory Computer Security BBS, Department of Commerce
NCUA	National Credit Union Administration
NDB BBS	Nutrient Data Bank Bulletin Board, United States Department of Agriculture
NDU	National Defense University
NEH	National Endowment for the Humanities
NEL	National Engineering Laboratory
NGDC BS	National Geophysical Data Center, Department of Commerce
NHI	National Highway Institute
NHPRC	National Historial Publications and Records Commission
NHTSA	National Highway Traffic Safety Administration
NIC	National Institute of Corrections
NIE	National Institute of Education
NIH	National Institutes of Health
NIJ	National Institute of Justice
NIS	Naval Investigative Service
NIST	National Institute of Standards and Technology
NLM	National Library of Medicine
NLRB	National Labor Relations Board
NMCS	National Military Command System
NML	National Measurement Laboratory
NOAA	National Oceanic and Atmospheric Administration
NOS	National Ocean Survey
NRC	Nuclear Regulatory Commission
NRWA	National Rural Water Association
NSA	National Security Agency
NSC	National Security Council
NSF	National Science Foundation

NSSDC ODIS	National Space Science Data Center, Online Data and Information Service, National Aeronautics and Space Administration
NSTL	National Space Technology Laboratories
NTIA	National Telecommunications and Information Administration
NTIAUNIX1	Information Infrastructure Task Force Gopher, Department of Commerce
NTID	National Technical Institute for the Deaf
NTIS	National Technical Information Service (Commerce)
NTSB	National Transportation Safety Board
NWC	National War College
OA	Office of Administration
OAS	Organization of American States
OASTP	Office of the Assistant Secretary for Technology Policy
OCHAMUS	Office of Civilian Health and Medical Program of the Uniformed Services
OCS	Office of Community Services; Officer Candidate School; Outer Continental Shelf
OCSE	Office of Child Support Enforcement
OECD	Organization for Economic Cooperation and Development
OERI BB	Office of Educational Research and Improvement Electronic Bulletin Board, Department of Education
OES	Office of Employment Security
OFCC	Office of Federal Contract Compliance
OFM	Office of Financial Management
OFPP	Office of Federal Procurement Policy
OFR	Office of the Federal Register
OGE	Office of Government Ethics
OGPS	Office of Grants and Program Systems
OICD	Office of International Cooperation and Development
OJJDP	Office of Juvenile Justice and Delinquency Prevention
OJP	Office of Justice Programs
OLMS	Office of Labor-Management Standards
OMB	Office of Management and Budget

OMIS	Office of Management and Information Systems
OPFI	Office of Program and Fiscal Integrity
OPIC	Overseas Private Investment Corporation
OPM	Office of Personnel Management
OPM Express	Office of Personnel Management Express, Office of Personnel Management
OPM Mainstreet	Office of Personnel Management Mainstreet BBS, Office of Personnel Management
OPO's	Organ Procurement Organizations
ORM	Office of Regional Management
ORR	Office of Refugee Relief; Office of Refugee Resettlement
OSC	Office of Special Counsel
OSCE	Office of Child Support Enforcement
OSDBU	Office of Small and Disadvantaged Business Utilization
OSF	Office of Space Flight
OSHA	Occupational Safety and Health Administration
OSHRC	Occupational Safety and Health Review Commission
OSM	Office of Surface Mining Reclamation and Enforcement
OSS	Online Schedules System, General Services Administration
OSSD	Office of Space Systems Development
OSTP	Office of Science and Technology Policy
OT	Office of Transportation
OTA	Office of Technology Assessment
OTAA	Office of Trade Adjustment Assistance
OTS	Office of Thrift Supervision
OVC	Office for Victims of Crime
OVI	Office of Voluntarism Initiatives
OWBO	Office of Women's Business Ownership
PADC	Pennsylvania Avenue Development Corporation
PAHO	Pan American Health Organization
PAL	Public Access Link, Federal Communications Commission
PayPerNet BBS	Federal Pay & Performance Management BBS, Office of Personnel Management
PBGC	Pension Benefit Guaranty Corporation

PBS	Public Buildings Service
PCC	Panama Canal Commission
PHA's	Public Housing Agencies
PHS	Public Health Service
PLBB	Patent Licensing Bulletin Board
PRC	Postal Rate Commission
PTO	Patent and Trademark Office
PWBA	Pension and Welfare Benefits Administration
RDA	Rural Development Administration
REA	Rural Electrification Administration
REFCORP	Resolution Funding Corporation
RETRF	Rural Electrification and Telephone Revolving Fund
RFE	Radio Free Europe
RIBBS	Rapid Information BBS, U.S. Postal Service
RICO	Racketeer Influenced and Corrupt Organizations
RIT	Rochester Institute of Technology
RL	Radio Liberty
ROTC	Reserve Officer Training Corps
RRB	Railroad Retirement Board
RSA	Rehabilitation Services Administration
RSPA	Research and Special Programs Administration
RTB	Rural Telephone Bank
RTC	Resolution Trust Corporation
SAIF	Savings Association Insurance Fund
SAMHS	Substance Abuse and Mental Health Services Administration
SAO	Smithsonian Astrophysical Observatory
SAVE	Systematic Alien Verification for Entitlement
SBA	Small Business Administration
SBA Online	Small Business Administration Online, Small Business Administration
SCS	Soil Conservation Service
SEC	Securities and Exchange Commission
SERC	Smithsonian Environmental Research Center
SGLI	Servicemen's Group Life Insurance

SIDS	Sudden Infant Death Syndrome
SITES	Smithsonian Institution Traveling Exhibition Service
SLAC	Stanford Linear Accelerator
SLS	Saint Lawrence Seaway Development Corporation
SPC	South Pacific Commission
SRDC	State Rural Development Councils
SSA	Social Security Administration
SSI	Supplemental Security Income Program
SSS	Selective Service System
SSURG	County Soil Survey Database
START	Strategic Arms Reduction Talks
Stat.	United States Statutes at Large
STATSG	State Soil Survey Database
TDA	Trade and Development Agency
TFCS	Treasury Financial Communication System
TSI	Transportation Safety Institute
TVA	Tennessee Valley Authority
U.N.	United Nations
U.S.C.	United States Code
UDAG	Urban Development Action Grants
UIS	Unemployment Insurance Service
UNESC	United Nations Educational, Scientific and Cultural Organization
UNICEF	United Nations Children's Fund (formerly United Nations International Children's Emergency Fund)
UNICOR	Federal Prison Industries, Inc.
UPU	Universal Postal Union
USA	United States Army
USAF	United States Air Force
USCG	United States Coast Guard
USDA	United States Department of Agriculture
USES	United States Employment Service
USGS	United States Geological Survey
USGS BS	United States Geological Survey Bulletin Board System, Department of the Interior

USIA	United States Information Agency
USITC	United States International Trade Commission
USMC	United States Marine Corps
USN	United States Navy
USNCB	United States National Central Bureau
USRA	United States Railway Association
USTTA	United States Travel and Tourism Administration
VA	Department of Veterans Affairs
VA Vendor BS	VA Vendor Bulletin Board, Department of Veterans Affairs
VETS	Veterans' Employment and Training Service
VGLI	Veterans Group Life Insurance
VISTA	Volunteers in Service to America
VOA	Voice of America
WAPA	Western Area Power Administration
WHO	World Health Organization
WHS	Washington Headquarters Services
WIC	Special supplemental food program for Women, Infants, and Children
WIN	Work Incentive Program
WMO	World Meteorological Organization
WTO	World Tourism Organization
WWMCCS	Worldwide Military Command and Control System
YCC	Youth Conservation Corps

BIBLIOGRAPHY

Braun, Eric. *The Internet Directory*. New York: Balantine Books, 1994.

Butler, Mark. *How to Use the Internet*. Emeryville, CA: Ziff-Davis Press, 1994.

Gibbs, Mark, and Richard Smith. *Navigating the Internet*. Carmel, IN: Sams Publishing, 1993.

Godin, Seth. *E-Mail Addresses of the Rich and Famous*. Reading, MA: Addison-Wesley Publishing Company, 1994.

Kent, Peter. *10 Minute Guide to the Internet*. Indianapolis, IN: Alpha Books, 1994.

Krol, Ed. *The Whole Internet*. Sebastopol, CA: O'Reilly & Associates, 1992.

LaQuey, Tracy. *The Internet Companion*. Reading, MA: Addison-Wesley, 1993.

Levine, John R., and Carol Barudi. *Internet for Dummies*. San Mateo, CA: IDG Books, 1993.

Levine, John R., and Margaret Levine. *Unix for Dummies*. San Mateo, CA: IDG Books, 1993.

Levine, John R., and Margaret Levine Young. *More Internet for Dummies*. San Mateo, CA: IDG Books, 1994.

Marine, April, *et al. Internet: Getting Started*. Englewood Cliffs, NJ: Prentice Hall, 1993.

Rittner, Don. *Whole Earth Online Almanac*. New York: Brady Publishing, 1993.

The United States Government Manual. Washington, DC: U.S. Government Printing Office, 1993–94. (Always out-of-date, poorly bound, and yet, an essential reference.)

Index

Rizzo, John, 11
Roanoke, VA, 231
Robb, Charles, 45
Roberts, Pat, 48
Rochester, NY, 227
Rose, Charlie, 46, 48
RSA-BBS, 96, 118–119
Rutgers Cooperative Extension
    Bulletin Board System,
    84–85

Sacramento, CA, 221
Safety Data Exchange Bulletin
    Board, 150–151
St. Olaf College Internet and BIT-
    NET Distribution Point,
    144–145
SALEMDUG-BBS, 94, 180–181
Sample Weather Data, 94
San Angelo, TX, 231
San Antonio, TX, 231
San Bernadino, CA, bankruptcy
    courts, 71
Sanders, Bernie, 47
Sandpoint, ID, 223
San Jose, CA, 221, 247–248
San Luis Obispo, CA, 248
San Pablo, CA, 248
San Ramon, CA, 248
Santa Ana, CA, bankruptcy courts,
    71
Santa Barbara, CA
    bankruptcy courts, 71
    RAIN, 221
Santa Fe, NM, 227
Sarasota, FL, 222
Savings Bond Division, 92
SBAI-BBS, 94, 209–210
SBA Online, 94, 208–209
SBB-BBS, 94, 154
SBIR-BBS, 94
SC_92, 55
SC_93, 55
Science and Technology Policy,
    Office of, 65–66
Science & Technology Information
    System, 198–200
SC_92ORD, 55
SC_93ORD, 55
SCRAM BBS, 174–175, 176
SCS, 85–86

Seal Beach, CA, 221
SEARCH, 68
Searching tools, Internet, 24
Seattle, WA, 231, 268
Secretary for Health, Assistant,
    Office of, 132–133
Security, 13
SEL, 104–105
Senate, U.S., 45–46
    Gopher, 45
    SENATE_01, 55
    Senators online, 45
    WWW Pages, 46
SENDIT, 228
SEORF, 229
Shawnee, IL, 223
Shays, Christopher, 48
Shepard's McGraw-Hill, 69
Silicon Valley Public Access Link,
    221, 245–246, 247–248
Simon, Paul, 45
SINCE_LAST_ON, 55
Skaggs, David, 48
SLONET, 221, 248
Small Business Administration,
    208–210
    Online, 208–209
    Software Clearinghouse BBS,
    209–210
Small Business Innovation
    Research, 190–191
Smartcom, 11
Smartcom II, 11
SMART-Sarasota, 222
Software, telecommunication, 10,
    11–12
SOI BBS, 153–154
Soil Conservation Service, 85–86
South Carolina, 230
    bankruptcy courts, 73, 76
    district courts, 79
South Dakota, bankruptcy courts,
    73, 76
Southern Tier, 227
Space Environment Laboratory,
    104–105
Space Telescope Electronic
    Information Service,
    194–195
Special Internet Connections, 274
Spokane, WA, 232

Springfield, MO, 226
Stanford Linear Accelerator
    Center, 119–120
Stark, Pete, 48
STATE, 55
STATE01, 55
STATE02, 55
State and Local Emergency
    Management Data Users
    Group, 180–181
State and Local Online Services.
    See individual states
STATE_CDROM, 55
State commercial online informa-
    tion providers, 35–37
State Department, 142–145
Statistics of Income Division,
    153–154
Stearns, Cliff, 48
STEIS, 194–195
STIS, 94, 198–200
STN International, 34
Stuart, FL, 222
Suncoast-Tampa Bay, 222
Support Center for Regulatory Air
    Models, 174–175, 176
Surety Bond Branch, 154
SV-PAL, 221, 245–246, 247–248
SWICH BBS, 95
SWIF-NET, 223
Sylvester, GA, 223
SYSOPS, xxvii, 15–17, 181

Tallahassee, FL, 222
Tampa Bay, FL, 222
Tarrant Co., TX, 231
Taylor, Charles, 48
TEBBS, 95, 202–203
Technology Assessment, Office of,
    57–58
    FTP Server, 57–58
Technology Transfer Network,
    175–176
TECH SPEC BBS, 94, 201
    PLUS, 201
Telecommunication software, 10,
    11–12
TELENEWS, 94
Telephone service, 10
TELNET, 20, 24
Tempe, AZ, 220

WITHDRAWAL